LIFE SCIENCES *in the* TWENTIETH CENTURY

BIOGRAPHICAL PORTRAITS

Editor

Professor Everett Mendelsohn teaches the history of science at Harvard University, where he has been on the faculty since 1960. He founded the *Journal of the History of Biology* in 1968 and served as its editor for the first 31 years. He has specialized his research in the history of the modern life sciences and the relations between science and society. His first book, *Heat and Life: The Theory of Animal Heat,* was published in 1964. His most recent book is an edited collection titled *The Practices of Human Genetics* (1999).

Consulting Editor

Brian S. Baigrie
University of Toronto

THE SCRIBNER SCIENCE REFERENCE SERIES

VOLUME 2

LIFE SCIENCES *in the* TWENTIETH CENTURY

BIOGRAPHICAL PORTRAITS

Everett Mendelsohn, *Editor*

Brian S. Baigrie, *Consulting Editor*

3 1333 01884 0031

Charles Scribner's Sons

an imprint of the Gale Group

New York • Detroit • San Francisco • London • Boston • Woodbridge, CT

Developed for Charles Scribner's Sons by Visual Education Corporation, Princeton, N.J.

For Scribners
PUBLISHER: Karen Day
COVER DESIGN: Pamela Galbreath

For Visual Education
EDITORIAL DIRECTOR: Darryl Kestler
PROJECT DIRECTOR: Meera Vaidyanathan
WRITERS: Guy Austrian, Tish Davidson, John Haley, Charles Roebuck, Rebecca Stefoff
ASSOCIATE EDITORS: John Kennedy, Sussannah Walsh
COPYEDITING SUPERVISOR: Helen Castro
COPY EDITOR: Eleanor Hero
INDEXER: Cynthia Landeen
PHOTO RESEARCH: Susan Buschhorn
PRODUCTION SUPERVISOR: Paula Deverell
PRODUCTION ASSISTANTS: Susan Buschhorn, Brian Suskin
INTERIOR DESIGN: Maxson Crandall, Rob Ehlers, Lisa Evans-Skopas
ELECTRONIC PREPARATION: Fiona Torphy
ELECTRONIC PRODUCTION: Rob Ehlers, Lisa Evans-Skopas

Library of Congress Cataloging-in-Publication Data

Life sciences in the twentieth century : biographical portraits / Everett Mendelsohn, editor.
     p. cm. — (Scribner science reference series ; v. 2)
  Includes bibliographical references (p.).
  ISBN 0-684-80647-9
  1. Life scientists—Biography. 2. Life sciences—History—20th century.
 I. Title: Life sciences in the 20th century. II. Mendelsohn, Everett. III. Series.

QH26 .L53 2000
570'.92'2—dc21
[B]

00-063789

TABLE OF CONTENTS

Table of Contents

INTRODUCTION

BY EVERETT MENDELSOHN

The twentieth century was a period of intense activity in all the sciences. From the new world of space and time created in the opening years of the century by the physicist Albert Einstein, through the discovery of radiation and radioactive materials and their ultimate use in the atomic bombs of 1945, to plastics and synthetic fibers, scientists understood and mastered matter. New scientific specializations, such as solid-state physics, came into being, enabling such developments as microchips and computers. In turn, these new developments helped scientists make advances in molecular biology and biotechnology that promise the ability to alter the genetic composition of living organisms.

Changes in Twentieth-Century Science. During the twentieth century, the United States became a major contributor to the advancement of science for the first time. In part, this represented the natural growth of a young nation developing its universities and research centers and encouraging its youth to pursue scholarly and scientific careers as well as industrial and economic activities. Up to this time, the United States had borrowed its science from Europe, but this began to change during the early decades of the 1900s. The development of American science was accelerated in the years after World War I (1914–1918) and came to full force during and after World War II (1939–1945). During the 1930s and 1940s, American science was further enriched by the migration of many scientists fleeing from European countries menaced by the forces of Nazism and Fascism. Among these refugees were several ingenious researchers and talented teachers, including the anthropologist Franz BOAS, geneticist Theodosius DOBZHANSKY, physiologist Otto LOEWI, and biochemist Otto MEYERHOF.

Public regard for scientific achievement received a strong boost when the Swedish chemist, industrialist, and inventor of explosives Alfred Nobel established a fund in his will to award prizes in the natural sciences, medicine, literature, and peacemaking. From the beginning of the century, the Nobel Prizes in the sciences singled out individuals and their fields of work for generous rewards. The awards have become the most prestigious ones in science, and by recognizing new areas of research they have stimulated new fields.

The twentieth century was also a period in which women, who had been largely excluded from scientific work during the previous centuries, were integrated into the scientific community. This inclusion was part of a wider change in which new careers and advanced education and training became available to women. The entry of women into the sciences came faster and more prominently in the many subfields of biology than in the physical sciences. Despite these advances, which occurred early in the 1900s, women are still underrepresented in all areas of scientific endeavor.

Another important element in the growth of science in the twentieth century was government investment, which began after World War II. The investment came at first from recognition of the role that the sciences played in developing new weapons of warfare. It quickly spilled over to other areas of science when it became apparent that scientific knowledge and technique were essential for industrial development and growth. As each country established its own methods to support science, there was an increase in scientific activity and in the number of practicing scientists. This trend persisted during the Cold War between the former Soviet Union and the United States and Western Europe, which lasted from 1946 to 1991.

Evolution and Biochemistry. The individuals whose biographies are recorded in this volume all worked in and around the field of biology. They represent a sampling of the activities and achievements in the life sciences during the 1900s. From their stories we can reconstruct the history of biology during that period.

Of all the fields of science, biology has always been the most diverse. But there have been several strong movements toward unification. There can be no doubt that the theory of evolution proposed by the Englishman Charles Darwin in his influential book *On the*

Introduction

Origin of Species (1859) offered the most important unifying theory in biology. Darwin's theory serves as the basis for the integration of all fields of biology and of all explanations in the life sciences, including those for the origins and development of humanity. During the twentieth century, his theory of evolution was often used to explain many biological phenomena, and its influence has been extended to other domains ranging from human society to the heavens. As a scientific theory, evolution has been added to and refined during the past 100 years, especially through its merger with genetic theory in the early decades of the century.

Darwin's theory of evolution has faced considerable opposition. In the United States, there has been a continuing skirmish between the science of evolution and fundamentalist Christian groups. These groups are intent on undermining or severely limiting the role of evolution in explaining human origins and development and the role of natural processes in explaining the basic structures and functions of living systems. Critics of evolution have instead proposed reliance on God's hand, design, or intelligence to account for diversity and change through time of organic species. In other countries, antievolution efforts either have not existed or have been subdued.

A second important unifying element in twentieth-century biology has been the extensive development of biochemistry, the study of biologically active chemical molecules and processes. In some ways biochemistry stands in contrast to evolution, focusing on the minute parts rather than on the whole organism. Although the fundamental building blocks of living organisms, such as proteins, had been identified in the second half of the 1800s, their chemical composition, structure, and function became a focus for intense study beginning in the early 1900s. Through focused biochemical research it became increasingly apparent that, at a basic level, organisms can be understood as a complex set of interactions of molecules that are continuously formed and broken down. In the process the molecules provide the organism with energy and create the structures that give it form.

The growing understanding and importance of biochemistry led some to adopt a reductionist view: that life is nothing more than molecules, matter, and energy. Others, who adopted an antireductionist or organismic point of view, argue that molecules are essential. However, they contend that through the course of evolution organisms have developed levels of organization that are not easily reducible to simple chemical reactions.

Biology and the Physical Sciences. The increasing recognition of the chemical and physical bases of life led to greater interaction between biology and the physical sciences. This interaction not only contributed to understanding and explaining biological processes but also helped develop the means (technologies) of conducting biological research. For instance, biologists expanded their use of X rays, discovered at the beginning of the century, from looking beneath the surface of the body to analyzing the structure of molecules. During the mid- to late 1900s, this technology gave rise to more sophisticated equipment and apparatuses. The electron microscope enabled scientists to observe the structures of organisms far smaller than those permitted by even the most powerful light microscopes. The use of radioactive atoms for tagging molecules in biochemical processes enabled scientists to perform detailed analyses of the formation and breakdown of molecules in the numerous interactions of systems in living organisms.

Influence of Genetics. Writing in 1865, the Austrian monk Gregor Mendel related the results of experiments he had carried out on the garden pea plant. His report consisted of a series of rules that govern how the characteristics of the pea plant—color, height, texture—behave during crossbreeding experiments and how these traits are passed from one generation to the next. His work went unrecognized until 1900, when three European biologists rediscovered it. The response to Mendel's work was immediate, and a new field of research—genetics—was established. Mendel's original rules of heredity were extended and refined and were rapidly applied in plant and animal breeding.

The new field of genetics provided a boost to eugenics, a discipline that attempted to apply the rules of genetics to create better human beings. Although the fundamental outlines of eugenics were developed in the late 1800s by Francis Galton, many eugenicists saw the new genetics as providing support for Galton's ideas. Most geneticists and some biologists and physicians became supporters of eugenics, and numerous studies were undertaken and proposals made to utilize genetic information about humans to control human hereditary development.

Eugenicists identified human traits in Mendelian terms, from simple characteristics such as eye and hair color to complex behavioral traits, such as alcoholism, shiftlessness, criminality, imbecility, musical ability, intelligence, and industriousness. For individuals with traits considered negative, the eugenicists recommended harsh remedies, including sterilization, immigration bans, and imprisonment.

During the early decades of the century, eugenics enjoyed support across the political spectrum with only minor opposition. But the excesses committed by the Nazi regime in Germany in the 1930s in implementing the policies of eugenics quickly undermined support in much of Europe and the United States. Nonetheless, the belief that basic human traits are biologically determined and affected by the environment (education and upbringing) in only minor ways has remained strong and has been the focus of much discussion and debate. The late twentieth-century advances in genetics and behavioral biology have rekindled these controversies and have emerged in debates about sociobiology and human genetics.

DNA and Genetic Engineering. In the mid-1900s, scientists recognized deoxyribonucleic acid (DNA) as the basic component of the hereditary material of chromosomes in all cell nuclei. Its structure was delineated in 1953 in a classic pair of papers by James WATSON and Francis CRICK. That launched a race to identify how genes worked. The simple code carried by the DNA molecules was quickly deciphered, and after 20 years of intense research genetics began to achieve its final goal—genetic engineering, or altering the genetic code of organisms in a specific and direct manner.

The insertion of new genetic material into the genome (existing genetic content of an organism) using a technique called recombinant DNA marked a critical turning point, opening the way for genetic engineering. This feat, only a dream early in the century, became the basis of the construction of altered organisms. For example, genes inserted into bacteria gave them the ability to metabolize (digest) oil spills. Since that time, many plants have been genetically modified to improve yield, increase nutritional elements, or provide resistance to disease. Cows have been genetically engineered to increase milk production and pigs to increase the protein content of their meat. Notwithstanding these remarkable advances, the path from genetic structure to a mature plant or animal remains the focus of much biological research.

The steps from creating a fertilized egg (by merging two nuclei and their genetic content) to developing a viable adult organism also underwent striking changes in the closing decade of the twentieth century. The creation of the lamb "Dolly" by Ian WILMUT and Keith CAMPBELL in Edinburgh's Roslin Institute in 1997 was only the most dramatic of a series of challenging experiments in the cloning of animals. (Dolly was the first animal to be cloned from a mature, fully differentiated cell of another animal.) However, the ability to develop identical copies of genetic material through cloning presents biology and medicine with both promise and problem. The major promise involves providing embryos into which new genetic information can be inserted. Such a procedure might involve providing a sheep with human proteins in its milk or equipping a pig with genes that would help it to develop organs that would not be rejected in transplants into humans. But cloning has also been the basis of much fiction and other writing in which human clones were viewed as replacements for the dead or as a way of maximizing certain genetic traits in the population.

New Frontiers. Although cloning is scientifically challenging, exciting, and ethically problematic, it is only one of a number of research frontiers in animal and human reproduction. The next few decades will almost certainly refine the techniques in use and focus on genetic reengineering of organisms, particularly higher organisms.

At the end of the 1900s, the pace of biological research was at an all-time high. At the beginning of the century, important new fields for research in the life sciences emerged. At the end of the century and the opening years of the twenty-first century, research was transformed into production and the growth of commercial enterprise. Biotechnology has been among the fastest-growing areas of industrial development. The promises for medicine have been noted, as well as the capacity to change agriculture and eventually alter human beings themselves. But with all the new development has come an excitement in the reporting of science and an overstatement of the claims being made for what has already been achieved or that can be achieved in the near future. Achieving a balance among scientific discovery, technological capacity, and ethical responsibility is perhaps the most important research front for the life sciences at this time.

TIME LINE

1889   Santiago **RAMÓN Y CAJAL** discovers than neurons are the basic units of the nervous system.

1891   Waldemar **HAFFKINE** develops a vaccine against bubonic plague.
Charles **SHERRINGTON** discovers the knee-jerk reflex.

1895   German physicist Wilhelm Röntgen discovers X rays.

1896   George Washington **CARVER** becomes director of the agricultural research department at the Tuskegee Institute.

1897   Ronald **ROSS** demonstrates that malaria is transmitted by mosquito bites.

1901   Karl **LANDSTEINER** discovers that human blood is divided into three types—A, B, and O.

1902   Florence Rena **SABIN** becomes the first female faculty member at Johns Hopkins University's medical school.
Charles **RICHET** discovers anaphylaxis, the abnormal sensitivity to external substances, or an extreme allergy.

1903   Ivan **PAVLOV** describes the nature of the conditioned reflex.

1905   John Scott **HALDANE** demonstrates that breathing is controlled by the partial pressure of carbon dioxide in blood.
Edmund **WILSON** uncovers the connection between chromosomes and sex-linked characteristics.

1906   Frederick Gowland **HOPKINS** discovers that vitamins are essential for life even though required in small amounts.
Jules **BORDET** discovers the bacterium that causes whooping cough.

1909   Charles **NICOLLE** demonstrates that lice spread the contagious disease typhus.

1910   Thomas Hunt **MORGAN** discovers the central role of chromosomes in heredity.

1911   Elizabeth **KENNY** introduces muscle therapy to treat polio.
Henry Hallett **DALE** discovers histamines.

1914   Alexis **CARREL** performs the first successful heart surgery on a dog.

1914–1918   World War I.

1917   Oswald **AVERY** announces the growth of pneumococcus bacteria outside the body.
Sigmund **FREUD** publishes *Introduction to Psychoanalysis*.
Julius **WAGNER VON JAUREGG** treats syphilitic paralysis by injecting patients with the malarial parasite.

1918–1919   Epidemic of Spanish flu causes 40 million deaths in Europe.

1919   Alice **HAMILTON** becomes the first female faculty member at Harvard University.
Morgan publishes *The Physical Basis of Heredity*.

1920   Harvey **CUSHING** develops new techniques in brain surgery.

1921   Morgan proposes the chromosome theory of heredity.
        Joseph **ERLANGER** begins research that turns into the field of neurophysiology.
        Otto **LOEWI** discovers how chemicals mediate impulses from nerve cells.

1922   Frederick **BANTING** begins the first clinical trials of insulin.

1924   Otto **WARBURG** discovers the main enzyme responsible for cellular respiration (iron oxygenase).

1925   Cushing discovers a method of destroying tumors using electricity.

1926   George **MINOT** treats pernicious anemia with liver extract.

1927   Antonio **EGAS MONIZ** develops a new method of locating brain tumors.
        Hermann **MULLER** discovers that X rays produce mutations in the genes of fruit flies.

1928   Alexander **FLEMING** discovers penicillin.

1929   Robert **YERKES** establishes a laboratory to study nonhuman primates.
        Gerty **CORI** explains carbohydrate metabolism.

1930   Helen **TAUSSIG** begins to develop new methods to prevent pediatric heart problems.

1931   Louis **LEAKEY** makes his first expedition to Olduvai Gorge in present-day Tanzania (East Africa).

1932   John Burdon Sanderson **HALDANE** publishes *The Causes of Evolution*.

1933   Gladys **EMERSON** begins the study of wheat germ oil that leads to the isolation of vitamin E.
        Dorothy **HODGKIN** makes the first X-ray diffraction photograph of a protein.

1935   Gerhard **DOMAGK** discovers prontosil, the first sulfa drug to treat streptococcal infections.

1936   Egas Moniz performs the first prefrontal lobotomy.
        Percy **JULIAN** begins work extracting useful compounds from soybeans.
        Carrel develops an artificial heart.

1937   Erlanger discovers the electrical nature of nerve transmission.
        Theodosius **DOBZHANSKY** publishes *Genetics and the Origin of Species*.

1938   Franz **BOAS** publishes *General Anthropology*.

1939   Paul **MÜLLER** synthesizes dichlorodiphenyltrichloroethane (DDT).

1939–1945   World War II.

1940s   Hattie **ALEXANDER** uses rabbit serum to develop a treatment for influenzal meningitis.

1940   Howard **FLOREY** and Ernst **CHAIN** develop penicillin as an antibiotic.
        Hans **KREBS** discovers the Krebs or citric acid cycle of metabolism.
        Landsteiner discovers the Rh factor in blood.

1941   George **BEADLE** and Edward **TATUM** discover the role of genes in controlling chemical reactions in cells.
        Charles **DREW** develops improved methods for the storage of blood.

1946   Beadle and Tatum begin studies that lead to the one gene, one enzyme theory.

1948   Mary **LEAKEY** discovers the skull of *Proconsul africanus* in Kenya.
        Rita **LEVI-MONTALCINI** discovers nerve growth factor in embryos.
        World Health Organization (WHO) is formed.

1949   Edward **KENDALL** discovers that cortisone relieves the pain of rheumatoid arthritis.

Time Line

1950   Jacques-Yves **COUSTEAU** launches the oceanographic research and exploration vessel *Calypso.*

1951   Rosalind **FRANKLIN** produces clear images of DNA using X-ray diffraction.
Rachel **CARSON** publishes *The Sea Around Us.*
Gertrude **ELION** synthesizes 6-MP to treat leukemia.
Barbara **MCCLINTOCK** discovers "jumping genes."

1952   Joshua **LEDERBERG** proves that bacteria are capable of sexual reproduction.
Maurice **WILKINS** shares his X-ray diffraction work on the molecular structure of DNA with James **WATSON** and Francis **CRICK.**
First successful sex-change operation is performed.

1953   Watson and Crick discover the structure of DNA and publish their findings in *Nature.*
First successful open-heart surgery is performed.

1954   Jonas **SALK**'s polio vaccine is administered to nearly 2 million schoolchildren in the United States.

1955   Cousteau releases *The Silent World,* a film about the undersea world.

1957   Albert **SABIN** develops the oral polio vaccine.

1959   Mary Leakey discovers a 1.75 million-year-old fossil that is believed to be the "missing link" between the apelike *Australopithecus* and the ancestors of modern humans.

1960   Jane **GOODALL** begins research in Africa to study wild chimpanzees.

1962   Carson publishes *Silent Spring.*

1963   First human lung transplant surgery is performed.

1964   Alexander becomes the first female president of the American Pediatric Society.

1967   Dian **FOSSEY** begins her studies of mountain gorillas in Africa.
Christiaan **BARNARD** performs the first successful human heart transplant operation.

1970   Environmental Protection Agency (EPA) is created in the United States.

1971   Computerized axial tomography (CAT) is used to study internal organs.

1972   DDT is banned in the United States.

1978   The first human "test tube baby" is born in England.

1979   Smallpox is eradicated.

1980   Christiane **NÜSSLEIN-VOLHARD** demonstrates that specific genes control the early development of embryos.

1981   Acquired Immune Deficiency Syndrome (AIDS) is observed for the first time.

1984   Richard **LEAKEY** finds the fossil skeleton *Homo erectus* in Africa.
Human immunodeficiency virus (HIV) is found to cause AIDS.

1988   Scientists announce plans to map the human genome.

1996   Ian **WILMUT** and Keith **CAMPBELL** clone a lamb from the cells of an adult sheep.

2000   Scientists announce completion of the human genome project.

BIOGRAPHICAL PORTRAITS

Othenio ABEL

1875–1946

PALEONTOLOGY, PALEOBIOLOGY

* **paleontology** study of extinct or prehistoric life, usually through the examination of fossils

Othenio Abel's greatest achievement was founding the new science of paleobiology, the biology of fossil organisms. Abel was born in Vienna, Austria, into a family with a tradition of interest in the sciences, particularly botany. As a teenager, he became interested in paleontology* and eagerly collected fossils. To please his parents he studied law, but he soon returned to botany and published several papers on orchids.

In 1898, while still a student, Abel became an assistant at the Geological Institute of the University of Vienna. The following year he received a doctoral degree in geology and paleontology. For the next seven years, he served on the staff of the Imperial-Royal Geological State Institute in Vienna. During this time he studied the fossil whales of Belgium and worked with the staff of the Royal Museum of Natural History. In 1907 Abel accepted a professorship at the University of Vienna.

Stimulated by the writings of fellow paleontologists, such as Louis Dollo, Vladimir Kovalevsky, and Henry Fairfield Osborn, Abel developed a new field of research called paleobiology. The subject is a branch of paleontology and is concerned with the biology of fossil animals. In 1917 the university made him director of a new department of paleobiology, which later became the Paleobiological Institute of the university.

Abel had been at the University of Vienna for 28 years and published more than 250 papers. During these years, he received awards from the Geological Society of London, the National Academy of Sciences in Washington, D.C., and the Zoological-Botanical Society of Vienna. He was also a member of many distinguished scientific academies and learned societies. Beginning in 1935 he taught for five years at the University of Göttingen in Germany, where he investigated new areas of research within the larger subject of paleontology. In 1940 Abel retired to Austria, where he continued his scientific activities until shortly before his death.

Hattie Elizabeth ALEXANDER

1901–1968

BACTERIOLOGY

* **serum** clear liquid that separates from the blood after the blood cells clot

* **antibiotic** any chemical substance produced by various microscopic organisms that hinders the growth of or destroys other harmful microorganisms

Hattie Elizabeth Alexander was a pioneer in bacteriology, the science that deals with microscopic organisms called bacteria that can cause infection and disease. She was also a pediatrician, and she applied her research to defeat influenzal meningitis, a lethal disease that affected infants.

Born and raised in Baltimore, Maryland, Alexander was educated at Goucher College in Towson, Maryland. After her graduation from college in 1923, she worked as a bacteriologist at the U.S. Public Health Service laboratory in Washington, D.C., and with the Maryland Public Health Service. Alexander earned her medical degree from Johns Hopkins University in Baltimore in 1930 and interned at the Babies Hospital in New York City. While there she saw the devastating effects of influenzal meningitis, a serious disease that causes swelling of the membranes around the brain and spinal cord.

Knowing that researchers had recently used rabbit serum* to boost the human immune system against pneumonia, Alexander applied this technique to influenzal meningitis in the early 1940s. Using the serum treatment in combination with antibiotics*, she reduced the hospital's death rate for infants with influenzal meningitis by 80 percent. As the

* **mutation** relatively permanent change in the structure of a material
* **DNA** deoxyribonucleic acid, the material in chromosomes that carries genetic information from ancestor to offspring

treatments were improved and standardized over the years, the death rate fell even further.

During the course of her research, Alexander saw that some influenzal meningitis–causing bacteria had become resistant to antibiotics through the mutation* of their genes. Her research into this process was among the early work conducted on DNA*.

A member of many scientific societies, Alexander became the first female president of the American Pediatric Society. She was frequently honored for her achievements as a teacher, researcher, and doctor. During her career, Alexander published nearly 150 papers and was the author of many textbooks on pediatrics. She served as a lecturer and consultant even after her retirement. Alexander died of cancer at the age of 67.

Agnes Robertson
ARBER

1879–1960
BOTANY

* **paleobotanist** scientist who studies extinct or prehistoric plants

Agnes Robertson Arber was a botanist and a pioneer for women interested in careers in scientific research. Born Agnes Robertson in London, England, she attended University College in London and the Botany School at the University of Cambridge. A teacher encouraged her interest in comparative plant anatomy, the study of how the structures of different plants are different from and similar to each other.

In 1909 Robertson married paleobotanist* Edward A.N. Arber. She devoted the next few years to the study of herbals, books about the medicinal uses of herbs. Three years later, she published a pioneer volume in the field, *Herbals, Their Origin and Evolution,* which included many important botanical illustrations. Her later works include anatomical studies of water plants, grasses, and a class of plants called monocotyledons (plants with one seed leaf).

Although Arber worked alone and had few contacts with university scientists, she earned considerable recognition. Always at the forefront of the movement of women in scientific research, Arber became the first female botanist fellow of England's Royal Society. She also received the Gold Medal of the Linnean Society. In the later years of her life, Arber wrote three books about science and philosophy.

Oswald Theodore
AVERY

1877–1955
BIOLOGY

* **genetics** branch of biology that deals with heredity
* **DNA** deoxyribonucleic acid, the material in chromosomes that carries genetic information from ancestor to offspring

The Biologist Oswald Theodore Avery spent many years studying the *pneumococcus* bacteria that cause pneumonia. His work helped establish the science of immunochemistry, which examines the chemical basis for resistance to and protection from disease. Avery also contributed to the scientific understanding of genetics* and of DNA*.

Avery was born in the Canadian province of Nova Scotia, but his family moved to New York State in 1887. After attending Colgate University, he went to the Columbia University College of Physicians and Surgeons and received his medical degree in 1904. He began a career as a physician but soon joined the staff of a research laboratory in Brooklyn, New York, where he specialized in bacteriology, the study of bacteria. From 1913 to 1948, Avery worked at the Rockefeller Institute Hospital in

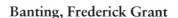

New York, continuing his research on bacteria. Seven years later he died in Nashville, Tennessee.

When Avery came to the Rockefeller Institute Hospital, he joined the investigation of lobar pneumonia that was already in progress. In 1917 he and some other researchers announced that they had grown the *pneumococcus* bacteria outside the body, and that the bacteria had produced a substance that gave organisms immunity to the disease. Avery proved that this substance was a product of bacterial growth and that it was present in the blood and urine of people and animals suffering from pneumonia.

The immunological substances that Avery discovered were capsules of complex carbohydrates called polysaccharides that surround the bacteria. He showed that each type of bacterium produces a specific chemical type of polysaccharide envelope. He also proved that immunology* could be analyzed in terms of the biochemical composition of cell parts—a discovery that contributed to the development of immunochemistry.

Beginning in 1932, Avery investigated a process called transformation, in which infection by disease-causing bacteria converts a non–disease-causing strain of *pneumococcus* into one that *does* cause disease. Cells that have been transformed pass the disease-causing trait to later generations of cells. Avery and his fellow researchers found that the transformation occurred in the DNA of the cells. At the time, most scientists believed that the proteins in the cells carried genetic information, but Avery's discovery turned their attention to DNA. Avery's work was essential for the studies conducted several years later. It helped such scientists as James Watson and Francis Crick accurately describe the structure of DNA and lay the basis for the new field of molecular biology. (*See also* **Watson and Crick.**)

* **immunology** science that deals with the immune system, which protects the body from foreign substances, cells, and tissue by causing an immune response

---

Frederick Grant
BANTING

1891–1941

ENDOCRINOLOGY

* **hormone** internally secreted substance transported by body fluids to stimulate the functions of organs or tissues

* **extract** solution that contains the essential components of a more complex material

The Canadian physician Frederick Grant Banting was one of the discoverers of insulin, a hormone* produced by the pancreas that is used in the treatment of diabetes. For years, many scientists had attempted to use extracts* from the pancreas for such a purpose, but Banting and his colleagues were the first to achieve success in their efforts.

Life and Career. The youngest of five children, Banting was born and raised on a farm in Ontario, Canada. He enrolled at the University of Toronto with the intention of studying for the clergy. However, during his second year, he switched to medicine and specialized in orthopedic surgery to correct deformities of the bones, spine, joints, muscles, and other parts of the skeletal system. In 1916 during World War I, called to serve in the Canadian Army Medical Corps, he was assigned to a hospital in England and was soon sent to the front lines in France. Two years later, he received the Military Cross after he was wounded in action.

When the war ended, Banting returned to Canada and established a surgical practice in the city of London, Ontario, the site of Western University (now the University of Western Ontario). But the practice struggled and Banting was forced to accept a position at the university's medical

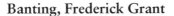

* **physiology** science that deals with the functions of living organisms and their parts

school, teaching anatomy and physiology*. The day before he was scheduled to lecture to his students on the function of the pancreas, he read an article in a medical journal about the relation between diabetes and structures in the pancreas called the islets of Langerhans. The article inspired him to conduct a series of investigations that ultimately resulted in his discovery of insulin. For this achievement, he shared the 1923 Nobel Prize in physiology or medicine with J.J.R. Macleod, a scientist from the University of Toronto.

Soon Banting gained worldwide fame and was awarded membership in many of the world's major medical and scientific societies. The University of Toronto later opened the Banting Institute for medical research in his honor. He spent the remainder of his career as head of the Banting and Best Department of Medical Research, which was named in honor of Banting and one of his research assistants, C.H. Best. In this position he conducted research on cancer, coronary thrombosis*, and silicosis*. During World War II he served as chairman of national medical committees in Canada, particularly in the area of aviation medical research. This required Banting to make periodic visits to England to work with his British colleagues. He died in a plane crash during one of these journeys.

* **coronary thrombosis** blood clot that develops in a cavity of the heart
* **silicosis** buildup of fibrous tissue in the lungs caused by inhaling silica dust over a long period of time

Discovering Insulin. The journal article that inspired Banting reported the results of experiments in which the pancreatic ducts of animals had

Frederick Banting improved the lives of millions of people with his discovery of the hormone insulin. He became famous during the so-called "insulin rush," when diabetics from all over the world came to Toronto to receive insulin treatment.

been tied off. The pancreas gradually degenerated, but the islets of Langerhans seemed unaffected. Earlier researchers believed these structures were the source of a hormone that could prevent diabetes. The hormone that was believed to be effective against diabetes was also the hormone required to convert sugar in the body into usable energy (a process known as glycolysis). Animals used in the experiments continued to convert sugar into energy, even though the only intact portions of the pancreas were the islets of Langerhans. This suggested that the islets were the source of a hormone responsible for glycolysis. The finding was reinforced by an 1889 study in which the removal of a dog's entire pancreas resulted in symptoms of severe diabetes.

Banting believed that extracts from the islets could be used to prepare an effective drug to combat diabetes. He thought that these extracts should be made from glands in which the ducts had been tied off before they were removed from the animal. This would prevent secretions of other tissues within the pancreas from destroying any useful component of an extract taken from the whole pancreas. To this end, Banting devised the idea of tying off the pancreatic ducts of dogs, waiting six to eight weeks, then removing the entire pancreas.

Although Banting was not the first to investigate the possibility of creating an antidiabetic drug from pancreatic excretions, all previous efforts had failed to produce effective results. Banting, though, was unaware of most of these research studies when he began his work. In fact, he later said that he would not have pursued his investigations if he had been familiar with the earlier research.

Banting approached Professor Macleod of the University of Toronto with his idea. Macleod was skeptical of the notion that the pancreas secreted a hormone, and that the islets of Langerhans were anything but a structure for removing poisons from the body. Nevertheless, he agreed to give Banting access to a laboratory for eight weeks, a research assistant, and ten dogs with which to pursue his investigations. Banting's research assistant was Best, a recent graduate whose student research on diabetes qualified him to work with Banting. They were later joined by E.C. Noble, another advanced student who had worked with Best in his studies of diabetes.

Banting, Best, and Noble began their work tying off the pancreatic ducts of dogs and developing techniques to remove the pancreas. But because of surgical problems, the pancreatic tissues of most of the dogs did not degenerate. In some animals the ducts were tied off too loosely to block pancreatic secretions into the body. In others the ducts were tied so tightly that the ducts established new canals through which to carry their secretions. Banting operated on the dogs again, in some cases tying the ducts several times at different tensions. After several weeks he removed the pancreas from one dog, chopped it into pieces, and froze it in a salt solution. As he had expected, the dog developed symptoms of diabetes. Banting then prepared an extract from the ground pancreas and injected it into the same dog. Within two hours the animal's abnormally high blood sugar level had fallen by nearly 50 percent and its condition improved markedly.

The experimenters then turned their efforts to eliminating possible sources of error in their work and finding other ways to produce the extract,

Giving Credit Where It's Due

Banting was an unlikely person to conduct research into the secretions of the pancreas. He was trained as a surgeon, not a clinician, and therefore he had little standing in the medical research community. Moreover, because he was neither a chemist nor a physiologist, he lacked expertise in those fields as well. Consequently, despite his outstanding contribution to the discovery of insulin, Banting played no part in writing the initial research reports on the work. Nevertheless, the success of insulin as a treatment for diabetes ensured that he received the recognition he deserved.

which they called isletin (named after the islets of Langerhans). Over the next several months, the group ran into and overcame several difficulties related to reproducing and purifying the pancreatic extract when they attempted to prepare solutions from the whole gland. Their work eventually produced an effective extract. Macleod then brought in another researcher, a biochemist* named J.B. Collip, who developed a method that enabled him to prepare a relatively pure extract that could be used in clinical* trials.

The first trials of the drug (now called insulin—Macleod introduced the name but it had been suggested as early as 1910) began in 1922 at the Toronto General Hospital. A 14-year-old boy with diabetes received daily injections of pancreatic extract that produced an immediate improvement, including greatly reduced sugar levels in his urine. The injections were then stopped for ten days, during which time sugar reappeared in the urine. Smaller doses of the extract were then administered and sugar in the urine was again lowered. The results of the clinical trials led doctors to adopt insulin as the main resource in treating diabetes. In fact, before insulin was widely available, diabetic patients from other countries went to Toronto for treatment, in what was called the "insulin rush."

Banting and Macleod received the Nobel Prize for the discovery, and they shared the monetary award from the prize with Best and Collip. Although problems of purification and production of insulin remained, they were soon solved by individual researchers as well as by the Eli Lilly pharmaceutical company. By the late 1920s the remaining difficulties had been overcome, and insulin was established as an effective treatment for diabetes.

Robert
BÁRÁNY
1876–1936
OTOLOGY

Robert Bárány is best known for a series of experiments in which he demonstrated how the sensation of dizziness is created in the inner ear. Born in Vienna, Austria, he attended the University of Vienna and began working for its ear clinic in 1903. He treated patients and conducted systematic research in a field known as otology, or the study of the ear.

Before Bárány began his research, problems of equilibrium (balance), such as dizziness, had been studied only in pigeons and rabbits. It was only during Bárány's time that a French scientist named Prosper Ménière related these problems to the equilibrium system in the inner ear. That scientist had revealed that the organ of equilibrium was a small, fluid-filled space in the inner ear.

Bárány applied these discoveries, as well as the findings of earlier scientists, to his experiments with humans. He identified how the act of spinning around affects the organ of equilibrium, recorded how a person's eyes and muscles react to dizziness, and discovered that the organ of equilibrium is affected by temperature. Bárány proved that the organ of equilibrium is connected to the brain through the nervous system. As a result, the sensation of dizziness, which had always been described in various subjective ways, could now be described as a precise physical condition related to the nervous system.

In 1914, at the height of his career, Bárány enlisted for service in World War I, despite a serious condition that caused his knee to stiffen. As

a military doctor he hoped to test his ideas on patients who suffered brain wounds in battle. But he was captured by the Russians and held prisoner. In 1915, when Bárány was awarded the Nobel Prize in physiology* or medicine for his work, he was released.

Two years later Bárány went on to direct a medical clinic in Sweden that specialized in the treatment of ear, nose, and throat problems. He remained there until his death in 1936.

A quiet, reserved researcher who worked diligently, Bárány was awarded honorary memberships in many medical and scientific societies, and the University of Stockholm presented him with an honorary doctorate in 1924.

Christiaan Neethling
BARNARD

born 1922

CARDIAC SURGERY

In 1967 Christiaan Neethling Barnard performed the first successful transplant of a heart from one human to another. Barnard was born in Beauford West, South Africa. He studied medicine in Cape Town and later in the United States at the University of Minnesota. While in the United States, he assisted researchers who were working on a heart-lung machine, and shortly thereafter he changed his specialty from general surgery to cardiothoracic (heart-lung) surgery and cardiology*.

In 1958 he returned to Cape Town, where he became a surgeon at the Groote Schuur Hospital. He introduced open-heart surgery to South Africa and developed a new design for artificial heart valves. Barnard also experimented with heart transplants in dogs, and as early as 1954, he succeeded in kidney transplant operations.

When Barnard was satisfied with the extent to which he had developed his transplant techniques, he recommended the procedure to one of his patients, a 55-year-old grocer named Louis Washkansky. Shortly thereafter, a donor heart became available when a young woman died in an automobile accident. Leading a team of 20 surgeons in a five-hour operation, Barnard removed Washkansky's diseased heart and replaced it with the donor organ. Unfortunately, the drugs administered to prevent Washkansky from rejecting the new heart weakened his immune system. He died of double pneumonia 18 days after the transplant surgery.

Despite the patient's death, the operation was celebrated as a major success. Barnard's next transplant patient lived for more than a year after the operation. But the technical risks and difficulties and the ethical issues have continued to make heart transplants an often problematic procedure. Arthritis forced Barnard to retire from surgery in 1983. He is the author of a textbook, an autobiography titled *One Life,* and several novels.

George Wells
BEADLE

1903–1989

GENETICS

George Wells Beadle was one of the discoverers of the method by which genes determine the characteristics of organisms. Working with fruit flies *(Drosophila)* and bread mold *(Neurospora),* Beadle found that genes influence heredity chemically.

Born on a farm in Nebraska, Beadle studied at the University of Nebraska and Cornell University. To earn his doctoral degree, he studied the

* **genetics** branch of biology that deals with heredity

* **biochemist** person who specializes in the science that deals with chemical compounds and processes occurring in living organisms

* **enzyme** any of numerous complex proteins that are produced by living cells and catalyze specific biochemical reactions at body temperature

* **mutation** relatively permanent change in the structure of a material

* **physiology** science that deals with the functions of living organisms and their parts

genetics* of the fruit fly in the laboratory of the well-known geneticist Thomas Hunt MORGAN. Later, he worked in Paris, where he and a colleague studied fruit flies and found that specific genes activated certain chemical reactions to determine the eye color of the flies.

Several years later, Beadle was at Stanford University, where he worked with the biochemist* Edward Lawrie TATUM. They turned their attention to simpler organisms—red bread molds—and together Beadle and Tatum concluded that each gene in the mold was responsible for producing a particular enzyme*. Each enzyme in turn promoted a chain of biochemical reactions that generated amino acids (the building blocks of proteins), which were necessary for the growth of the organism. Beadle and Tatum then used X rays to create mutations* in the genes of the molds, and they discovered that the mutated genes were unable to produce the enzymes, thereby interrupting the chain of biochemical reactions. Next, they experimented by adding the necessary amino acids to the environment in which they grew the mold. They were able to ascertain which genes produced the specific enzymes that promoted the biochemical reactions necessary for the production of the amino acids. These experiments led to the development of what was then called the "one gene–one enzyme" concept—each gene determines the structure of a particular enzyme, which then allows a single chemical reaction to take place.

Their discovery that genetics acted through biochemical reactions earned Beadle and Tatum the Nobel Prize in physiology* or medicine in 1958. This concept transformed genetics from the observation of physical traits to the chemical study of genes and gene action.

Beadle's professional career took him to several other universities, including the California Institute of Technology and the University of Chicago. In 1968 he became director of the American Medical Association's Institute for Biomedical Research. He died in California in 1989.

John Desmond BERNAL

1901–1971

CRYSTALLOGRAPHY,
MOLECULAR BIOLOGY

* **crystalline** composed of tiny crystals

* **DNA** deoxyribonucleic acid, the material in chromosomes that carries genetic information from ancestor to offspring

John Desmond Bernal was one of the most brilliant and unusual scientists of the 1900s and a leading figure in the field of crystallography, the study of the structure of crystalline* substances. Bernal is also considered among the founders of molecular biology because his techniques were essential to the work of the early discoverers of the structure of DNA*, including James Watson, Francis Crick, Rosalind FRANKLIN, and Maurice WILKINS. Bernal led an unconventional life that gave rise to many tall tales and myths. Loved by many, disliked by others, and only partially understood by anyone, Bernal was a singular figure in the history of science.

Early Life and Career

Bernal was born in Nenagh, Ireland, the son of a squireen (a farmer and an Irish Catholic gentleman) and an American, college-educated journalist. Although it would have been beyond the financial means of an ordinary Irish farmer, Bernal's family was able to send him to private boarding schools in England. It was there that he showed early signs of both his intellectual brilliance and his unusual personality.

School Days. Bernal's first private school was Stonyhurst, a Catholic institution that he entered at the early age of ten. In an example of his unusual nature, Bernal formed the Society of Perpetual Adoration at Stonyhurst, in which small groups of boys, organized into shifts, prayed throughout the night. After two years he left Stonyhurst and spent a short time in Ireland. Bernal then enrolled at Bedford, a middle-class Protestant school where he likely endured the taunts and abuse of his classmates because of his odd appearance and manners. However, his schoolmasters recognized his talent, and he won a mathematics scholarship to Emmanuel College at Cambridge University at age 18. It was an unfortunate match for Bernal, who was not only a faithful Catholic attending a Puritan* school but a devoted Marxist* as well. Unable to resolve the contradictions between Marxism and Catholicism, Bernal abandoned his religion. Throughout his life, however, he devoted himself to campaigning for peace and the perfectibility of humankind with something strongly resembling religious faith.

Despite his great intelligence Bernal's academic record in college was spotty. He was a fine mathematician, but he did poorly on his mathematical examinations. He excelled in chemistry, mineralogy, and geology but performed poorly in physics. This may well have been due to his extracurricular activities and, specifically, to the time he spent working out complex problems in crystallography. Although his interest in crystalline substances eventually won him a research position at London's Royal Institution, the administrators at Emmanuel College failed to appreciate his genius, and because of his poor grades, the school did not renew his fellowship.

Work and Play. At the Royal Institution, Bernal earned a reputation as the foremost crystallographer in England. His accomplishments included the successful analysis of the structure of graphite and the creation of a diagram for interpreting X-ray photographs of crystals. In 1927 after Bernal had spent several years at the Royal Institution, he was invited to Cambridge University to interview for a job as director of the university's new department of crystallography. During the interview Bernal behaved oddly; he said very little and answered most questions with just a word or two. However, when asked how he would run the department, Bernal spoke without pause for half an hour. Charmed and impressed, the interview board hired Bernal for the post.

Bernal's early years at Cambridge were the most productive of his career. Despite his scientific brilliance, however, he was not popular among the university community, perhaps because of his openly Communist* beliefs. Nevertheless, he received several scientific honors and was elected to England's Royal Society at the early age of 36.

It was during his time at Cambridge that Bernal undertook the work that influenced the development of the field of molecular biology. With his students, he used X rays to perform crystallographic studies of important biological molecules, such as proteins and the amino acids* of which they are composed. He was convinced that the structure of these molecules provided the key to the origins of life and the processes that support it. His investigations were important to the work that led to the discovery of the structure of the DNA molecule by Watson, Crick, Franklin, and Wilkins

* **Puritan** of or relating to the Puritans, a Protestant group of the 1500s and 1600s that advocated reformation of the Church of England and a strict moral code

* **Marxist** person who follows the social, political, and economic principles advocated by Karl Marx

* **Communist** referring to Communism, a social system in which land, goods, and the means of production are owned by the state or community rather than by individuals

* **amino acid** class of compounds that function as the building blocks of proteins

Bernal, John Desmond

* **nucleic acid** class of complex chemicals, including DNA and RNA, that is found in all living cells and viruses

Bernal and the Bomb

A story from World War II offers an illustration of Bernal's courage and his eccentric personality. A German bomb had landed on the train station at Liverpool Street but failed to explode. Although Bernal had no training in bomb disposal, he decided to deactivate it. No one stepped in to discourage him from this dangerous exercise. Nevertheless, after a short time Bernal succeeded in his task and declared: "Mr. Stationmaster, now you can announce that your station is open."

some 20 years later. When Bernal began his work on the molecules of biologically active materials, many of the techniques needed to discover the structure of nucleic acids* were not yet available. He did have access to them later, but his temperament was always more suited to envisioning and beginning new projects than to following them through to conclusion. Although his record at following through on scientific projects was mixed, he did inspire others to do outstanding work. Two of his students, Max Perutz and Dorothy HODGKIN, received the Nobel Prize in chemistry in 1962 and 1964.

Later Life and Career

Bernal's devotion to Communism was challenged at the outset of World War II, when the Soviet Union signed a treaty with Germany to divide Poland. However, when Hitler invaded the Soviet Union two years later, Bernal threw himself into the Allied war effort.

World War II and After. During the war Bernal took on projects to protect English civilians from bombing, to advise top British officers on special operations, and to plan the invasion of Europe. He was among the group of scientists that invented operations research. After the war he served on government committees while conducting and guiding scientific research, most notably on the structure of liquids, including water. A year after the end of the war, he received the Royal Medal, one of the English Royal Society's highest honors. He also became heavily involved in Communist causes, convinced that Communist philosophy was devoted to preserving peace and furthering the advancement of humankind. He was among the most widely respected and admired Western intellectuals who supported Communism. His personal charm and sense of humor set him apart from the typical Communist, who was generally overly serious and narrowly focused on political matters. Although Bernal served in high positions in many Communist organizations and committees, he continued to maintain excellent relations with friends and colleagues who were ardently anti-Communist.

The Science of Science. In the 1930s Bernal took a leading role in explaining the role of science in contemporary society. His wide-ranging intellectual interests and activities by this time had earned him the nickname "Sage," because many of his colleagues considered him to be uncommonly wise. With his reputation as an accomplished scientist secure, Bernal expanded his scope to include politics, philosophy, and the history of science.

A scientific conference held in England in 1931 influenced Bernal greatly. Several Soviet scientists arrived unexpectedly to explain their ideas about the history and philosophy of science. The unified vision and social purpose of the Soviet delegates, which to Bernal seemed different from the detached and remote character of British science, impressed him.

Over the next few years, Bernal became increasingly active in left-wing politics in Europe. At one point he served on more than 60 committees at the same time. Still, he found time to write *The Social Function of Science,* which quickly became a classic in its field. The book, published in 1939, argued that science was a powerful force in human history and was destined to become even more powerful. But Bernal thought that the capitalist economic system prevented science from reaching its full potential. Socialism*, he believed, was the only system that could allow science to advance, yet still maintain social order. In the book Bernal compared the state of British science with that of science in the Soviet Union. He concluded that the new socialist order, represented by the Soviet Union, held the key to the future of science.

Bernal, however, discovered things about socialism that troubled him deeply as time passed, particularly the fate of scientific colleagues who fell out of favor with the Soviet rulers. Still, he held tightly to his vision of a world in which the methods and approach of science conquered social problems.

Bernal's active support of and participation in Communist causes kept him constantly on the move. When he was not flying to Communist capitals, such as Moscow or Peking, he was reviewing scientific papers in the car on the way to and from the airport. Bernal was a physically strong man, but his health was not equal to the hectic schedule he maintained. At age 62 he suffered the first of several strokes that proved disastrous to his health. At first he refused to let this slow his activities, but the combined effects of several strokes caused him to be almost completely paralyzed. He was unable to move any muscles and his speech was barely audible, even with an amplifier. Despite his physical limitations, Bernal remained mentally alert and active until his death at age 70. (*See also* **Watson and Crick.**)

* **socialism** economic or political system based on the idea that the state or groups of workers should own and control the means of production and distribution of goods

Franz
BOAS

1858–1942
ANTHROPOLOGY

Franz Boas stands as one of the leading figures in twentieth century anthropology, the study of human beings, especially in relation to origins and cultural characteristics. He is considered the founder of the cultural or relativist school of anthropology, which supports the theory that the criteria of evaluation and judgment vary with individuals and their environment. Through his writings and teaching, he shaped several generations of American anthropologists.

Life and Career

As early as the age of five, Boas was drawn to the physical sciences, such as geography and astronomy. During his high school years, he developed a strong interest in the history and development of culture. His career was an outgrowth of his childhood interests and the scientific training he received.

Background and Education. Boas was born into a Jewish family in Minden, a city in the Westphalia region of Germany. His father was a merchant, and his mother founded a kindergarten. At an early age Boas declared his interest in traveling to far-off lands to study the lives and customs of other peoples. At school at the Gymnasium in Minden, however, he

Boas, Franz

Although born in Germany, Franz Boas spent nearly his entire career in the United States, and he is considered the founder of the American culture-centered school of anthropology. Boas was a popular and effective teacher, and many of his students were responsible for developing anthropology in the United States.

* **naturalist** one who studies objects in their natural settings

* **physiologist** one who specializes in physiology, the science that deals with the functions of living organisms and their parts

* **anthropometrist** one who studies measurements of the human body to determine differences and similarities among cultural groups

came to focus on mathematics and physics. Thereafter, Boas studied these subjects at the Universities of Heidelberg, Bonn, and Kiel, major German centers of education. At the age of 23, he received a doctoral degree in physics and geography from the University of Kiel, but his childhood interest in faraway places remained. This desire and his need to experience "nature as a whole" was renewed, probably by the inspiration of the naturalist* and geographer Alexander von Humboldt. A friendship with the geographer Theobald Fischer also helped turn Boas toward anthropology.

Early Career. In 1882 Boas attended the meeting of the Berlin Anthropological Society, where he met Rudolf Virchow, a famous physiologist* and anthropometrist*, and Adolf Bastian, Germany's leading practitioner of ethnology—the study of the division of humans into races and their origin, distribution, relations, and characteristics. Virchow trained Boas in anthropometric measurements, and Bastian encouraged him to pursue a career in the geographic and human sciences rather than in physics.

The following year Boas fulfilled his childhood dream of traveling to a remote and exotic location by visiting Baffin Island in the Canadian Arctic on the polar research vessel *Germania*. His goal was to gather geographic and anthropological material, and he had prepared for the expedition by reading about the culture of the Eskimo (Inuit) people of the region and by studying their language. Boas's geographic work was a success. He mapped 250 miles of Baffin Island's forbidding coastline, often at great personal danger, and he corrected many mistaken ideas about the island. More importantly, the expedition was a crucial point in Boas's shift to anthropology. He not only came to admire the Eskimo people but also saw that—contrary to what some people believed at the time—their culture was not shaped primarily by geographic forces. Boas agreed with Bastian's belief that human mental processes, rather than external conditions, were the primary elements that shaped theirs and other cultures. He devoted the rest of his career to understanding cultures and how they are formed.

After he returned to Germany, Boas worked at a museum and became a lecturer in geography at the University of Berlin. Shortly thereafter, he encountered some Bella Coola Native Americans, who had come to Berlin as part of an "exhibit" on the Northwest Coast Indians. They aroused Boas's interest in the Northwest Coast cultures. He scraped together funds to live among them in their homeland for a few months. This marked the first of the 13 field trips that Boas made to the Northwest Coast over a period of more than 40 years. In all, he spent about two and a half years among the Native Americans of that region.

In 1886 after that first field trip, Boas left the Northwest Coast for New York. At a meeting of the American Association for the Advancement of Science, he made contacts that grew into new opportunities for work. Boas had been uncertain about pursuing his career in Germany, where he suffered discrimination and insults because he was Jewish. Instead of returning to Germany, he decided to remain in the United States. He went to work on the magazine *Science*, married a woman from New York whom he had met in Germany, and began building a career in his adopted country.

Professional Achievements. For several years, Boas taught anthropology at Clark University in Worcester, Massachusetts. He then moved to Chicago to help organize the anthropological exhibits for a large fair called the Columbian Exposition, held in 1893. When the exposition closed, he worked at the newly founded Field Museum in Chicago, built to house some of the exhibits from the Exposition.

Three years later, Boas returned to New York City, where he became curator of ethnology at the American Museum of Natural History. He also lectured at New York's Columbia University, where he became a professor in 1899. Boas held his position at the museum until 1905 and his professorship until 1937.

One of Boas's most ambitious projects was the American Museum of Natural History's Jesup North Pacific Expedition, which ran from 1897 to 1900. He organized the far-ranging fieldwork of this expedition, which was designed to explore the relationships between the people of Siberia in northeastern Asia and the Native Americans of Alaska and the Northwest Coast. Because Boas was certain that the cultures in both regions faced extinction, he sent teams into many regions to collect artifacts, make observations, and record the local myths, stories, and histories.

In 1911 Boas tried to establish an American school of archaeology* and ethnology in Mexico. The Mexican Revolution, which had begun the previous year, doomed this effort to failure. However, Boas was able to

Voices from the Past

In 1897 Franz Boas wrote to the Native American Kwakiutl people of British Columbia to explain that one of the North Pacific Expedition's goals was to preserve things that might be lost to cultural change. "It is not good that . . . stories are forgotten," he wrote. "Friends, you are telling them from mouth to ear, and when your old men die they will be forgotten. It is good that you should have . . . a book that I have written on what I saw and heard when I was with you two years ago. It is a good book, for in it are your laws and your stories. Now they will not be forgotten."

* **archaeology** scientific study of material remains of past human cultures, usually by excavating ruins

introduce some of his anthropological methods to the school for the purposes of defining the sequence of cultures in the Valley of Mexico.

A New School of Anthropology

Between 1890 and 1925, anthropology took a new direction due largely to the efforts of Boas. He labored to make anthropology a true science, with demanding standards and a high degree of precision.

Overturning Old Ideas. In the late 1800s and early 1900s, most anthropologists agreed that the different races of human beings belonged to a single species. Not all of them believed, however, that the races were equally capable of cultural development. Before Boas's time, the main school of anthropological thought was the evolutionary school, which viewed human groups hierarchically, from lowest to highest. According to this view, some human cultures were considered primitive, and other, more highly evolved cultures, were civilized. Scholars in Europe and the United States dominated the study of anthropology at this time. Not surprisingly, the anthropologists who supported the evolutionary view of human culture tended to regard white Euro-American cultures as the most civilized. Other cultures were considered less civilized, or more primitive.

Boas did not set out specifically to destroy the evolutionary position in anthropology. Rather, he opposed any approach that began with a theory or preconception and then selected facts to fit that theory. He believed that only by careful and thorough collection of the facts could an anthropologist hope to understand a culture. Boas urged researchers to abandon their preconceived ideas about primitivism and civilization, about simplicity and complexity. Instead he encouraged them to ask critical questions: What standards of measurement do we use when we say that one culture is simple compared with another? How do we classify cultures that have simple technology but complex social organizations? How can an anthropologist study other cultures without being tainted by the prejudices and biases built into his own culture?

Boas's own fieldwork and research, combined with wide reading and study, led him to the conclusion that all human cultures are equally evolved, although in different ways. This position became known as cultural relativism, and it dominated anthropology, especially in the United States, for much of the 1900s.

Scientific Principles. Boas's most significant contributions to anthropology came from his desire to change the method of study from a set of comparisons and judgments shaped by the observers' own values into an exact science. Instead of adopting the evolutionary model, he called for anthropologists to use a historical approach. By plotting the elements of culture—language, folklore, myths, and customs—as they occurred geographically, he believed that an anthropologist could detect how different peoples adapted these elements to their own traditions.

From the resulting pattern, an anthropologist would be able to reconstruct the history of cultural development. Boas also believed that

Preservation or Exploitation?

Ever since Boas, anthropologists have tried to define their role. Are they guardians of vanishing cultural heritages, or merely outsiders using people's lives and creations for their own purposes? Researchers have been criticized for carrying off artifacts and for digging up the dead—as Boas did—to study skeletons and burial customs. Yet their work sometimes benefits the peoples they have studied. In recent years, several Siberian groups have used materials from the North Pacific Expedition to teach young people traditions and crafts that have almost vanished.

anthropologists could then demonstrate how elements had taken hold and been organized by various groups over time. Using these methods, Boas discovered that within a certain geographic area, some societies showed closely related elements. This suggested the existence of natural culture regions, such as that of the Native Americans of the Northwest Coast.

Boas's fundamental belief was that anthropologists could not simply assume or take for granted the laws by which cultures form, change, and influence individuals. An anthropologist has to discover these laws, and Boas believed that the historical approach offered the best tool with which to do so. However, he also recognized the limits of the scientific, historical approach. Unlike mathematics or physics, history is difficult to express in uncomplicated terms. Much of it can only be inferred or deduced from the evidence that existed.

Boas was convinced that an anthropologist's best approach is to collect as much information and to describe as many phenomena of human society as possible. He encouraged his fellow anthropologists to focus on what he believed were the most informative areas—language, folklore, myths, art, and physical characteristics.

Boas helped formulate some of the basic principles of modern anthropology. One is that all classifications are relative—something can be simple or complex only when compared with something else. Another is that an anthropologist must strive to avoid forcing his own values and categories of thought onto the culture being studied.

Major Contributions. In the course of laying out an entirely new approach to anthropology, Boas made many contributions to the field. One of these was his multiyear study of the Eskimo and Northwest Coast peoples. He established a close cultural relationship between the northern Native American peoples and those of Siberia—a relationship confirmed by modern DNA* testing. Boas believed that the Native Americans had crossed to North America from Asia using a land bridge that no longer exists. Modern scientists accept this as true, although they are still investigating the details of how the Americas were populated.

One of Boas's most influential books was *The Mind of Primitive Man,* published in 1911. A collection of his lectures on the subjects of race and culture, the work demonstrated that race, culture, and language are independent of one another. In other words, no race or ethnic group is naturally more or less developed or cultured than any other. During the 1920s, when the United States government restricted immigration based on presumed ethnic and racial differences, those opposed to such limits cited Boas's work as evidence that racial differences are nonexistent. This concept became increasingly unpopular in Boas's native Germany as the Nazis rose to power. Their philosophical and political ideas were based on notions of German (Aryan) racial superiority. During the 1930s the Nazis burned Boas's book and revoked his doctoral degree.

Another of Boas's important contributions was in the field of anthropometrics, which he had studied under Virchow. Boas was the first scientist to launch studies of human growth in North America, and he produced the first chart of standard heights and weights for American children according to age.

* **DNA** deoxyribonucleic acid, the material in chromosomes that carries genetic information from ancestor to offspring

Boas was also one of the first anthropologists to recognize that an individual's experience and knowledge as a member of a particular society is an important subject for scientific investigation. Under his guidance, his students Ruth Benedict and Margaret Mead began to break new ground in studying how culture influenced personality. Other students made significant progress in the study of folklore, linguistics, and anthropology. His influence on two generations of anthropologists was perhaps his greatest contribution to the field.

Boas is widely recognized and honored as one of the leading scientific figures of his day. He belonged to many American and European anthropological associations and served as president of the American Anthropological Association, the New York Academy of Science, the American Folklore Society, and the American Academy for the Advancement of Science. He edited the *Journal of American Folklore* from 1908 to 1924. He also made significant contributions to the field of linguistics. He edited the *Handbook of American Indian Linguistics* from 1911 to 1941. In it, he outlined methods for linguistic research. In 1917 he founded the *International Journal of American Linguistics*, which he maintained with personal funds and edited until his death in 1942.

Jules BORDET

1870–1961

BACTERIOLOGY, IMMUNOLOGY

* **antibody** protein produced by the immune system to neutralize the presence of a foreign protein in the body

* **serum** clear liquid that separates from the blood after the blood cells clot

The Belgian scientist Jules Bordet made important discoveries about how bacteria are destroyed in the blood of immunized animals. His studies enabled him and others to identify specific types of bacteria and to develop vaccines to combat their harmful effects.

The son of a schoolteacher, Bordet received his M.D. in his early 20s. In 1894 he won a scholarship to the Pasteur Institute in Paris, France, where he conducted a series of experiments on the mechanics of bacteriolysis, the destruction of bacterial cells. He injected the bacteria that cause cholera into the abdomens of mammals and noticed that the immune systems in the animals created particles called antibodies* in response to the antigen (foreign bacteria) in their bodies. When he heated the animals' blood serum* to temperatures greater than 55°C, the serum lost its ability to dissolve or destroy the bacteria, and the antibodies, although ineffective, remained in the system. Bordet found that it was possible to destroy the antigen by adding fresh, unheated serum with antibodies to the heated serum.

He concluded that bacteriolysis required two substances. One—the antibody—is specific to the antigen. He called it the sensibilizer. The other is a nonspecific substance found in all serum that does not become unstable even when heated. He called the second substance the complement. Bordet showed that the same process that destroyed bacteria destroyed the body's healthy red blood cells—a major factor in disease.

This work made Bordet famous. In 1901 he founded and became director of a new research institute in Brussels, Belgium, called the Pasteur Institute of Brabant. There he demonstrated that when antibodies unite with antigens to form a new complex particle, this particle combines with the complement in serum. Once the complement is captured, it cannot contribute to the destruction of red blood cells. This was an important diagnostic aid because knowledge of the presence of either the antigen or the antibody could be used to identify the other agent.

Working with his brother-in-law, Octave Gengou, Bordet used his discoveries to identify specific antibodies and antigens. This information was essential for vaccines to combat certain diseases. Their study of serum enabled the two scientists to identify the bacteria that cause typhoid fever, hog cholera, and other diseases. They also prepared a vaccine for whooping cough. A few years later, other scientists used their procedure to make a vaccine for syphilis, a sexually transmitted disease.

Bordet then devoted himself to the study of blood clotting, while also directing the Institute. He rose to the top of his field, winning the Nobel Prize in physiology* or medicine in 1919. The next year, he wrote a summary of current knowledge in the field of immunology*. He also began to study bacteriophages, substances that destroy bacteria. Other scientists identified these as viruses, but Bordet wrongly believed them to be toxins rather than organisms. Bordet continued his study of bacteriophages as the director of the Pasteur Institute until he retired in 1940.

* **physiology** science that deals with the functions of living organisms and their parts

* **immunology** science that deals with the immune system, which protects the body from foreign substances, cells, and tissue by causing an immune response

Emma Lucy
BRAUN

1889–1971

BOTANY, PLANT ECOLOGY, CONSERVATION

Emma Lucy Braun—or "Dr. Lucy" as she was known to her colleagues and students—was an original and dedicated scientist in the fields of plant ecology and botany. She fought to protect and preserve the forests and prairies of Ohio and Kentucky. As a botanist, she tirelessly studied and cataloged plant life in detail.

Braun was born in Cincinnati, Ohio, and was educated at a local school, where her father was the principal and her mother a teacher. Encouraged by her mother, Braun began an extensive collection of plant specimens. She received a Ph.D. in botany from the University of Cincinnati in 1914 and taught there as a professor for the rest of her career. Braun and her sister, Annette, lived together their whole lives, making a room of their house into a laboratory and transforming the lawn into an experimental garden.

Braun's scientific work took her throughout the Appalachian Mountain regions of Ohio and Kentucky. In 1934 she published a meticulous description of the flora that existed around Cincinnati both at that time and 100 years earlier. This work became a model for comparing changes in regional flora over time. In 1950 Braun's studies led to her landmark publication, *Deciduous Forests of Eastern North America.*

In addition to her fieldwork, Braun actively supported the national movement to conserve wilderness areas from destruction. She wrote many papers and articles to support forest preservation. Because of her efforts, the National Park Service and the state of Ohio have designated thousands of acres of wooded land for conservation.

A leader in her field and her community, Braun was the first woman to serve as president of the Ohio Academy of Science and the Ecological Society of America. She remained active, leading field trips and presenting public lectures, until her death due to heart failure at the age of 81.

David
BRUCE

MICROBIOLOGY

Mary Bruce's Contribution

David Bruce's wife, Mary, was a capable and resourceful partner in his medical research. Before they left for Africa, she learned the latest techniques for using a microscope and other laboratory skills so that she could help in his work. She assisted him in their laboratory in Zululand, and during the Boer War she was a nurse in his operating theater—work that won her a Royal Red Cross. She died four days before her husband. On his deathbed Bruce requested that his wife's assistance be emphasized in any accounts of his life.

* **corpuscle** blood cell
* **platelet** minute particle in blood that assists in clotting

David Bruce spent his career in Great Britain's Army Medical Service and Royal Army Medical Corps. He became famous for his research into the cause and control of two deadly diseases—Malta fever on the Mediterranean island of Malta and trypanosomiasis in Africa.

Shaping a Medical Career. David Bruce was born in Melbourne, Australia, to a Scottish couple who went to that continent during the gold rush of the early 1850s. When he was five years old, the family returned to Scotland and settled in Stirling. Bruce attended high school until the age of 14 and then worked in a warehouse. He was strong and healthy and dreamed of becoming a professional athlete, but when he was 17, he suffered an attack of pneumonia that weakened him, ending those dreams. He returned to school and entered the University of Edinburgh in 1876.

Bruce became interested in ornithology, the scientific study of birds, and planned to study zoology. After one year at the university, however, he was convinced by a physician friend to study medicine. He left the university in 1881 and went to work assisting a doctor in the town of Reigate, where he met and married Mary Elizabeth Steele.

Conquering Malta Fever. Bruce discovered that he did not care for general medical practice, so in 1883 he joined the Army Medical Service with the rank of surgeon captain. The following year he was sent to Malta, a Mediterranean island where the army maintained troops.

Bruce decided to investigate Malta fever, a disease whose symptoms included sweating, weakness, and body pains. The disease caused about 100 British soldiers to be hospitalized each year for an average of three months each. Because the hospital where Bruce was stationed had no research laboratory, he brought in a microscope and began examining tissue from the spleens of sick patients. In adults, the spleen acts as a storage organ for red blood corpuscles* and platelets*, and as a filter for blood. In 1887 he announced that he had isolated the microorganism that caused Malta fever. Years later the microorganism and its close relatives were named *Brucella*, in honor of Bruce. Malta fever and other diseases caused by these organisms, such as Mediterranean fever and undulant fever, were renamed brucellosis.

Two years later Bruce left Malta, but in 1905, he returned to the island as the head of a 12-person commission to study the fever, which continued to plague the soldiers stationed there. No one knew how this fever was transmitted or how to prevent it. A member of Bruce's commission proposed that the disease microorganisms were carried in goat's milk. After goat's milk was eliminated from the soldiers' diet, they noticed that the disease disappeared.

African Researches. Between his two periods of work on Malta, Bruce conducted medical research in Zululand in South Africa, and in Uganda in East Africa. Great Britain controlled both regions and hoped to bring under control certain widespread African diseases that affected people and livestock and interfered with its colonization efforts.

In addition to his experience from his stay in Malta, Bruce gained knowledge and expertise at the Army Medical School in Netley, England,

* **bacteriological** related to the study of bacteria, microscopic organisms that can cause infection and disease

where he practiced and taught the methods of bacteriological* experimentation, a field pioneered by such prominent scientists as Louis Pasteur and Joseph Lister. In 1894 the army sent Bruce to Natal, a British province in South Africa, to investigate a disease called nagana that was affecting cattle in northern Zululand.

Bruce and his wife traveled for five weeks by ox wagon to reach the settlement of Ubombo, where they set up a laboratory on the porch of their hut. After his initial examinations of infected cattle, Bruce suspected bacterial infection, but he found nothing in their blood to support this suspicion. Eventually he discovered a moving, vibrating microorganism that he determined was a trypanosome, a type of microscopic one-celled animal that lives in larger animals and usually enters the host through an insect bite. (It is similar to the organism that causes malaria in humans.)

Bruce and his wife spent almost two years in their isolated hut. He published the results of his research in papers that described the trypanosome and established the tsetse fly as its carrier. He suggested that wild game animals, such as antelope and buffalo, which were immune to nagana infection, served as reservoirs for the disease.

In 1899 the Boer War, a conflict between the British and the descendants of earlier Dutch settlers in South Africa, interrupted Bruce's research. During the war he directed a hospital and performed surgery. In 1901 Bruce and his wife returned to Great Britain.

They again traveled to Africa in 1903 after Bruce had been chosen to head a commission to investigate sleeping sickness, a disease that claimed many human victims in Uganda. Although other researchers had already

Although considered by some colleagues to be abrupt, blunt, and egotistical, David Bruce devoted his talent and energy to improving public health. "The advance of knowledge," he said, "is not for the benefit of any one country, but for all."

discovered trypanosomes in the blood of fever patients in various regions in Africa, no one yet suspected a connection between these fevers and Ugandan sleeping sickness. Aldo Castellani, a doctor who had been working in Uganda before Bruce's arrival, was added to the commission. He was the first physician to propose that trypanosomes caused sleeping sickness in humans. Castellani taught Bruce the technique of drawing fluid from patients' spines and examining the fluid for trypanosomes. By the time Bruce returned to England later the same year, sleeping sickness was recognized as a form of trypanosomiasis, a disease caused by trypanosomes.

After his second period of work in Malta, Bruce returned to Uganda in 1908. He spent two years researching methods to control the spread of sleeping sickness which, like nagana, is carried by the tsetse fly. Afterward, he spent two years investigating sleeping sickness in Nyasaland, the present-day nation of Malawi.

Bruce was knighted in 1908 and received many other honors from universities and learned societies around the world, including fellowships in the Royal Society of England and the Royal College of Physicians of London. He also received honorary doctorates from the Universities of Glasgow, Liverpool, Dublin, and Toronto. From 1914 until 1919 he was commandant of the Royal Medical College. During World War I he directed research in a number of diseases, such as tetanus* and trench fever, which affected soldiers. In his later years, because he suffered from frequent lung infections, he spent his winters in the warmer climate of the Portuguese island of Madeira. He died of cancer in London at the age of 77.

* **tetanus** infectious disease marked by contractions of the voluntary muscles; also known as lockjaw

Keith
CAMPBELL

born 1955

CELL BIOLOGY, EMBRYOLOGY

* **embryologist** scientist who studies the development of an egg and sperm into an embryo, an organism at the early stages of development before birth or hatching

* **microbiology** study of microscopic organisms

* **DNA** deoxyribonucleic acid, the material in chromosomes that carries genetic information from ancestor to offspring

Keith Campbell, a British embryologist* and cell biologist, was a key member of the team that achieved one of the major breakthroughs of the 1990s—cloning. As a member of the group headed by the Scotsman Ian WILMUT at the Roslin Institute in Scotland, Campbell helped develop and use the techniques that made cloning possible. The result was a sheep named Dolly—the first mammal to be cloned from the cell of a fully developed adult mammal.

Campbell was born and raised in Birmingham, England. After he graduated from high school, he worked as a medical technician but was bored with the work. He moved to London to study microbiology* at Queen Elizabeth College in London, and he went on to earn a doctorate from the University of Sussex.

In 1991 Campbell joined Wilmut at the Roslin Institute to work on cloning. At that time, however, work on cloning had come to a standstill. Most biologists were convinced that it was impossible because once an egg is fertilized, it differentiates, or divides into the specialized cells that eventually make up the different tissues of an organism, such as muscle, brain, and skin. Therefore, any adult cell DNA* that a researcher used for cloning would have to be able to reverse its differentiation (specialization) to express *all* the genes that were active when it was still an embryo, and not just those it had expressed in becoming specialized cells, such as those of the nerves, muscles, or tissues.

When scientists attempted to clone organisms such as frogs and mice, the resulting animals did not live very long. In other cases, they were unable to reproduce the same result in later experiments. Wilmut had heard that Steen Willadsen, a Danish embryologist, had successfully produced clones from differentiated embryo cells from cattle but had not reported his results. (An embryo is an animal at the early stages of development before birth or hatching.) The news convinced Wilmut and Campbell that cloning animals from differentiated cells might be worth investigating.

Wilmut and Campbell developed a process in which they transferred the nucleus of a mature cell into an egg cell whose genetic* material had been removed. (An organism's chromosomes* are located in the nuclei of its cells and contain all the genetic information necessary for development.) They believed that the egg cell would then undergo successive divisions and develop into a genetic replica of the organism from which the mature cell had been obtained. But they encountered a problem. Because cells are continually undergoing a cycle of growth and division, the chromosomes of the parent cell are copied and distributed to the new cells it generates. They had to find a way to ensure that the mature cell from which the genetic material was taken and the egg cell to which it was transferred were in the same stage in the cycle of cell division.

Campbell, who had written his doctoral thesis on the cell cycle, devised a solution to this problem. He knew that if cells do not receive adequate nutrients, they enter a stage known as G0, or gap zero, in which all cellular activity is suspended. He was also aware that egg cells enter that stage after fertilization to incorporate the new genetic material they had just received. Campbell reasoned that if he could get the donor cells to enter the G0 state, he could ensure that the egg cell would divide without interference to its chromosomes.

Wilmut and Campbell used this technique to transfer genetic material from sheep embryo cells to fertilized egg cells whose genetic material had been removed. In 1995 their attempts succeeded and they cloned two sheep, Megan and Morag. During the six-week period preceding the lambs' birth, Campbell slept on the floor of his office at the Roslin Institute so that he could monitor the pregnant ewes on an hourly basis.

The following year, Wilmut and Campbell published their results, but their paper received only modest attention because they were working with embryos and not mature cells. This prompted them to investigate the more difficult possibility of cloning sheep from the differentiated cells of a fully developed sheep, not merely the partially differentiated cells of an embryo.

Campbell was confident that they would succeed. He knew that differentiated cells did not express all the genes contained in their chromosomes because certain proteins inhibited (repressed) nearly 90 percent of those genes. Consequently, only the genes necessary for the cell to exist as a specialized tissue in a particular part of an organism were active. Campbell used a technique that he believed could force those proteins to unbind from the DNA in the chromosomes, freeing the cell's genetic material to serve as the basis for generating a new organism with the same genes. In 1996 Wilmut and Campbell fused the genetic material of sheep udder cells

* **genetic** relating to genes, the basic units of heredity that carry traits from ancestors to offspring

* **chromosome** structure in the cell that contains the DNA (genes) that transmit unique genetic information

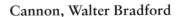

with sheep egg cells. They succeeded in making one embryo undergo development out of their 277 attempts. On July 5, 1996, Dolly, the first animal to be cloned from a mature, fully differentiated cell of another animal, was born.

Since cloning Dolly, Wilmut and Campbell have further advanced cloning techniques. In 1997 they cloned Polly, a sheep whose genetic material was altered to contain a human gene. Three years later Campbell accepted a professorship at Nottingham University and moved his laboratory there. His goal is to find applications for cloning technology in human medicine. He continues to work on understanding the mechanisms that lead to embryonic development and cellular differentiation.

Walter Bradford CANNON

1871–1945

PHYSIOLOGY

* **physiology** science that deals with the functions of living organisms and their parts

* **hormone** internally secreted substance transported by body fluids to stimulate the functions of organs or tissues

* **traumatic shock** disturbances in the body's circulation and metabolism in response to severe physical injury

* **sympathetic nervous system** part of the nervous system that excites the body, increasing breathing and pulse rate to prepare an animal to fight or flee danger

* **neurology** study of the structure, function, and disorders of the nervous system

The American scientist Walter Bradford Cannon was the first person to use X rays in the study of the physiology* of digestion. Cannon's early work was dominated by his studies on digestion, but he later turned to studies of the nervous system and the ways in which bodily functions are controlled by hormones*. He worked on treatments for traumatic shock* and engaged in investigations of the sympathetic nervous system*, demonstrating the manner in which internal organs are affected during periods of stress. A believer in the universality of science, Cannon linked his work in science to the conviction that scientists had an obligation to defend freedom, an essential element for productive scholarship and research.

Early Life and Education. Cannon was born in Prairie du Chien, Wisconsin. His father, a railroad worker, and his mother, a schoolteacher, were descendants of early settlers in colonial Massachusetts. Cannon attended primary and grammar schools in Milwaukee, Wisconsin, and St. Paul, Minnesota. Because Cannon did not work hard in school, his father put him to work in a railroad office at age 14. Cannon worked at the job for two years before returning to school. His experience with a dull railroad job stimulated him to take high school seriously. He finished the four-year course in three years and graduated first in his class.

One of Cannon's high school English teachers persuaded him to apply to Harvard College in Cambridge, Massachusetts, and helped him obtain financial aid to attend the school. The assistance was especially important because Cannon's family could not afford a college education. Cannon became interested in the biological sciences. He studied under influential teachers including the well-known philosopher and psychologist William James and the zoologist George Henry Parker. Cannon graduated from Harvard in 1896 and received a master's degree from the college the following year.

Cannon at Medical School. While at Harvard, Cannon had also become interested in neurology* and psychology, subjects he hoped to pursue in medical school. He wished to attend Johns Hopkins Medical School in Baltimore, Maryland, but his letters requesting financial aid went unanswered by the school officials. Instead he enrolled in Harvard Medical School in 1896.

Although Walter Cannon performed path-breaking research in several fields—including radiology, gastroenterology, neurophysiology, pharmacology, endocrinology, and psychology—he is best described as a physiologist. He was a valued member of many professional organizations and the recipient of several honors.

At Harvard, Cannon worked with the biologist Charles Davenport, from whom he gained considerable insight into the nature of scientific research. Cannon wrote his first research paper, titled "On the Determination of the Direction and Rate of Movement of Organisms by Light," with Davenport. These research experiences led him into the physiology laboratory, where Henry Pickering Bowditch, a professor of physiology, suggested that Cannon and another student, Albert Moser, use X rays to examine the mechanism of swallowing. X rays had been discovered only a year earlier by German physicist Wilhelm Röntgen, and this marked the first time that they were used to study a physiological phenomenon.

Cannon and Moser devised an experiment in which they observed the passage of gelatin (gummy material obtained from animal tissues) capsules through the throat of a frog and a goose. Soon after this investigation, the process was presented at a meeting of the American Physiological Society. This was the first public demonstration of movements of the digestive tract using the new X-ray method.

As a student Cannon was not only an innovator in research but also in medical education. In the late 1890s medical students had to sit through long hours of lectures each day. The experience made Cannon question the effectiveness of the lecture method. Observing the eagerness and zest with which law students discussed and argued legal cases, he believed that this approach could also work for medical students. In 1900 Cannon developed a case method for medicine, using printed data from actual case histories gathered from various hospitals. The data were to be studied and analyzed by students and discussed in detail at a conference with the instructor. The method was enthusiastically adopted by the various departments of the medical school.

During his final year as a medical student, Cannon taught comparative anatomy to undergraduate students. After receiving his M.D. he accepted a position as instructor of physiology at Harvard Medical School and was promoted to assistant professor in 1902. Cannon was a popular teacher and students responded positively to his teaching methods. In 1906 Cannon received an offer to move to Cornell Medical School in Ithaca, New York. In response Harvard offered him a position as full professor and head of the physiology department. Cannon accepted the offer from Harvard and remained chair of the department until his retirement in 1942.

Medical Researcher. After his new appointment Cannon continued his studies of the gastrointestinal* tract. His principal tool was the fluoroscope, an instrument that adapts X-ray technology for viewing the internal structures of bodies. He studied swallowing, contraction, and relaxation of the digestive tract as well as the time it takes various foods to pass from the stomach into the intestines. In 1911 Cannon summarized this work in the first of his influential books, *The Mechanical Factors of Digestion.* Cannon's research also laid the groundwork for the development of gastrointestinal radiology*.

Cannon's research did not always develop in a straightforward manner. It often emerged from chance observations that other investigators might have ignored. For example, during his investigations into digestion, he noticed that movements in the animals' stomach and intestines stopped when they became excited. These observations stimulated Cannon to study the effect of strong emotions on bodily functions and disease states—studies that led to an examination of the sympathetic nervous system, the part of the nervous system that responds involuntarily and excites the body. He summarized his findings in *Bodily Changes in Pain, Hunger, Fear and Rage,* published in 1915.

Cannon argued that during emergencies—such as those created by pain, cold, emotional stress, or injury—the adrenal gland releases a substance that helps the body react to and deal with the problem. Initially some physiologists criticized Cannon's idea, but they were more receptive when he was able to offer experimental proof to support his claims.

Further Studies. In 1916 the National Research Council named Cannon a member of a committee on traumatic shock. When the United States entered World War I, he went to Europe and arranged to join a group of physicians and surgeons who were dealing with soldiers suffering from shock as result of their injuries. In 1923 he reported his findings in a book titled *Traumatic Shock.*

After the war Cannon returned to his investigation on the sympathetic nervous system and studied heart action as an indicator of sympathetic nerve activity. His extraordinary skill as a surgeon enabled him to remove the entire sympathetic nervous system from the body. This procedure led

* **gastrointestinal** relating to or affecting the stomach and intestines

* **radiology** branch of medicine that uses radiant energy, in the form of X rays and radium, to diagnose and treat disease

to a series of studies that continued for almost ten years and showed that the function of the autonomic sympathetic nervous system is to maintain a uniform condition in internal bodily fluids and to control involuntary actions. Cannon called this condition homeostasis, from Greek words meaning "similar" and "condition." His work paralleled research that had been done by the French physiologist Claude Bernard in the 1800s and had led to the development of the concept of the internal environment *(milieu intérieur)*.

Cannon extended his findings on homeostasis to other physiological functions. He concluded that an organism automatically adjusts its internal mechanisms when threatened with a disturbance that endangers its equilibrium. In 1926, at a meeting of the Congress of American Physicians, he developed this idea further, proposing that certain physiological factors help maintain steady states within the body. These ideas were the basis of his widely read book *The Wisdom of the Body,* published in 1932.

Beginning in the 1930s, Cannon and his colleagues began to devote their attention to the study of chemical transmission of nerve impulses. Their work resulted in pioneering advances in physiology, including the idea of the existence of two substances in the nerves—one that excites (activates) impulses in the nervous system and the other that inhibits (stops) them. Later research identified these substances as the hormones epinephrine (adrenaline) and norepinephrine (noradrenaline).

Fight or Flight

In his studies of the nervous system, Cannon helped explain the mechanism now known as "fight or flight." When faced with danger, stress, or other threatening situation, humans and animals respond by fighting the danger or fleeing from it. As the body prepares for "fight or flight," the heart rate and blood pressure increase, the lungs enhance the breathing rate to put more oxygen into the blood, and the blood sugar concentrates. The pupils of the eye enlarge and various glands release chemical substances to help the body cope with the situation at hand. All of these responses are triggered automatically by the nervous system to prepare for an emergency, whether real or imagined.

Cannon and Russia. Cannon's work on digestion took him to Russia and the school of physiology founded by Ivan PAVLOV. Familiar with each other's research, Pavlov and Cannon became friends. In 1935 Cannon visited Moscow to attend the International Physiological Congress, where he spoke out on the relation of freedom to scientific research.

In 1937 Cannon refused an offer of the presidency of the American Russian Institute, largely because he wished to avoid political arguments. But he continued to express his ideas about political freedom and scientific research. In 1943, during World War II, Cannon became president of the American-Soviet Medical Society, the purpose of which was to organize the exchange of medical information between the United States and the Soviet Union.

Cannon and Spain. Cannon also had strong ties with the medical and scientific community in Spain. Some individuals had trained with him at Harvard, while others had become his friends during a visit to Spain in 1930. His interest in Spain was motivated by the same concerns that shaped his interest in Russia—a concern with the development of science.

When the monarchy of Spain was overthrown and a republic formed in 1931, Cannon considered the event a triumph for freedom. Soon after, however, the Spanish Civil War erupted and threatened to topple the newly established Spanish republic, an extension of the spread of political ideas from Europe. In 1936 Cannon joined a group of distinguished American physicians in organizing the Medical Bureau to Aid Spanish Democracy. The purpose of this organization was to help the women, children, and elderly of Spain during wartime. Because of his involvement with the bureau, Cannon was caught up in bitter political controversies,

Carrel, Alexis

* **Communist** referring to Communism, a social system in which land, goods, and the means of production are owned by the state or community rather than by individuals

especially when many newspapers and journals declared that the bureau was a Communist* organization and that Cannon was a Communist.

Despite the criticism, Cannon worked tirelessly to help the Spanish loyalists—those who supported the republic. He spoke at rallies and persuaded pharmaceutical companies to send drugs and materials to Spain. In 1937 when the U.S. State Department banned nurses and physicians from offering their services, Cannon joined a protest of intellectuals that led to a change in that policy.

In 1939, however, the loyalists were defeated and Cannon directed his efforts to rescuing scientists and physicians who had fought in the war. He found positions for many of them at universities in the United States and in South America. These activities were later broadened to include physicians and scientists whose lives and careers were threatened by the Nazis in Germany and Austria, as well as Chinese scientists who had been uprooted by war between China and Japan. In 1935 Cannon had traveled to China to work at the Peking Union Medical College, and subsequently he was involved in the formation of the American Bureau for Medical Aid to China.

Later Life. When World War II began, Cannon again devoted himself to the problems of traumatic shock. This time, however, he did not act as a scientific investigator. Instead he served as head of the Committee on Shock and Transfusion of the National Research Council. The organization helped develop methods to separate and preserve blood, which was very important in the prevention and treatment of traumatic shock.

In 1942 Cannon retired from Harvard Medical School. He served briefly as a visiting professor at the New York University Medical School and conducted research in Mexico. By this time his health was failing, largely because of illnesses related to his early research with X rays. He had been diagnosed with mycosis fungoides, a disease caused by overexposure to X rays, which took his life in 1945.

During his lifetime, Cannon received many honors. He was elected to several learned scientific societies including the American Philosophical Society, the National Academy of Sciences, and England's Royal Society. He also received numerous medals and honorary degrees.

Alexis
CARREL
1873–1944
SURGERY, EXPERIMENTAL BIOLOGY

* **physiology** science that deals with the functions of living organisms and their parts

Alexis Carrel pioneered techniques used in heart surgery and in organ and tissue transplants. His achievements, which include a method of repairing cut or torn blood vessels, earned him the 1912 Nobel Prize in physiology* or medicine.

Carrel was born and educated in Lyons, France. As a youth his interest in dissecting birds demonstrated his aptitude for biology. Encouraged by an uncle, Carrel also experimented with chemistry. In 1890 he entered the University of Lyons as a medical student. Three years later he began to work at various hospitals in the city and became interested in anatomy and surgery. He received his medical degree in 1900.

By that time, Carrel had been working for about six years on problems connected with surgery on the blood vessels. He may have been influenced

in his work by the circumstances surrounding the death of French president Sadi Carnot, who was shot by an assassin. The bullet cut one of Carnot's major arteries—a type of wound that doctors at the time could not repair. Carrel perfected suturing—a method of using very fine needles to sew together the ends of torn blood vessels. He coated his needles, thread, and instruments with paraffin jelly to prevent the blood from clotting and blocking the vessel, and he practiced strict cleanliness to avoid infection. He announced his first success with this method in 1902.

Two years later Carrel traveled to the United States, where he taught physiology at the University of Chicago. Later he joined the Rockefeller Institute for Medical Research (now Rockefeller University) in New York, where he continued to perform experimental surgeries on blood vessels. By applying his methods to difficult surgeries, such as kidney transplants in animals, he gained a reputation for his surgical skill, original techniques, and bold experimentation. He also laid the foundation for later progress in heart and blood vessel surgeries and in organ transplants.

Prompted by his early successes with organ transplants, Carrel began to dream of growing human tissues and organs to replace diseased or damaged parts. Using heart tissue from chick embryos*, he experimented with ways of keeping tissue alive outside the body. One such specimen remained alive for many years, outliving Carrel himself. His work also inspired later scientists to grow virus cultures* in animal cells and to make vaccines.

During World War I, Carrel returned to France and directed a hospital and research center near the front lines in that country. His wife assisted him as a surgical nurse. During this time, working with a chemist named Henry A. Dakin, Carrel developed a method for preventing infection in severe wounds—bathing the wounds with an antiseptic solution. Antibiotic drugs later replaced this technique.

Carrel later began a research program aimed at maintaining entire organs outside the body. Using a sterilized glass pump invented by American aviator Charles Lindbergh, Carrel was able to keep organs alive for days or weeks—a milestone in the advancement of modern surgical equipment. This was a pioneer step in the development of an apparatus used today in surgery of the heart and great vessels.

In a widely read book, *Man the Unknown,* published in 1935, Carrel speculated about the future of the human race and the benefits that scientific enlightenment could bring, including freedom from disease, long life, and spiritual advancement. During World War II he returned to Paris, where he ran a research institute. He died of heart failure during the war.

* **embryo** organism at the early stages of development before birth or hatching

* **culture** microorganisms, such as bacteria or tissue, grown in a specially prepared nutrient substance for scientific study

Rachel Louise CARSON

1907–1964

ECOLOGY, NATURAL HISTORY,
MARINE BIOLOGY

Rachel Louise Carson was a marine biologist who achieved fame as the author of several popular books on scientific subjects. Her best-known work is *Silent Spring,* which alerted the public to the environmental damage caused by the unrestricted use of pesticides. *Silent Spring* became one of the most influential books of its time and served as an important stimulus for the organized environmental movement in the United States.

Early Life and Career. Carson grew up on a farm in Pennsylvania as the youngest child in a family that experienced financial difficulties. During her childhood, she spent much of her time in the woods near her home and developed a great affection for animals and the natural world. The young Carson also enjoyed writing, and a children's magazine recognized her talent by publishing a story that she wrote at the age of ten. The article won a prize called the Silver Badge, which Carson later called the greatest joy of her publishing career. The same magazine bought two more of her stories the following year, which encouraged her to study writing. Despite her family's financial problems, Carson was able to attend Pennsylvania College for Women (now Chatham College) with the help of a scholarship. She studied English and biology and graduated in 1928 with high honors.

The following summer, Carson began to work at the Marine Biological Laboratory in Woods Hole, Massachusetts. There she saw the ocean for the first time, beginning her lifelong fascination with the sea. She enrolled in graduate school at Johns Hopkins University in Baltimore, Maryland, and earned her master's degree in zoology in 1932. For the next five years, she taught at Johns Hopkins and the University of Maryland while writing articles for the *Baltimore Sun* newspaper. Her father died when Carson was 28, and she was forced to support her widowed mother. At that time the country was in the worst period of the Great Depression, and money was scarce. To supplement her income, Carson began to write public information materials for the United States Bureau of Fisheries on a

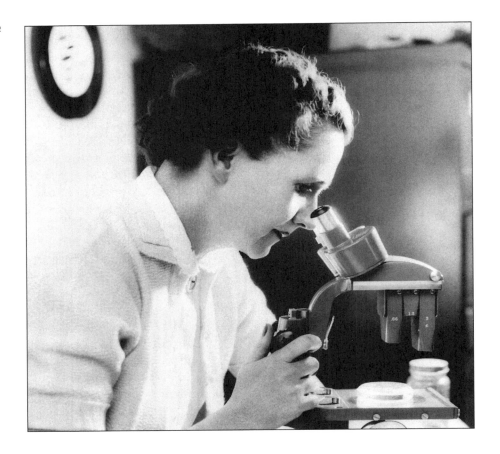

Rachel Carson published her first story at the age of ten in the same magazine that introduced the works of such writers as William Faulkner, F. Scott Fitzgerald, and E.B. White. She enrolled in college intending to study literature, but a biology course awakened her "sense of wonder" and she changed her major to zoology and became a marine biologist.

part-time basis. A year later her sister died, leaving her two children in Carson's care. Fortunately, the following year, the Division of Scientific Inquiry was looking for a full-time junior aquatic biologist. Carson was the only woman to take the civil service examination, and she won the job after receiving the highest score.

Professional Writer and Researcher. Carson's duties in her new job included writing radio broadcast texts, pamphlets, and reports on fisheries research and oceanography*. One of her earliest assignments was to write a script for a radio program about the sea. Although the piece caught the attention of her supervisor, he rejected it because he considered it too literary. But he recognized the quality of the work and encouraged her to send it to *Atlantic Monthly* magazine. The article, which explained how animals live in the ocean, was published in 1937 with the title "Undersea." An editor for a large publishing house read the article and encouraged Carson to expand it to a book. A few years later Carson published her first book—*Under the Sea-Wind.* Unlike most scientific books of the time, *Under the Sea-Wind* explored the habits and lives of sea creatures in a very personal manner. Its main theme was that all species are dependent on each other and the environment around them. The book was published just before the United States entered World War II and, perhaps as a result, did not sell well despite favorable reviews.

Around the same time as the publication of *Under the Sea-Wind,* Carson transferred to the information section of the Fish and Wildlife Service, which had been created when the Bureau of Fisheries merged with the Biological Survey. During World War II, Carson's duties at the Fish and Wildlife Service focused on producing public service information. She wrote pieces explaining how to prepare meals with fish, and she promoted the conservation of some species of edible fish. In 1949 she was promoted to the position of editor in chief and was responsible for developing and promoting programs on oceanography, conservation, and the service's new wildlife refuge network. Near the end of the war, she asked *Reader's Digest* magazine to run a story about the effects of the insecticide DDT. The editors rejected the idea, but the subject later became the focus of Carson's greatest success as a writer and scientist.

In the late 1940s, Carson won the Eugene F. Saxton Memorial Fellowship, which enabled her to take a leave of absence to pursue writing. The result, *The Sea Around Us,* was a book that traced the origin and history of the oceans and explored the ecological relations between the environment and marine and human life. Chapters appeared in the *New Yorker* magazine, and when the book was released in 1951, it became an instant best-seller. It stayed on the best-seller list for 86 weeks and won the National Book Award and the John Burroughs Medal. *The Sea Around Us* made Carson famous, earning her honorary doctoral degrees and creating a demand for her as a lecturer. She also won a Guggenheim fellowship for another book, which gave her the financial freedom to leave her job and write full-time.

Her next book was *The Edge of the Sea,* another best-seller about the natural history of seashore life. Writing this work took Carson along the

* **oceanography** science that deals with oceans and marine biology

eastern coast of the United States, and she fell so much in love with Maine that she bought a summer home there. *The Edge of the Sea* stayed on the best-seller list for 20 weeks and earned Carson awards and recognition. Although Carson's writing brought her fame, she did not adopt the life of a celebrity. She lived quietly at home, caring for her mother and grand-nephew and corresponding with professional writers and scientists.

For the next few years, Carson spent her time working on smaller projects. These included the script for a television program as well as articles for nonscientific magazines. One of the articles, titled "Help Your Child to Wonder," was based on her personal experiences. The article urged parents to encourage their children's explorations of the natural world. She argued that one does not need scientific training to observe the world around oneself, just the appreciation for beauty that every child possesses. After her death the article was expanded to book length and published under the title *The Sense of Wonder*.

Silver Screen Success

Although most people knew of Rachel Carson through her writing, many learned of her work through film. One of her best-selling books, *The Edge of the Sea,* was adapted as a motion picture by RKO Radio Studios. However, the film took many liberties with facts and had scientific inaccuracies. Despite the studio's distortion and romanticizing of the subject (or maybe because of it), the movie won the 1953 Academy Award for best full-length documentary.

Investigation of Pesticide Use. One of the people with whom Carson corresponded regularly was a woman in Massachusetts named Olga Owens Huckins. In 1958 Owens wrote to Carson about the destruction of her bird sanctuary caused by excessive use of the insecticide DDT. Despite increasingly poor health, Carson plunged ahead with research into the subject. Her reputation influenced many well-respected biologists, chemists, and other scientists to help her in her work. Over the course of four years, she compiled a large body of evidence that showed that chemical contamination had affected the earth's ecological balance. Among other things, she uncovered groundwater contamination by pesticides and high concentrations of chemicals in animals high up the food chain. She also recognized that the widespread use of pesticides was reducing the number of natural predators and increasing the rate at which pests developed resistance to such pesticides.

The resulting book, *Silent Spring,* first appeared as a series of articles in the *New Yorker* magazine. It was the object of attacks from the agricultural and chemical industries even before it was published in book form. Although Carson did not oppose all pesticide use, her opponents characterized her as an environmental fanatic who was against pest control. Carson countered by arguing that she objected to the reckless use of pesticides without regard to the effects it might have on the environment and the natural ecological balance. Nevertheless, her opponents criticized the book as biased, unscientific, and factually incorrect. Controversy surrounded the book, even though its arguments were based on sound principles advanced by respected scientists and the book itself contained a 50-page section of scientific sources.

Several months after the book appeared, the CBS television network aired a program called "The Silent Spring of Rachel Carson." On the show, Carson spoke against a representative of the chemical industry. She displayed a calm, rational, and scientific approach that won her many fans and made pesticide use a national issue. That year she won a host of awards for *Silent Spring* and was elected into the American Academy of Arts and Sciences. This book was another best-seller that had as much

There she found strong support from her professors, and she excelled in her studies of biology.

Research into Skin Cancer. Cobb pursued graduate work at New York University. She then conducted research at several hospitals and universities in Illinois and New York. Her work at these institutions showed that the chemicals that destroyed cancer cells worked similarly in test tubes and in human bodies. A talented organizer and administrator, she founded the Tissue Culture Research Laboratory during her time at the University of Illinois and served as its director for two years.

In one of her most important studies, Cobb examined the effects of radiation on skin cells. At the time, scientists suspected that ultraviolet radiation from the sun caused skin cancer. They also knew that X rays and other forms of radiation destroyed cancerous cells. In her experiment Cobb took cancerous skin cells from mice and exposed them to X rays and radium, a radioactive element. She found that darker skin cells—those with more melanin—were less affected by the radiation than pale skin cells. This meant that people with darker skin were less likely to get skin cancer from the sun than those with lighter skin. But if they did get cancer, they would need higher doses of radiation treatment.

Aiding Minority Students. In 1960 Cobb left New York University to join the staff of Sarah Lawrence College. Nine years later she accepted an appointment as dean at Connecticut College, where she established a program to encourage minority students to enter the health sciences. Her career as an administrator took her to Rutgers University in New Jersey and to two branches of the California State University system. She did less teaching and research, and focused more on helping minority students and women advance their education and careers. In 1979 she published a major critique of the obstacles faced by women in the sciences, titled "Filters for Women in Science." In 1981 Cobb was named president of California State University in Fullerton, and nine years later she accepted the honorary title of president emeritus of the university.

The CORIS

Carl Ferdinand Cori
1896–1984
BIOCHEMISTRY

Gerty Theresa Cori
1896–1957
BIOCHEMISTRY

The husband and wife team of Carl Ferdinand and Gerty Theresa Cori were pioneers in the study of the metabolism* of carbohydrates such as sugar. Their work highlighted the important role that enzymes* play in normal metabolism and stimulated the work of many later researchers. Against the advice of colleagues, and despite the existing bias against female scientists, the Coris collaborated on their most important studies. For their efforts they shared the 1947 Nobel Prize in physiology* or medicine.

Lives and Careers

Carl and Gerty Cori took quite different paths to their careers in science. Carl Cori's choice of a medical career followed a family tradition of scientific accomplishment. But in the male-dominated medical world of the

* **metabolism** physical and chemical processes involved in maintaining life

* **enzyme** any of numerous complex proteins that are produced by living cells and catalyze specific biochemical reactions at body temperature

* **physiology** science that deals with the functions of living organisms and their parts

* **biochemist** person who specializes in the science that deals with chemical compounds and processes occurring in living organisms

* **pathologist** specialist in the study of diseases and their effects on organisms

early 1900s, Gerty Cori's ambitions were more unusual and her road to success more difficult.

Early Lives. Carl Cori was born in the city of Prague, then part of the empire of Austria-Hungary. His grandfather was a professor of theoretical physics, and his father was the director of the Marine Biological Station located in the city of Trieste on the Adriatic coast. As a youth, Carl spent a great deal of time at the station, and he visited his grandfather during the summers. These experiences stimulated his interest in science, and at the age of 18 he entered the University of Prague as a medical student.

Gerty Cori, born Gerty Theresa Radnitz, was born in Prague the same year as her future husband. She was schooled at home until age ten, at which time she entered a school for girls. After graduating six years later, she wished to enter the University of Prague. However, she was weak in several subjects, so she studied for a year to prepare for the school's entrance examination. She passed the exam and enrolled in the university's medical school, where she met Carl Cori.

Shortly after Carl and Gerty enrolled at the university, World War I began and Carl spent several years as an officer in the Austrian Army's Sanitary Corps. After completing his service, he returned to the university, where both he and Gerty earned their medical degrees in 1920. They were married the same year. Carl spent the next two years teaching and doing research at the Universities of Vienna and Graz. Meanwhile, Gerty took a position as an assistant at the Karolinen Children's Hospital in Vienna. This marked the first instance of a pattern that repeated itself throughout their lives. Although Gerty's research work and skills were comparable to Carl's, he received better job offers and more recognition.

Life in the United States. World War I caused the collapse of the Austria-Hungary empire and the devastation of much of Europe. In this atmosphere opportunities for doing important scientific work were scarce. Fortunately, in 1922 Carl received an offer to move to the United States to join the New York State Institute for the Study of Malignant Diseases in Buffalo as a biochemist*. Gerty joined him at the institute a few months later as an assistant pathologist*. The Coris were pressured to do research on harmful diseases, especially cancer, and were unable to pursue their work on metabolism of carbohydrates in animals. They were also advised by their fellow researchers to avoid working together, which many felt would hinder Carl's career. Consequently, their early work at the institute focused on the metabolism of tumors. But they later returned to the study of carbohydrate metabolism and jointly published several influential papers on cancer research.

After nine years in Buffalo, Carl took a post as research associate at the Washington University School of Medicine in St. Louis, Missouri. The university hired Gerty as a research assistant in biochemistry so the two could continue their work together. It was in St. Louis that the Coris undertook the research that resulted in their most important findings on sugar metabolism. Their laboratory gained worldwide recognition and attracted many outstanding students. Five scientists who later won Nobel

* **pharmacology** science dealing with the preparation, uses, and effects of drugs

* **hormone** internally secreted substance transported by body fluids to stimulate the functions of organs or tissues

* **polymer** chemical compound composed of small molecules linked together to form larger molecules with repeating structures

* **glucose** natural sugar found in many fruits and animal tissues

Prizes worked under the Coris during this time. The Coris spent the remainder of their professional lives at Washington University, where Carl eventually became chair of the Department of Biological Chemistry. Gerty served as an associate professor of research in biochemistry and pharmacology*.

At the age of 51, Gerty developed symptoms of a fatal cancer of the bone marrow. For the next ten years she continued with her research but underwent many blood transfusions to combat the disease. When she died in 1957 she was one of the most respected biochemists in the world. She had been elected a member of the National Academy of Sciences and received awards and honorary degrees from many scientific societies and universities. Carl shared many of the same awards and honors as his wife, whom he outlived by 27 years. He remarried three years after Gerty's death and died in 1984 in Cambridge, Massachusetts.

Scientific Accomplishments

Gerty Cori's work in the Karolinen Hospital focused on the function and disorders of the thyroid gland, which plays a key role in regulating metabolism. She continued this work after moving to the United States. Together with her husband she also investigated the effect of insulin, a hormone* that is essential for the metabolism of carbohydrates, on chemicals produced by the body.

Early Studies. When the Coris began their research, the mechanism behind carbohydrate metabolism was poorly understood. It was known that the body stores sugar in the form of a polymer* called glycogen, which is made up of many individual sugar molecules joined together. Most scientists at the time believed that the body hydrolyzes (adds water molecules to) glycogen to produce glucose*, a carbohydrate that the body burns to produce energy. Glycogen acts as a reserve of stored glucose, which the body can draw upon as needed. Carbohydrate metabolism was thus thought to be a very simple process that involved only carbohydrates and water. The Coris' work proved, however, that the then-current understanding of carbohydrate metabolism was flawed.

Gerty's research on the thyroid stimulated her interest in the action of hormones on biological processes. After the discovery of insulin in 1921, she began to conduct studies on its role in sugar metabolism. She and Carl later examined the effects of insulin on blood sugar levels and conducted studies to determine why tumors use large amounts of glucose. Their research showed that the process by which glycogen becomes glucose is much more complicated than previously thought. The Coris started the next phase of their research by measuring the rate at which the body absorbs various types of sugar in the intestine. They measured some of the substances produced by the body as a result of carbohydrate metabolism, including glycogen and lactic acid. They were particularly interested in determining the effect of insulin on the conversion of sugar into lactic acid in the muscles and liver. Their work overturned long-held ideas about carbohydrate metabolism. It also showed that the process was dependent on the action of several enzymes, which they were the first to identify.

The Cori Cycle. The Coris proposed a new mechanism—later named the Cori cycle—to explain carbohydrate metabolism, which occurs in four stages. In the first stage, glucose in the blood is transformed into muscle glycogen, which is then converted into lactic acid. The lactic acid then forms liver glycogen, which is again converted into glucose that the body then burns to produce energy. Having uncovered this process, the Coris set out to discover the specific agents and actions underlying it.

It was apparent to the Coris that simple hydrolysis of glycogen to produce glucose would involve a great loss of energy that would later have to be restored before glucose could be reconverted into glycogen. Such a process would be a very inefficient way for the body to produce energy. Their first breakthrough was the discovery of a substance in muscle tissue called glucose-1-phosphate that is produced when a certain enzyme acts on glucose. The formation of glucose-1-phosphate enables the efficient transformation of glycogen into glucose and helps conserve energy. The Coris also found that another enzyme changes glucose-1-phosphate into a related compound called glucose-6-phosphate. Yet another enzyme converts glucose-6-phosphate into glucose, which in turn becomes lactic acid because of the action of still another enzyme.

The Coris were the first to identify these specific compounds and each of the enzymes responsible for their conversion into the products involved in carbohydrate metabolism. They also determined where the production of each compound occurred during the metabolic cycle. Scientists soon changed the way they thought about reactions in the body. The Coris' research gave rise to the idea that specific enzymes may control many of the body's biochemical reactions. For this work, the Coris shared the 1947 Nobel Prize in physiology or medicine with the Argentine physician Bernardo HOUSSAY, who had also carried out important studies in the field.

The Coris achieved a number of other historic firsts in their work with enzymes. They were the first to synthesize* glycogen in a test tube by combining glucose-1-phosphate, phosphorylase, and glucose. This marked the first time a natural polymer was produced outside of living tissue, and it offered supporting proof for the Coris' proposed structure of glycogen. The Coris' work led to the identification and isolation of a number of other important enzymes.

Later Studies. Following their groundbreaking work on the role of enzymes in carbohydrate metabolism, Gerty began to investigate several childhood diseases that are caused by the failure of the body to store glycogen properly. Her studies on the interaction between enzymes and glycogen proved quite valuable in this new research. She discovered that these so-called glycogen storage disorders could be classified into two separate groups. One group of disorders resulted from the production of excess glycogen, and the other involved abnormal glycogen molecules. Gerty demonstrated that both groups of disorders resulted from either a shortage of certain enzymes or because of changes in the enzymes during the process of metabolism. She became the first person to show that the lack of a particular enzyme could cause a disease. Her research into the glycogen storage disorders also made clear that, by studying enzymes, scientists

* **synthesize** to create artificially

38

could better understand the disruption of metabolic processes that depend on those enzymes.

After Gerty's death, Carl continued to study carbohydrate metabolism in muscles. In 1966 he joined the staff of Harvard Medical School and remained there until the end of his career. The Coris' combined efforts in the study of carbohydrate metabolism made a significant impact in the field of biochemistry. Together, Carl and Gerty Cori not only made important discoveries but also stimulated new research and helped train a new generation of biochemists.

Jacques-Yves COUSTEAU

1910–1997

OCEANOGRAPHY,
ENVIRONMENTALISM

* **oceanography** science that deals with oceans and marine biology

During a career that spanned more than 40 years, Jacques-Yves Cousteau established himself as the world's most recognizable figure in the field of underwater exploration and oceanography*. As the inventor of an underwater breathing apparatus and portable manned submarines, Cousteau enabled divers to go deeper underwater with greater freedom than ever before. As an explorer, filmmaker, and champion of environmental causes, he introduced millions of people to the wonders of the world beneath the sea and inspired many more to follow in his footsteps, forever linking his name to the exploration of the oceans.

Early Life and Career. Cousteau's life story is as unlikely as it is impressive. Although he eventually became a leading figure in ocean research, Cousteau had no formal scientific training. Still, he developed a love for the ocean that he transformed into a career of significant accomplishments. Cousteau was born in the French village of St. André de Cubzac, north of the city of Bordeaux and near the Atlantic coast. He suffered from health problems as a boy, but this did not prevent him from spending a great deal of time at the beach and learning how to swim. He also suffered from impatience with formal schooling, and he was expelled from high school for breaking windows there. Cousteau's father, a lawyer, traveled a great deal, and his family moved frequently. When Cousteau was ten, his family lived in New York City for a short while. It was during that time that he made his first real dive in a lake in Vermont, where he was attending summer camp. But his ambitions did not yet include ocean exploration. Instead, he hoped to become a pilot in the French Navy.

At age 20 Cousteau entered the French Naval Academy and spent several years serving aboard a cruiser in Asia. He entered the academy's school for naval aviators and trained to become a pilot. However, a serious automobile accident in which he broke both of his arms cut short his career as a pilot. To rehabilitate his arms he swam regularly, and it was during this time that he first used a pair of underwater goggles. He was amazed by the underwater world that revealed itself to him, and he fell in love with the sea. Cousteau had found his life's calling.

The Aqua-Lung. Cousteau served France both as a gunnery officer and as a member of the Resistance, the organization that opposed the Nazis during their occupation of France during World War II. After the war he

39

---

received France's highest award, the Legion of Honor, for his Resistance activities. However, his most significant achievements during the war did not occur on the battlefield. In 1943 he teamed up with an engineer named Emile Gagnan to develop the Aqua-Lung, the world's first practical portable underwater breathing apparatus.

Cousteau and Gagnan were not the first to come up with this idea, however. By the late 1800s, French inventors had developed devices to enable divers to carry compressed air with them, freeing them from bulky diving suits connected to the surface by air hoses. This early equipment, however, was inefficient and difficult to use. Divers had to open a valve manually to grab a quick breath of air before closing the valve again. Cousteau and Gagnan set out to improve on this concept. Gagnan had previously devised a way for automobiles and trucks to run on compressed gas, and he and Cousteau modified that invention for diving. The new device, which Cousteau called the Aqua-Lung, featured a regulator that automatically delivered air to the divers, enabling them to breathe normally without having to open and close valves for air.

The Aqua-Lung, made available to the public after the war, revolutionized the field of diving. For the first time, divers could explore underwater without being connected to the surface or struggling with their equipment to get fresh air. The device was not only portable, but it was also rugged and far less expensive than other diving equipment. This caused an explosion of popular interest in sport diving, and today about half a million people earn their diving certificates each year because of Cousteau and Gagnan's invention.

Exploring the Deep. During the war, Cousteau also invented movie cameras that were capable of filming beneath the surface of the water, and he conducted pioneering experiments with underwater filmmaking. After the war he founded the French Undersea Research Group to continue his work with filming beneath the sea. He soon had the opportunity to combine his two wartime inventions. In 1950 Cousteau and two friends acquired the American-built minesweeper *Calypso*. This warship was designed to remove underwater mines. They transformed the ship into a vessel for oceanographic exploration and research. With financial support from scientific, academic, and commercial sources, Cousteau and his crew set out to explore and film the wonders of the world's oceans. On one of his earliest voyages in *Calypso,* Cousteau shot the first color film footage ever taken at a depth of 150 feet and conducted the first-ever offshore oil survey. In 1996 the *Calypso* sank as the result of a collision, but Cousteau's family plans to replace it with a larger vessel, the *Calypso II.* The new vessel will be powered by a combination of diesel engines and the Turbosail wind-propulsion device, another Cousteau invention.

In 1959 Cousteau added another vessel to his personal fleet. Along with French engineer Jean Mollard, Cousteau built the *Diving Saucer,* a two-person submarine that could descend to depths of 1,000 feet. The *Sea Fleas,* a pair of single-person submarines that could probe 500 feet deeper than the *Diving Saucer,* followed in 1965. Cousteau also conducted a series of underwater experiments known as the Conshelf Saturation Dive

Jacques-Yves Cousteau is shown here descending into the waters of the Persian Gulf in a shark-proof cage. Working from the research vessel *Calypso,* Cousteau and a team of divers examined the seabed in waters up to 250 feet deep. They brought up specimens of the undersea world for detailed examination and study.

Program. In the Conshelf experiments, teams of divers lived and worked underwater for extended periods of time, breathing a mixture of helium and oxygen. Conshelf III, the final component of these experiments, featured six divers living and working 300 feet underwater for three weeks.

Popularizing the Deep. Cousteau built his reputation on his wartime inventions and postwar experiments in ocean exploration. However, his fame was a result of the many films that he made to record his voyages and discoveries. His first feature film, *The Silent World,* was released in 1955. It won both the Academy Award for best documentary film and the Golden Palm at the International Film Festival in Cannes, France. He won a second Academy Award nine years later for the film *World Without Sun.* In addition to feature films, Cousteau produced more than 70 films for television.

Cousteau is perhaps most famous to viewers in the United States for his long-running television series *The Undersea World of Jacques Cousteau.* Other Cousteau television specials include the Public Broadcasting System

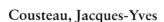

Getting into Hot (and Cold) Water

Jacques Cousteau's first dive was not for fun or adventure—it was a punishment for his youthful disobedience. When Cousteau refused to ride horses at summer camp in Vermont, the counselor in charge ordered him to dive into Lake Harvey to remove branches from around the boat dock. The water was ice-cold, and Cousteau was a skinny child, but he soon grew used to the task. Throughout the summer he spent more and more time under the water, holding his breath so he could explore the lake as long as possible. Little did he or anyone else realize that it would be a preview of the way he would spend most of his life.

series *Cousteau Odyssey* and the series *Cousteau Amazon*. Besides film and television, Cousteau also wrote many books, including *Through 18 Meters of Water, The Silent World, The Living Sea, World Without Sun,* and *The Ocean World*. Cousteau's films and books have been translated into many languages, and through them he has transmitted his fascination with the sea to generations of viewers and readers around the world. By touching so many people, Cousteau became one of the leading figures in popularizing the worldwide environmental movement.

During his career Cousteau developed a strong commitment to preserving and protecting the marine environment he observed. In 1974 he formed the Cousteau Society, a nonprofit environmental organization whose focus is marine conservation. In 1988 he resigned the position he had held for 31 years as director of Monaco's Musée Océanographique to pursue his ecological interests. In his later years, he was an official guest at the 1992 United Nations Conference on Environment and Development. He was also appointed to the United Nations High Level Advisory Board, on which he served as an adviser on environmental issues to the World Bank. In 1993 the president of France, François Mitterrand, appointed him Chairman of the Council on the Rights of Future Generations, a post from which Cousteau resigned two years later to protest France's nuclear testing in the Pacific Ocean. Cousteau denounced the effects of ocean pollution, nuclear energy, and overfishing in many of his published works. Before his death he professed to be most proud of his work in environmental conservation.

Worldwide Recognition. Because of his many accomplishments, scientific and academic institutions worldwide have honored Cousteau. In 1951 he was appointed director of the Oceanographic Institute of Monaco, a post he held for more than 30 years. He received honorary degrees from Harvard University, the University of California at Berkeley, and Brandeis University, among others. He also received the Presidential Medal of Freedom, the highest award presented by the United States government to a civilian. The French Navy promoted him to commander for his achievements, and he was elected to the Académie Française, France's highest honor for lifetime contributions to the national culture.

Cousteau's other awards include the United Nations' International Environmental Prize, the National Geographic Society's Centennial Award, and the Smithsonian Institution's James Smithson Bicentennial Medal. The television industry recognized his contributions by electing him to the Television Academy of Fame and bestowing on him the Founders Award from the International Council of the National Academy of Television Arts and Sciences. Cousteau has also served on many international scientific and environmental panels and committees.

Cousteau's Legacy. Cousteau died in 1997, but his work is carried on today by the Cousteau Society, headed by his widow, Francine, and by environmentalist and yachtsman Peter Blake. Founded in 1973, the society includes many engineering, research, and marketing firms that were incorporated to provide funding and direction for Cousteau's research and exploration activities. The society continues the mission started by its founder—to educate people about the oceans and to champion the preservation of the natural world for future generations.

CRICK, *Francis*

See *Watson and Crick.*

Harvey Williams CUSHING

1869–1939

NEUROSURGERY, NEUROPHYSIOLOGY

* **neurosurgery** surgery performed on any part of the nervous system, including the brain, spinal cord, and nerves

* **anesthetic** substance that causes loss of sensation with or without loss of consciousness

* **thorax** part of the body between the neck and the diaphragm

* **pituitary gland** gland whose secretions control the actions of other glands and influence growth and metabolism

* **hormone** internally secreted substance transported by body fluids to stimulate the functions of organs or tissues

Harvey Williams Cushing is considered by many to be the foremost figure in the field of neurosurgery*. The tenth child of a physician, he attended Yale University and Harvard Medical School. After receiving his M.D. in 1895, Cushing joined the staff at Massachusetts General Hospital before becoming an assistant resident at Johns Hopkins Hospital in Baltimore, Maryland. He worked there under William Halsted, a prominent American surgeon. During this time Cushing devoted his full attention to studying neurosurgery. In 1912 he accepted a professorship at Harvard, where he served as chair of the Medical School's Department of Surgery. He was also chief surgeon at Boston's Peter Bent Brigham Hospital from its opening in 1913 until his retirement nearly 20 years later. He then returned to Yale as Sterling Professor of Neurology from 1933 to 1937. He died in 1939.

During his early career, Cushing studied a wide range of medical conditions and made several notable surgical accomplishments. In the early 1900s doctors had only a limited knowledge of how to handle certain anesthetics*, such as ether. This resulted in many unnecessary deaths during surgery. Cushing devised a chart on which to record the temperature and respiration of a patient undergoing an operation using ether, enabling surgeons to closely monitor their patients' vital signs. He later successfully experimented with the use of local anesthetics for amputations and hernia operations. During the Spanish-American War (1898), he became adept at surgically handling perforated intestines in soldiers with typhoid fever. Cushing also served as a battlefield surgeon during World War I, where he succeeded in reducing the rate of mortality from head wounds by 50 percent.

Cushing was the first to conduct experimental surgery on the thorax* and the heart. In the course of this work, he studied chronic wounds in the heart valves of dogs to find a cure for mitral stenosis, a condition characterized by the narrowing of the valve between the two chambers on the left side of the heart. The experimental operations that he conducted on the thorax convinced him that the lungs had to be kept inflated during surgery. He did so by opening the trachea (windpipe), developing a procedure that is still used in thoracic surgeries.

Cushing also made important contributions to the understanding of the pituitary gland*, proving that it has a major influence on many bodily processes. In his landmark book, *The Pituitary Body and Its Disorders*, published in 1912, Cushing described the effects of undersecretion and oversecretion of hormones* by the pituitary and showed how to recognize

the symptoms of such disorders. He was particularly interested in tumors of the pituitary. In addition, he made a connection between a certain type of pituitary tumor and a condition in which a patient develops a painful buildup of fatty tissue on the face and body, now known as Cushing's disease or Cushing's syndrome. The book describes and provides treatments for many types of tumors, including those affecting blood vessels, the tissues lining the skull, and the tissues that support nerve cells.

Cushing's greatest contributions came in the study and surgical treatment of tumors of the brain and spinal cord. When he began practicing medicine, the mortality rate for brain surgery patients was nearly 100 percent. Cushing found that brain surgery resulted in a slowing of the heartbeat followed by a sharp rise in blood pressure in the arteries. Based on this finding, he began to use the new blood pressure device developed in Europe to monitor his patients, making it safer to cut into a patient's skull without adverse effects. In 1925 he also devised a way to destroy tumors by using electricity, enabling him to operate on many patients who had tumors that he previously dared not attack.

Cushing was not only a brilliant researcher and surgeon but also an excellent writer. The author of more than 300 books and papers, Cushing also wrote a biography of the physician William Ostler that won a Pulitzer Prize. Cushing was also an avid collector of medical texts, leaving a library of more than 8,000 items to Yale University. More than 20 universities in America and around the world acknowledged his talents by presenting him with awards and honorary degrees. He was a member of more than 70 medical, surgical, and scientific societies. In 1932, the year of his retirement from Harvard, some of his young colleagues formed the Harvey Cushing Society, which later became the American Association of Neurological Surgeons.

Henry Hallett
DALE

1875–1968

PHYSIOLOGY, PHARMACOLOGY

* **histamine** compound found in mammalian tissues that is released during allergic reactions and causes the dilation of blood vessels, the contraction of smooth muscle, and the stimulation of gastric acid secretion

* **physiology** science that deals with the functions of living organisms and their parts

* **clinical** related to the observation and treatment of disease in actual patients rather than in artificial experiments

Henry Hallett Dale is best known for his work in two major areas of research—the action and distribution of histamine* in the body and the chemical transmission of nerve impulses. In 1936 he was awarded the Nobel Prize in physiology* or medicine for his work on nerve impulses.

The son of a businessman, Dale was born in London in 1875. He attended the Leys School in Cambridge, England. In 1894 he enrolled in Trinity College at Cambridge University and was instructed by some of the leading physiologists of the day. He graduated with honors and underwent clinical* training at St. Bartholomew's Hospital, earning his medical degree in 1909. Dale also studied physiology at University College in London and worked for several months in Frankfurt, Germany, with the renowned biological chemist Paul Ehrlich. In 1904 Dale became director of the Wellcome Physiological Research Laboratories in England. Although his colleagues advised against such a move, the job provided Dale with sufficient income to raise a family.

In 1914 Dale left Wellcome to join the staff of the Medical Research Committee, which later became the National Institute for Medical Research. In 1928 he became its first director and remained in the position until 1942.

For the next four years he was director of the Royal Institution of Great Britain. He also served as chairperson of the Scientific Advisory Committee to the War Cabinet, a position that he held through World War II.

Dale was actively concerned with the social role of science, and he played a leading part in the adoption of a plan for standardizing drugs and antitoxins. At the 1925 conference of the Health Organization of the League of Nations, he convinced his colleagues to adopt international standards for the quality of insulin* and extracts* from the pituitary gland*.

Although Dale was an important researcher, he never wrote a book, but collections of some of his papers were published late in his life. *Adventures in Physiology* was published in 1953, and *Autumn Gleanings* appeared the following year. In *Adventures in Physiology,* he included a commentary in which he emphasized the role that chance played in some of his work. One example of the effect of chance on Dale's discoveries is clear in his early research on an agricultural fungus known as ergot. Although Dale did not achieve his intended goal of evaluating the uses of ergot as a drug, his work in this area accidentally led to his first discoveries concerning histamine and the transmission of nerve impulses.

While investigating the physiological effects of ergot, Dale had attended a demonstration in 1907 at which an ergot extract was shown to cause the uterus of a pregnant cat to contract. In 1909 he discovered that extracts from the pituitary gland had the same effect on the cat uterus he was using as an experimental organ. This suggested to him that an unknown substance contaminated the ergot extract used in the demonstration. In 1910 he and George Barger, a colleague at Wellcome Laboratories, identified the substance as histamine, which became a primary focus of Dale's research.

Around 1911 Dale showed that histamine is a naturally occurring substance in the body. He also pointed out similarities between the effects of histamine poisoning and anaphylactic shock. However, Dale could not yet prove that there was a connection between the two. He was unable to demonstrate that histamine played a unique role in the body's physiology and was not a byproduct of the breakdown of some other substance.

Over the next 15 years, Dale conducted a series of classic experiments that ultimately established a connection between histamine poisoning and anaphylactic shock. In these experiments he injected the limb of an animal with histamine and found that blood plasma flowed into the tissues. The resulting loss of fluid caused the blood to stagnate and flow back to the heart at a greatly reduced rate, causing shock. In 1927 Dale and his colleagues also proved that histamine normally appears in the body, and it is not the product of the chemical decomposition of another compound. Two years later, in a series of lectures, he presented the overwhelming evidence for histamine being the cause of the symptoms of anaphylactic shock. Dale's experiments also showed that circulation is controlled by specific chemical and humoral* factors in the body.

Dale's work with histamine led to his research on acetylcholine (ACh), the substance that transmits nerve impulses and forms salts that lower blood pressure. He discovered ACh just as he discovered histamine, as a contaminant of the ergot extracts he was investigating. ACh is similar to

* **insulin** hormone produced by the pancreas that is used in the treatment of diabetes

* **extract** solution that contains the essential components of a more complex material

* **pituitary gland** gland whose secretions control the actions of other glands and influence growth and metabolism

* **humoral** having to do with bodily fluids

45

Dale, Henry Hallett

histamine in that it affects the contraction and relaxation of blood vessels. Some of Dale's contemporaries had also written papers on this property of ACh. In 1914 Dale outlined the physiological properties of ACh and explored its effects on blood vessels. He noted how the effects of ACh were similar to the results of stimulation of the parasympathetic nervous system (PNS), the part of the nervous system that calms the body, reducing breathing and slowing the pulse rate.

One of Dale's colleagues, T.R. Elliot, had demonstrated earlier that the action of the sympathetic nervous system* (SNS), when stimulated, could be reproduced by injecting a test subject with adrenaline. This effect had led Elliot to suggest that the SNS exerted its effects by releasing adrenaline at the ends of the nerves it governed. However, he did not follow up on this idea of the chemical transmission of nerve signals, and it was not pursued until Dale made his parallel observation regarding the PNS and ACh in 1914. But Dale could not make any assertions about the role that ACh might play in the PNS until the existence of ACh in body tissues could be proved.

Beginning in 1921 the work of German physiologist Otto LOEWI showed that chemicals in the body probably transmitted nerve impulses. In 1929 Dale found that ACh occurs naturally in the body, and in the following years he discovered that it is released at some nerve endings of the PNS and the SNS. His work, along with that of Loewi, proved that nerve impulses are transmitted chemically by ACh, adrenaline, and other substances released at nerve endings. For this discovery Dale and Loewi shared the 1936 Nobel Prize in physiology or medicine.

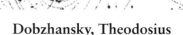

In addition to the Nobel Prize, Dale received many awards and honors, including a knighthood in 1932, appointment as secretary of the Royal Society from 1925 to 1935 and as its president from 1940 to 1945, and the Royal and Copley Medals in 1937. The Society for Endocrinology recognized his contributions by naming a medal after him in 1959. Two years later the Royal Society established a Henry Dale professorship. He died in 1968.

Theodosius DOBZHANSKY

1900–1975

GENETICS, EVOLUTION

* **genetics** branch of biology that deals with heredity

* **evolution** historical development of a biological group such as a species

* **entomologist** specialist in entomology, a branch of science dealing with insects

* **humanism** system of thought in which human interests and values are of primary importance

---

The Russian scientist Theodosius Dobzhansky had a major influence on modern ideas about genetics* and evolution*. Through his studies and research, Dobzhansky laid the groundwork for new ideas of how the evolution of species came about through adaptation. He discovered that species that adapt successfully tended to have a wider variety of genes. Many of these genes, although not necessarily useful to the organism in its present environment, provide the species with significant genetic diversity. This diversity enables the species to adapt effectively to changes in the surrounding environment.

Early Life and Career. Born in Nemirov in the Ukraine, Russia, Dobzhansky was the son of a high school mathematics teacher. In 1910 Dobzhansky's family moved from Nemirov to the outskirts of the city of Kiev. During his early years there, he became an avid butterfly collector. In 1915, following a meeting with a young entomologist*, Dobzhansky decided to study ladybugs. These became the subject of his first scientific work, which was published in 1918.

Dobzhansky entered the University of Kiev and graduated with a degree in biology in 1921. Before he graduated, he was hired as an instructor in zoology at the Polytechnic Institute in Kiev, where he taught until 1924. He then became an assistant to the head of the newly formed department of genetics at the University of Leningrad. While there, he investigated the ways that genes can affect the different features of an organism.

In 1927 Dobzhansky received a fellowship to work with American geneticist Thomas Hunt MORGAN at Columbia University in New York. The next year he moved with Morgan to the California Institute of Technology, where he became assistant professor of genetics. Dobzhansky returned to Columbia University in 1940 as a professor of zoology and remained there for the next 22 years, after which he was appointed professor at the Rockefeller Institute (now Rockefeller University) in New York. In 1971 Dobzhansky moved to the department of genetics at the University of California at Davis, where he remained until his death four years later.

Achievements. Dobzhansky was one of the most influential and productive biologists of the 1900s. He published nearly 600 works, which covered subjects ranging from experimental research in various biological disciplines to essays on humanism* and philosophy. Although his works are diverse, they are unified by the common theme of biological evolution.

Dobzhansky's success as a creator of new ideas and his skill at combining concepts to create new theories was based on his broad knowledge,

Theodosius Dobzhansky combined field-work and laboratory research to study genetics and evolution. He collected specimens from Alaska to Tierra del Fuego, and on every continent except Antarctica.

* **natural selection** theory that within a given species, individuals best adapted to the environment live longer and produce more offspring than other individuals, resulting in changes in the species over time

excellent memory, and sharp mind. He had a great ability to see how his ideas related to other theories or problems. His success as an experimental researcher depended on a wise blending of field and laboratory research. Whenever possible, Dobzhansky combined field and laboratory research to study a problem, using laboratory studies to identify or confirm processes involved in natural phenomena. He also worked with mathematicians, who helped him design theoretical models for experimental testing and to analyze his observations.

Dobzhansky generously recognized and praised the achievements of other scientists, and he admired the intellect of his colleagues. An excellent teacher and researcher, he acted as an adviser for many young students working toward their doctorates and as a mentor for young colleagues who visited him from other countries. Dobzhansky also spent long periods at foreign academic institutions and was largely responsible for the establishment or development of genetics and evolutionary biology in a number of countries. He received many honors and awards and was a member of many respected academic societies.

Contributions to Evolutionary Theory and Genetics. Dobzhansky's most significant contribution to science was his role in reformulating modern evolutionary theory. His book *Genetics and the Origin of Species,* published in 1937, is one of the most important books on evolutionary theory of the century. The theme of the book is the role of genetics in explaining the origin of species. Before this time, most scientists believed that the changes caused by natural selection* occurred rarely and slowly. Through his studies of the fruit fly *(Drosophila),* Dobzhansky modified this view by showing that a particular population of a species can display significant genetic changes in a relatively short period of time.

Dobzhansky explained that the genetic variation within and between populations was the result of the same basic evolutionary processes. He argued that certain genes become more widespread than others in a specific population and that these play an important role in adaptation and survival. With each new generation, these genes become more common because they produce a superior genetic makeup when combined with other genes that are not expressed in an organism. At the same time, however, the presence of these other genes enables the species to adapt rather quickly to changes in environmental conditions.

Another important aspect of Dobzhansky's work dealt with speciation, the process by which a species does not merely change its characteristics but actually evolves into two or more different species. Dobzhansky saw speciation as a dynamic process of gradual change. As part of his studies of speciation, he proposed the phrase *isolating mechanisms* to designate the phenomena that prevent or slow the exchange of genes between species. Throughout his life Dobzhansky identified, classified, and investigated the various kinds of isolating mechanisms.

Other Work. Dobzhansky also made significant contributions to other fields of biology, including ecology. Much of his genetic research was ecological in nature. For example, he studied the changes in species that were

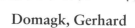

A Role for Religion

Although deeply religious, Dobzhansky rejected many of the fundamental beliefs of traditional religion, such as the existence of a personal god and of life after death. His spirituality was based on a strong conviction that there is meaning in the universe. Dobzhansky saw such meaning in evolution, which had produced the remarkable diversity of life-forms on earth. For Dobzhansky the existence of such diversity pointed toward some higher power, and he spent a great deal of time exploring the evolutionary basis of religion. At the same time, his strong belief in evolution made him quick to criticize the antievolutionist stands of conservative Catholics and Protestants.

* **anthropology** study of human beings, especially in relation to origins and cultural characteristics

a result of variations in geographic location, and he also investigated the ecological diversity of environments. He also studied species' diversity in tropical forests and developed theories to explain the presence of the large variety of species in tropical regions of the world.

In 1962 Dobzhansky published *Mankind Evolving*, a book some consider to be as important as *Genetics and the Origin of Species*. This book, which extended the ideas of English evolutionist Charles Darwin and others to an understanding of human nature, remains unsurpassed in the way it combines genetics, evolutionary theory, anthropology*, and sociology. Dobzhansky stated that human nature has two dimensions: the biological, which humankind shares with the rest of the world, and the cultural, which is exclusive to humans. According to Dobzhansky, these two dimensions result from two interconnected processes—biological evolution and cultural evolution.

Dobzhansky's interest in the interconnectedness of biology and human problems was evident in many of his publications after the mid-1940s. This interest was probably triggered by such factors as the persecution of Jews during World War II, the suppression of genetics and geneticists in the former Soviet Union, and the influence of his friend and colleague Leslie C. Dunn, who was involved with providing shelter in the United States for scientists fleeing from the Nazis. Dobzhansky was also concerned with the role of religion in human life, and he explored the evolutionary basis of religion in articles that he published in the 1960s and 1970s. In the later years of his life, he also wrote a number of essays dealing with various philosophical questions.

Gerhard DOMAGK

1895–1964

MEDICINE, CHEMISTRY

* **streptococcal** refers to the spherical *Streptococcus* bacterium that causes disease in humans and domestic animals

* **physiology** science that deals with the functions of living organisms and their parts

The German scientist Gerhard Domagk helped introduce the era of chemical medicine when he found that a red industrial dye could kill the bacteria that caused streptococcal* infections. He discovered similar chemicals to treat tuberculosis and cancer. In 1939 Domagk was awarded the Nobel Prize in physiology* or medicine for his work on drugs.

Inspiration in School. Domagk was born in 1895 in the German state of Brandenburg. The son of a teacher, he attended an elementary school that emphasized the sciences. At a young age he decided to be a doctor. But the outbreak of World War I in 1914 interrupted Domagk's college studies, and he entered the armed forces. Domagk was wounded in battle. He then transferred to the army medical corps and received medical training. He earned his M.D. from the University of Kiel in 1921.

Domagk worked as a professor at several German universities. During this time, he published a paper on cells in the human body that attack and dissolve foreign cells and particles in parts of the body other than the blood. This paper attracted the attention of a major German chemical factory, I.G. Farbenindustrie. At the age of 32 he was hired to head the company's medical research laboratory.

Industry and Medicine. Domagk also developed an interest in chemotherapy, the treatment of illness with chemicals. The connection between industrial chemicals and the treatment of disease had been suggested in

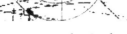

Rise of the Wonder Drugs

Gerhard Domagk launched the era of so-called wonder drugs when he used a chemical dye to save the life of a British prime minister and the son of an American president, who were both suffering from infections. Doctors, scientists, and ordinary people all hoped that a single chemical could cure a deadly disease just by entering the body. Other wonder drugs, such as penicillin and aspirin, fueled people's optimism that science and technology could invent instant solutions to complex natural problems.

---

* **antibacterial** referring to substances that hinder the growth of bacteria, microscopic organisms that can cause infection and disease

* **antibiotic** any chemical substance produced by various microscopic organisms that hinders the growth of or destroys other harmful microorganisms

1909, when the German scientist Paul Ehrlich discovered a chemical called arsphenamine that could kill certain bacteria. Since that time, other scientists had made progress with chemotherapy in certain instances, but they had had little success against common bacterial infections in humans.

Guided by Ehrlich's work, Domagk focused his attention on a group of dyes called azo dyes. Two chemists at the firm produced a red dye from that group that they called Prontosil rubrum, intended for treating leather. Domagk, who had been systematically examining the medical effects of dyes, experimented with Prontosil and found that it defended against bacteria in mice and unlike many dyes, was only slightly toxic (poisonous).

Fame and the Führer. An opportunity to test Prontosil in humans came when Domagk's daughter fell ill with a streptococcal infection. Several treatments that had been tried failed. Desperate for a cure, Domagk injected his daughter with a massive dose of his experimental new drug and she recovered completely. Domagk published his findings in 1935 in a paper that became a model of how to evaluate new drugs. The new treatment was hailed around the world when it saved the lives of British Prime Minister Winston Churchill and Franklin D. Roosevelt Jr., the son of President Roosevelt of the United States.

Other scientists took up Domagk's work. They found that Prontosil's active antibacterial* ingredient, a molecule called sulfonamide, separated from the rest of the chemical when inside the human body. Sulfonamide could be produced much more cheaply than Prontosil. In 1938 another scientist manufactured a related chemical called sulfapyridine, which was effective against types of pneumonia caused by bacterial infections of the lungs. This work gave rise to a whole category of chemotherapy drugs known as the sulfa drugs. These chemicals were later replaced by antibiotics*, but they are still used for some conditions, such as urinary tract infections. Before Domagk's discovery, chemical dyes had been used against infections caused by larger protozoa (single-celled, microscopic organisms, such as amoeba). His treatment, however, was the first to succeed against the common small bacterium.

Domagk's discovery enabled the successful treatment of several dangerous diseases that usually ended in death. These included pneumonia; meningitis—an infection that causes swelling of the membranes around the brain and spinal cord; and puerperal fever—an infection sometimes suffered by women during childbirth.

Domagk's work was rapidly recognized and he was awarded the 1939 Nobel Prize in physiology or medicine. Although Adolf Hitler, the dictator of Nazi Germany, had forbidden Germans to accept Nobel Prizes, Domagk accepted his award. He was arrested and spent a week in jail. He was forced to turn down the prize in a letter written for him by the Nazi authorities. In 1949, two years after the fall of the Nazis in 1947, Domagk accepted the medal he had earned.

Taking on New Targets. In his postwar career, Domagk turned his attention to tuberculosis, a lung infection. Doctors had recently been encouraged by a new drug called streptomycin, which was effective against the tuberculosis bacteria. But their hopes were dashed when streptomycin proved to be highly toxic. Domagk investigated a group of chemicals called the thiosemicarbazones. These were also toxic, and doctors turned to them only when other treatments failed. Even so, Domagk's work led to other scientists' success in treating the disease in the 1950s. Domagk then tried to apply chemotherapy to fight cancer. Unfortunately his experiments were fruitless. Like many other scientists he grew pessimistic about the chances of a cure for cancer.

Domagk had a natural desire to help those suffering from illnesses, and his scientific curiosity wandered far. Toward the end of his life, he wrote: "If I could start again, I would perhaps become a psychiatrist and search for a causal therapy of Mental Disease which is the most terrifying problem of our times." Domagk died in Germany at the age of 68.

Charles Richard
DREW

1904–1950

PHYSIOLOGY

A great contributor to medical research and to humanity, Charles Drew developed techniques for processing and storing liquid and dried blood plasma for use in blood transfusions. Because he was an authority on separating plasma from whole blood, he was in charge of blood storage and supply for the U.S. Army and Navy and of the "Plasma for Britain" program.

---

* **pathology** study of diseases and their effects on organisms

* **platelet** minute particle in blood that assists in clotting

Charles Richard Drew is best known as the African American physician and surgeon who developed new ways to store blood for long periods. He also pioneered the establishment of blood banks to make blood available for transfusions to the injured and wounded, particularly soldiers in World War II. Despite his accomplishments, Drew had to fight racism and racist policies—especially those that got in the way of saving lives.

Excelling as a Young Man. Born in Washington, D.C., Drew attended Dunbar High School. Dunbar's students were all African American because the nation's schools at that time were segregated by race. Even so, Dunbar was one of the city's best schools, and Drew was among its most talented students and athletes. He also joined the United States Army Reserve Officer Training Corps. At Amherst College in Massachusetts, Drew was a star athlete and enjoyed his studies of chemistry and biology. Because of racism, however, he was excluded from many campus groups.

Surgery and the Study of Blood. In 1928 Drew enrolled in McGill University Medical School in Montreal, Canada. In 1935 he became an instructor in pathology* at Howard University, a historically black institution. Ten years later, Drew accepted a fellowship at Columbia University, where he studied the preservation of blood. He found that the fluid part of blood that carries nutrients, known as plasma, could be stored much longer than the solid cells—red cells, white cells, and platelets*. Because plasma was a good substitute for whole blood for most medical purposes, Drew's discovery greatly helped emergency treatment. For example, a person's body often goes into shock when too much blood is lost in a short time. Shock can lead to loss of consciousness and death. But Drew found that transfusing plasma stabilized the patient's body.

The Doctor in Wartime. In 1939 World War II broke out in Europe, with heavy losses to America's allies Britain and France. Drew organized efforts to collect blood in the United States and send it to Europe. He became recognized as an expert in blood storage. The American Red Cross

adopted his methods for plasma preservation and storage, and Drew became the director of the first blood bank set up by the American Red Cross. His efforts saved the lives of many soldiers and civilians.

Shortly after Drew accepted this new position, he had a disagreement with the Red Cross and the military. For years the Red Cross had refused to collect blood from African Americans for the nation's blood supply. During the war, however, the military announced that it would accept donations of blood from all Americans. But the Red Cross stored the blood of black and white Americans separately so that white soldiers would not receive transfusions of blood donated by black Americans. There was no scientific reason for this policy, and Drew argued unsuccessfully against it. He resigned his post in anger.

Drew returned to teaching and surgery at Howard University. He also served as chairperson of the Department of Surgery at the Freedmen's Hospital. In 1944 Drew received the Spingarn Medal from the National Association for the Advancement of Colored People for his work in training African American doctors. Despite his rocky relationship with the army, he joined a military project to improve medical care in Western Europe, which was being rebuilt after the war. In 1950 Drew was badly injured in a car accident. Although doctors tried to save him with a blood transfusion, he died two hours after arriving at the hospital.

Antonio
EGAS MONIZ

1874–1955
NEUROLOGY

* **physiology** science that deals with the functions of living organisms and their parts

* **cadaver** dead body, especially one intended for dissection

* **clinical** related to the observation and treatment of disease in actual patients rather than in artificial experiments

Antonio Egas Moniz is best known for developing two procedures—cerebral angiography and frontal leucotomy—to diagnose and treat diseases of the brain. A method of viewing the blood vessels in the brain, cerebral angiography remains in use but in a modified form. Frontal leucotomy, which is also known as a lobotomy, is the process in which nerve fibers between the frontal lobes of the brain are severed to cure certain types of mental disorders. For developing the latter procedure, Egas Moniz won the Nobel Prize in physiology* or medicine in 1949.

Egas Moniz was born in Portugal. In 1891 he entered the University of Coimbra to study mathematics. He later switched to medicine and specialized in neurology, the study of the structure, function, and disorders of the nervous system. In 1902, three years after he received his M.D., he became a professor at Coimbra. During the intervening years, Egas Moniz went to Paris and Bordeaux, France, to study with prominent neurologists and psychiatrists. In 1911 he accepted the chair of neurology at the newly opened University of Lisbon, a position he held until his retirement.

At the time Egas Moniz entered the field of neurology, doctors located brain tumors by injecting air into the brain cavity and taking an X ray of the patient's skull. But this technique proved to be imprecise and dangerous. Egas Moniz worked with cadavers* to develop a method of injecting a fluid into the cranial arteries that showed up clearly in X rays. After mapping the normal distribution of the blood vessels in the cranium, he introduced his method clinically* in 1927. He described his findings using X rays that indicated the location and size of a patient's brain tumor by the tumor's displacement of injected arteries. Using the cerebral angiography

developed by Egas Moniz, doctors could locate brain tumors easily and more safely by examining the flow of fluid through the arteries as shown in the X rays. This technique is used by doctors today to locate tumors and blood vessel disorders throughout the body.

When Egas Moniz began his career, no effective treatment existed for mental disorders in patients whose brains showed no organic disease. He was intrigued by studies in which researchers induced neuroses* in chimpanzees, then cut the nerves that connected the chimps' frontal lobes to the rest of their brains. The surgery, called a lobotomy, cured temper tantrums caused by the neuroses, yet the animals remained friendly, alert, and intelligent. Egas Moniz developed a similar procedure, frontal leucotomy, to treat psychiatric problems in humans, particularly those involving emotional tension. In the first trials, 14 of 20 patients were cured or improved and none died from the surgery. The technique was modified and used for about 20 years and it earned Egas Moniz the Nobel Prize. The invention of psychiatric drugs during the 1960s, however, led to a decline in the practice of frontal leucotomy, which is no longer in use.

In addition to the Nobel Prize, Egas Moniz received several other awards from the Portuguese, Spanish, Italian, and French governments. He also received honorary degrees from the Universities of Bordeaux and Lyons in France. He served as president of the Lisbon Academy of Sciences and was a member of such international scientific societies as the Royal Society of Medicine, the Academy of Medicine in Paris, and the American Neurological Association. His achievements extended beyond the boundaries of science. He was an accomplished historian, literary critic, and composer. He also had a distinguished political career, serving as a deputy in the Portuguese parliament, an ambassador to Spain, and foreign minister.

* **neurosis** mental disorder with no obvious organic cause that involves anxiety, phobia, or other abnormal behavior; *pl.* neuroses

Gertrude Belle
ELION

1918–1999
CHEMISTRY

* **nucleic acid** class of complex chemicals, including DNA and RNA, that is found in all living cells and viruses

* **biochemistry** science that deals with chemical compounds and processes occurring in living organisms

Gertrude Belle Elion pioneered the use of nucleic acids* to treat a variety of serious diseases from cancer to AIDS. Rather than simply testing chemicals on animals to see what effect they had, as many researchers did at the time, Elion adopted a different approach. She worked to understand the exact processes by which nucleic acids were linked to certain diseases and created chemical compounds to interfere with those processes.

Elion was born in New York City to parents who migrated from Russia and Lithuania. An excellent student, she attended Hunter College to study chemistry. After graduating she took classes at a secretarial school, worked as laboratory assistant at a hospital, and taught in a New York City high school because positions for women in the sciences were limited. She had great difficulty finding work in her field until World War II opened employment opportunities for women. She received a master's degree in biochemistry* from New York University in 1941.

The prospects for women scientists improved with the outbreak of the war. Employed as a quality control chemist, Elion was responsible for checking the color of mayonnaise and the acidity of pickles for a food company. One year later she received a research position at a large drug company, working on the healing potential of drugs containing sulfur.

* **synthesize** to create artificially

Elion did her major work at Wellcome Research Laboratories, a private corporation in Tuckahoe, New York. She studied nucleic acids, which were believed to govern many crucial operations of cells. Elion was assigned to synthesize* nucleic acids that could alter or interfere with other nucleic acids that caused undesirable effects. Other drugs developed by Elion and her research group improved treatment of such diseases as gout, chicken pox, and malaria.

The most significant new compound synthesized by Elion, called 6-MP, was used in the treatment of leukemia. When given to children suffering from the disease, their mean survival time increased from three months to a year. Another drug synthesized by Elion became a standard treatment for leukemia in adults. The success of 6-MP encouraged Elion to synthesize a variety of derivatives and to use newly developed radioactive techniques to explore the activity of the drugs in cells. Because leukemia cells closely resemble cells that form antibodies*, other researchers used 6-MP and its derivatives to assist transplant patients. The organ recipient's body often produces antibodies that reject the transplant tissue from an imperfectly matched donor, but the new drugs synthesized by Elion greatly diminished the production of antibodies. This produced much higher success rates for organ transplants.

* **antibody** protein produced by the immune system to neutralize the presence of a foreign protein in the body

Elion retired in 1983 but continued to lend her expertise to the effort to create AZT, a drug used to combat HIV and AIDS. Ironically, she never earned a Ph.D. because she was unable to attend school and work at the same time. Nevertheless, Elion's valuable work and innovative approach to creating beneficial drugs won her the Nobel Prize in physiology* or medicine in 1988. She also received the Garvan Medal from the American Chemical Society and numerous honorary degrees, as well as election to the National Inventors' Hall of Fame and the National Academy of Sciences. She advised many students, colleagues, and health organizations until her death in North Carolina in 1999.

* **physiology** science that deals with the functions of living organisms and their parts

Gladys Anderson
EMERSON

1903–1984

BIOCHEMISTRY, NUTRITION

* **biochemistry** science that deals with chemical compounds and processes occurring in living organisms

Gladys Anderson Emerson conducted pioneering research into the biochemistry* of nutrition and the links between nutrition and disease. She pursued her undergraduate education at the Oklahoma College for Women, majoring in both chemistry and English. She graduated from college in 1925 and the following year earned a master's degree in history from Stanford University. In 1932 she earned a Ph.D. in animal nutrition and biochemistry from the University of California at Berkeley. She then went to Germany where she studied chemistry under Nobel laureate Adolf Windaus.

Emerson returned to the United States in 1933 and took a research position at the Institute of Experimental Biology at Berkeley. During her time there, she made her first major discovery—she was the first person to isolate vitamin E, from wheat germ oil. After nine years she left Berkeley to take a post with the pharmaceutical firm Merck and Company. Rising to the head of its animal nutrition department, she led research that studied the vitamin B complex. Her research showed that a lack of vitamin B had severe negative health consequences for animals. For example, she found that rhesus monkeys deprived of vitamin B$_6$ developed hardening of the arteries.

Emerson later investigated the links between diet and cancer at the Sloan Kettering Institute in New York, where she worked from 1950 to 1953. In 1969 President Richard Nixon appointed her vice president of a national panel on food, nutrition, and health. In this position she testified at Food and Drug Administration (FDA) hearings on vitamin and mineral supplements and food additives. She also helped draft the U.S. Department of Agriculture's guidelines for dietary allowances. In addition to her scientific work, Emerson was an author, lecturer, and an award-winning photographer.

Joseph ERLANGER
1874–1965
PHYSIOLOGY

* **physiologist** one who specializes in physiology, the science that deals with the functions of living organisms and their parts
* **electrophysiology** branch of physiology that deals with the basic mechanisms by which electric currents are generated within living organisms
* **neurophysiology** branch of physiology that deals with the nervous system

* **cardiac** of, near, or related to the heart
* **pulse pressure** difference in blood pressure between when the heart contracts and when it relaxes
* **pulse wave** increase in arterial blood pressure that occurs when the heart contracts

The American physiologist* Joseph Erlanger made important contributions to the fields of electrophysiology* and neurophysiology*. His research into the functions of nerves greatly increased the understanding of the physiology of the central nervous system. This work won Erlanger and his colleague Herbert GASSER the 1944 Nobel Prize in physiology or medicine.

Early Life and Education. Born in San Francisco, California, Erlanger was the son of a German immigrant who came to California during the gold rush in the 1850s. He received his early education at the San Francisco Boys' High School. Thereafter, he studied chemistry at the University of California in preparation for a career in medicine. Erlanger then attended the newly founded Johns Hopkins Medical School in Baltimore, Maryland. He performed research during vacations, which he could not spend at home because of the cost of travel between Maryland and California. He focused his research on determining the relationship between specific nerves and muscles. His results provided the first decisive experimental confirmation of the view that each muscle is activated by definite motor nerve cells.

Scientific Researcher. Throughout his career Erlanger's research was marked by his interest in both physiology and medicine. In 1901 he published a paper titled "A Study of the Metabolism in Dogs with Shortened Small Intestines" in which he sought to determine the amount of intestine that could be surgically removed from dogs and yet let them survive. This paper came to the attention of William H. Howell, a professor of physiology at Johns Hopkins, who hired Erlanger as an assistant professor.

Thereafter, much of Erlanger's research was concentrated on circulation and cardiac* physiology. In 1904 he devised and built a sphygmomanometer (a device for measuring arterial blood pressure), which enabled him to demonstrate that pulse pressure* can give the precise volume of the pulse wave*. With this finding he could explain how pulse pressure affects kidney secretion of the protein albumin into the urine. This condition is known as albuminuria.

The same year Erlanger also began to study how impulses in the heart are transmitted, stimulating the organ's rhythmic beats. He proved that the Stokes-Adams syndrome, which is characterized by fainting spells, results from poor transmission of those impulses between different chambers and valves in the heart. These pioneering experiments formed the basis of much of the current knowledge about the conduction of impulses in the heart.

In 1906 Erlanger accepted a position as head of the physiology department at the University of Wisconsin. He was asked to set up a modern laboratory and was also responsible for teaching physiology. Four years later Erlanger moved to the medical school of Washington University in St. Louis, Missouri, where he became professor of physiology. Although World War I temporarily diverted Erlanger's activity he resumed his work on circulation after the war. He investigated the mechanism that produces the sounds that are detected by a stethoscope when placed on the skin over arteries during blood pressure measurement. Working with another researcher named J.C. Bramwell, Erlanger demonstrated that pulse waves in the arteries act much like the sea waves on a beach, breaking when they reach a certain magnitude. The crests and troughs of the waves correspond to sharp and dull sounds heard through a stethoscope.

In 1921 Erlanger and his former student Herbert Gasser began new research that developed into the field of modern neurophysiology. Using an early type of oscilloscope, a device that depicts periodic changes in electric voltage or current on a fluorescent screen, they obtained an exact picture of the electrical activity of nerve impulses. They discovered that the action potential* of a nerve is formed by several wave patterns traveling at different speeds. The results led Erlanger and Gasser to formulate the idea that the speed of nerve impulses is directly proportional to the thickness of the nerve fibers, and that each fiber requires a stimulus of different intensity to create an impulse. Erlanger and Gasser also discovered that different nerve fibers transmit different kinds of impulses, each represented by a different type of wave pattern. From these findings they concluded that different nerve fibers have different functions. They were jointly awarded the 1944 Nobel Prize in physiology or medicine for their discoveries.

When Erlanger reached retirement age, he did not stop working. He taught in the medical school of Washington University during World War II, when many of his younger colleagues were called to military service. After the war he maintained contact with members of his laboratory, providing them with the benefit of his knowledge of the field of physiology. An accomplished writer, he also focused on recording the history of physiology as a science. He died in St. Louis in 1965.

* **action potential** temporary change in the electric charge on the surface of a nerve or muscle cell that occurs when the cell is stimulated

Alice Catherine
EVANS
1881–1975
BACTERIOLOGY

The American bacteriologist* Alice Catherine Evans discovered that raw cow's milk contains a bacterium that causes spontaneous abortions in cows and a deadly fever in humans. She proved that humans contracted brucellosis—a dangerous bacterial disease—when they drank the milk of infected cows or handled infected animals. Her work led to the widespread use of pasteurization to ensure the safety of milk.

Evans was born in rural Pennsylvania. Her father was a surveyor, teacher, and farmer. She was educated at local schools but could not afford college and became a schoolteacher. She attended a free program for teachers at Cornell University. Scholarships and grants enabled her to study natural science and agriculture at the University of Wisconsin. The high quality of her work earned her a job with the U.S. Department of Agriculture. She studied bacteria in cow's milk and discovered that the *Brucellae* bacteria caused a condition known as undulant fever in cows or Malta fever in humans. She also proved that because this fever often resembles influenza and other diseases, it was frequently misdiagnosed. Evans herself fell ill with the disease, and she suffered from it for more than 20 years. The government and the dairy industry eventually accepted her argument for heat pasteurization to kill bacteria in milk.

Evans overcame much skepticism about her findings. Some scientists doubted her because she was a woman. Others questioned her findings because she lacked a Ph.D. Still others belittled her research because she worked for the United States government rather than for a university.

She received many awards and served as the first female president of the American Society of Bacteriologists. She retired in 1945 as senior bacteriologist at the National Institutes of Health. Evans died in a nursing home in Virginia following a stroke at the age of 94.

Niels Ryberg
FINSEN

1860–1904
PHOTOTHERAPY

Niels Ryberg Finsen understood that phototherapy, or the therapeutic use of light, could assist in healing. He may have gained his appreciation for light from his lifelong love of the outdoors. He was the son of the governor of the rugged Faeroe Islands in Denmark, where he was born and raised. He was schooled in Reykjavik, Iceland, and studied to be a doctor in Denmark's capital, Copenhagen.

Finsen's attention first turned to light when treating patients with smallpox. He saw that their irritated skin developed painful swelling and blisters from exposure to too much sunlight. He found that the harmful effects came from the blue, violet, and ultraviolet end of the light spectrum. The other end, which contains the red and infrared wavelengths, actually helped the patients' skin to heal. Finsen treated patients by putting them in rooms bathed in red light. He published his results in 1893 and 1894.

Meanwhile, another scientist had conducted experiments showing that bacteria could be killed by light. Inspired by this and other work on light, Finsen used a powerful lamp to produce intense ultraviolet light to kill the bacteria that caused lupus vulgaris, a disfiguring form of tuberculosis of the skin. His success made him famous in international medical circles and encouraged a wave of light treatments.

In 1896 private donors founded a Light Institute for phototherapy in Copenhagen and Finsen became its director. The institute was later named after him. Sadly, Finsen did not live to direct the institute for long. He had suffered from an infection of the tissues around his heart since the age of 23. The condition worsened over time, and Finsen died one year after accepting the 1903 Nobel Prize in physiology* or medicine.

Alexander
FLEMING

1881–1955
BACTERIOLOGY

* **physiology** science that deals with the functions of living organisms and their parts

* **bacteriologist** specialist who studies microscopic organisms called bacteria that can cause infection and disease

* **antibacterial** referring to substances that hinder the growth of bacteria, microscopic organisms that can cause infection and disease

The winner of the Nobel Prize in physiology* or medicine in 1945, Scottish bacteriologist* Alexander Fleming spent most of his professional career investigating the human body's defenses against bacterial infections. In 1928 he discovered the antibacterial* substance penicillin, paving the way for the effective treatment of life-threatening infectious diseases.

Life, Education, and Career. The descendant of Scottish farmers, Fleming was born in the tiny and remote rural village of Lochfield in Ayrshire, Scotland. His father died when Fleming was only seven years old. Fleming received his early education at several local schools, including the Dorval School and Kilmarnock Academy. During these years he learned to observe nature closely and to enjoy the simple pleasures of rural life.

At age 13 Fleming moved to London, where he lived with an older brother and sister and attended classes at the Regent Street Polytechnic school. Two years later Fleming became a clerk in a shipping company. In 1900 he enlisted in the London Scottish Regiment and planned to fight in the Boer War, a conflict between the British and the descendants of earlier Dutch settlers in South Africa. But the war ended before he had the opportunity to travel overseas.

About a year after Fleming joined the Scottish Regiment, he received a small inheritance, which he decided to use to study medicine. He did very well in his college entrance examinations and won a scholarship to St. Mary's Hospital Medical School, which was affiliated with the University of London. He graduated from the school in 1908.

Fleming maintained a lifelong association with St. Mary's and the university. Named assistant director of the Inoculation Department of the hospital in 1921, he became professor of bacteriology and head of the department seven years later. Fleming retired from his professorship in 1948. He then became head of the Wright-Fleming Institute, which was associated with the University of London, until his retirement in 1955. He died the same year.

Research and Accomplishments. Early in his career, Fleming became very interested in antiseptics (substance free of organisms that produce infection or disease) and the natural antibacterial action of blood. He supported the ideas of his mentor and colleague Sir Almroth Wright, who believed that vaccines could be used as immunization against bacterial infection. During World War I, Fleming joined the Royal Army Medical Corps and served under Wright at a wound-research laboratory in Boulogne, France. Using simple, ingenious techniques, Fleming demonstrated the antibacterial power of pus and the inability of chemical antiseptics to sterilize serious wounds. He also supported Wright in advocating the use of a saline solution to irrigate infected wounds.

After leaving the army in 1919, Fleming returned to St. Mary's and resumed his study of antibacterial mechanisms and substances. Over the next decade he did his best work in this discipline. One of his first accomplishments was to show that ordinary germicides (substance used to kill germs) damaged the white blood cells in infected blood. This finding led

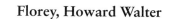

Fleming to condemn the practice of injecting chemical antiseptics directly into the bloodstream. He argued that the ideal antibacterial agent should hinder the growth of bacteria without affecting the body's normal tissues.

In 1921, while searching for ideal antibacterial substances, Fleming discovered a substance called lysozyme, an enzyme* found in certain body fluids, such as tears and saliva. The substance exhibited certain antibiotic* characteristics. Several years later, while working with a bacterium called *Staphylococcus,* Fleming noticed a bacteria-free circle around a mold growth in a laboratory testing dish. The mold was later identified as *Penicillium notatum.* Fleming studied this substance, which he named "penicillin." He reported that it did not harm blood cells and suggested that it might be an efficient antiseptic agent.

Because he lacked adequate skills in chemistry, Fleming was unable to isolate the antibacterial components of penicillin and obtain sufficient quantities for use in humans. Other scientists took up the challenge, however, and by the early 1940s, the remarkable antibiotic powers of penicillin had been established. As the discoverer of penicillin, Fleming received many tributes and honors, including a knighthood. In 1945 he shared the Nobel Prize with Ernst CHAIN and Howard FLOREY, the two scientists who isolated and purified penicillin for use as an antibiotic.

* **enzyme** any of numerous complex proteins that are produced by living cells and catalyze specific biochemical reactions at body temperature

* **antibiotic** any chemical substance produced by various microscopic organisms that hinders the growth of or destroys other harmful microorganisms

Howard Walter
FLOREY

1898–1968
PATHOLOGY

* **pathologist** specialist in the study of diseases and their effects on organisms

* **biochemist** person who specializes in the science that deals with chemical compounds and processes occurring in living organisms

* **clinical** related to the observation and treatment of disease in actual patients rather than in artificial experiments

* **antibacterial** referring to substances that hinder the growth of bacteria, microscopic organisms that can cause infection and disease

* **physiology** science that deals with the functions of living organisms and their parts

* **neurophysiologist** specialist in neurophysiology, a branch of physiology that deals with the nervous system

The Australian pathologist* Howard Walter Florey and British biochemist* Ernst CHAIN extracted and purified penicillin—discovered by Alexander FLEMING in 1928—and directed its production in quantities large enough to make it available as a clinical* drug. For their achievements with this antibacterial* drug, Florey, Chain, and Fleming shared the Nobel Prize in physiology* or medicine in 1945.

Early Life and Education. Born in Adelaide, Australia, Florey was the son of a prosperous factory owner. After attending St. Peter's Collegiate School, Florey had a brilliant scholastic career at the University of Adelaide. Interested in medicine and medical research from an early age, Florey enrolled in the Faculty of Medicine at the University in 1917. He graduated five years later with a bachelor's degree and a master's degree.

The award of a Rhodes scholarship allowed Florey to travel to Great Britain in 1922 to attend Oxford University, where he studied in the Honours Physiology School. There, he was taught by the great neurophysiologist* Charles SHERRINGTON, who had a profound effect on Florey's outlook on pathology. Florey was so impressed by the value of the Honours program that, when he later became professor of pathology at Oxford, he insisted that all candidates for the doctoral program in pathology study there before beginning experimental work.

After studying pathology and medicine at Oxford, Florey spent a year at Cambridge University and then went to the United States as a student at the Rockefeller Institute. After his return to Great Britain, Florey spent a short period at the London Hospital before returning to Cambridge, where he received a Ph.D. The most important influence on his career at

In addition to extracting, purifying, and making penicillin available as a useful clinical drug, Howard Florey was the president of England's Royal Society, the highest office in British science. During his tenure Florey established the Royal Society Population Study Group and acted as its chairman until his death.

* **microbe** microscopic organism

* **antibiotic** any chemical substance produced by various microscopic organisms that hinders the growth of or destroys other harmful microorganisms

Cambridge came from the famous biochemist Frederick Gowland HOP-KINS, who was then at the height of his career. In 1926 Florey married Mary Ethel Reed, who had been a fellow student at Adelaide University.

Teaching Career. In 1931 Florey was appointed professor of pathology at the University of Sheffield in England. Four years later he moved to Oxford as professor of pathology at the Sir William Dunn School of Pathology. Florey's appointment to this position marked a milestone in the history of pathology in Great Britain. For the first time, an individual with a background in physiology came to a position of influence in the teaching of pathology. Florey remained at the William Dunn School until 1962, when he resigned to become provost (director) of Queen's College, Oxford.

Florey created a very lively and stimulating atmosphere at the William Dunn School, encouraging interactions among department members. This cooperation later played an important role in the department's early work on penicillin. It also resulted in the Sir William Dunn School becoming the leading center of experimental pathology in Europe. Under Florey's leadership and inspiration, the university shaped the careers of a number of capable and brilliant young students.

Florey stayed in Britain for the remainder of his career, and his life was centered at Oxford after 1935. However, he maintained close ties with his Australian roots. In 1944 the prime minister of Australia invited him to Australia to report on the condition of medical research there. Florey's report led to the establishment of the Australian National University as a graduate university in 1946.

Florey remained closely connected with the Australian National University for the next decade as a senior adviser with a particular interest in the John Curtin School of Medical Research. He played a major role in establishing the school, and he visited the university as a consultant every year until 1957. In 1965 he was appointed chancellor of the university (an honorary post) and continued to take his annual trips.

Work and Research. Florey was unique among his contemporary pathologists in Great Britain because of his interests and approach. He was interested in studying the changes in the physiology and biochemistry that caused pathological changes in diseased cells, rather than in merely describing diseased tissues. He also had a great interest in the structure of tissues. In his later life, he made extensive use of electron microscopes to study tissue structure in great detail.

One of Florey's main interests was natural antibacterial substances. The idea of antibiosis—the antagonism that occurs between different types of microbes*—was not new in Florey's time. French chemist Louis Pasteur had made observations on the topic in the late 1800s. Alexander Fleming had discovered penicillin, but he had looked at it only as a useful antiseptic for treating specific infection sites and did not recognize that it could be used more generally as a powerful antibacterial substance. However, the work done by Florey and his colleague Ernst Chain transformed penicillin into a clinical tool of immense value, opening up the new industry of antibiotic* production.

Shortly after arriving at Oxford, Florey sought advice from Frederick HOPKINS to find a suitable person to lead a biochemical unit in the School of Pathology. Hopkins recommended Ernst Chain, a young refugee from Nazi Germany who was then working in Hopkins's laboratory. This recommendation proved to be critical as far as the development of penicillin was concerned, because Chain possessed the biochemical insight that enabled him to purify penicillin without the loss of its potency.

In 1930 Florey began a study of the antibacterial properties of lysozyme, an enzyme* discovered by Fleming in 1921. Florey pursued this work until he successfully purified the enzyme and determined its actions. Encouraged by the success of a contemporary scientist who was working in the same field, Florey and Chain then investigated the biological and chemical properties of the antibacterial substances that bacteria and molds produced.

By good fortune Florey and Chain selected penicillin as the first substance to study in detail. Their results were so promising that all the resources at the Oxford laboratory were turned to penicillin production on a scale that enabled Florey and Chain to conduct extensive clinical trials. Many tests were necessary before penicillin could be used in human medicine. However, because of the skills possessed by the scientists Florey had gathered around him, work proceeded rapidly.

In 1941 penicillin was used to treat nine cases of human bacterial infection. All patients responded very positively to the drug. But Britain's involvement in World War II at this time limited Florey's ability to produce enough of the drug for wartime use. He then went to the United States to stimulate interest in penicillin. His persistence paid off. After 1943 penicillin was available in sufficient quantities to treat war casualties as well as instances of diseases such as pneumonia, meningitis, syphilis, and diphtheria. In 1945 Florey, Chain, and Fleming all shared the Nobel Prize in physiology or medicine for their work on penicillin. Florey continued his research on antibiotics at Oxford for the next ten years.

After 1955 Florey returned to research in experimental pathology and remained active as a laboratory investigator for the rest of his life. His interests ranged widely, but they were generally concentrated on determining the structure and function of smaller blood vessels and their role in the process of inflammation. He did valuable research into the physiology of mucus secretion as well, clarifying its protective function in the respiratory and intestinal tracts. He also worked on the antibiotic known as micrococcin, the study of blood vessels, and the nature of atherosclerosis (hardening of the arteries). He remained active in science until his death, publishing two major works on the structure and function of blood vessel cells in 1967, the year before he died.

Florey received numerous honors during his career and was associated with a number of scientific organizations. He was knighted in 1944 and was awarded honorary degrees from British and Australian universities. He was president of the British Royal Society from 1960 to 1965, the first Australian and the first pathologist to hold this position. He was associated with the Royal College of Physicians in London and the Australian Academy of Sciences, and was elected an honorary member of the National Academy of Sciences of the United States.

* **enzyme** any of numerous complex proteins that are produced by living cells and catalyze specific biochemical reactions at body temperature

Dian FOSSEY

1932–1985

ANIMAL BEHAVIOR

* **anthropologist** scientist who specializes in the study of human beings, especially in relation to origins and cultural characteristics

Dian Fossey is famous for her studies of the mountain gorillas in Rwanda. She is seen here with her teammates with whose help she conducted her research.

Dian Fossey was the world's leading activist in the movement to preserve mountain gorillas, the rarest species of the great apes. She led a vigorous crusade against poachers and in support of gorilla habitat protection that ultimately led to her murder. She also studied these animals using the observational techniques pioneered by the animal behaviorist Jane GOODALL. That the mountain gorilla has not become extinct is largely due to the public awareness that Fossey brought to their plight.

The Early Years. Fossey was born in San Francisco, California. Her parents divorced when she was six, and her mother soon remarried. She considered her stepfather unloving and unnecessarily strict. Consequently her childhood was lonely and unhappy.

After graduating from high school, Fossey enrolled in a preveterinary program at the University of California at Davis, against the wishes of her stepfather. However, she was unable to handle the academic demands of the program and subsequently transferred to San Jose State College to study occupational therapy. She graduated in 1954 and took a job as the director of the occupational therapy department at Kosair Crippled Children's Hospital in Louisville, Kentucky.

Fossey became fascinated with the mountain gorillas in Africa when she read a book about them written by the zoologist George Shaller. In 1963 she borrowed $8,000 to finance a seven-week trip to Africa, where she met the anthropologist* Louis Leakey, who had supported Goodall's studies of chimpanzees in Tanzania. Fossey encountered her first mountain gorilla when she traveled to the Democratic Republic of Congo (formerly Zaire). Her observations of the mountain gorillas solidified her desire to study the great apes and ultimately changed her life.

Three years later, Leakey visited Kentucky on a lecture tour. Fossey convinced him to hire her to study mountain gorillas. He agreed but told her that she must first have her appendix removed. Not realizing that Leakey was only testing her desire to go to Africa and that he did not really expect her to undergo the operation, she immediately had her appendix removed.

Africa and Activism. Fossey arrived in Zaire in 1967. She intended to study the gorillas at the Parc National des Virungas, but a violent civil war forced her to relocate to nearby Rwanda, where she set up a site that she named the Karisoke Research Center. Fossey found the mountain gorillas difficult to observe because they had been hunted and harassed by poachers and indigenous Batusi tribesmen. After spending months approaching the gorillas slowly and imitating their behavior, she finally earned their trust and was able to observe them at close range.

Before Fossey began observing mountain gorillas little was known about them because of their remote habitat. Fossey's studies revealed that the gorillas were gentle vegetarian creatures with strong family bonds. Realizing that she would need an advanced degree to attract funding for her research, Fossey left Africa after three years to complete a Ph.D. in zoology at Cambridge University. Thereafter she returned to Karisoke and became more militant in her campaign to protect the gorillas from poachers. In 1977 her favorite gorilla, Digit, was killed. Six months later poachers shot two more gorillas. These deaths made national news in the United States and increased public awareness of the plight of the mountain gorillas.

As the years passed Fossey grew increasingly aggressive in her war against poachers. She withdrew from people and identified more and more with the gorillas. Between 1980 and 1983, however, Fossey was forced to leave Africa for health reasons. She returned to America and accepted a position at Cornell University. During this time she published a book about her experiences, *Gorillas in the Mist,* which was later made into a movie of the same name.

By the time Fossey returned to Karisoke in 1983, she had been transformed from a scientist and observer into an animal activist. At one point she kidnapped the child of a poacher so that she could exchange the child for a gorilla the poacher had captured. Two years later she was found murdered at her camp. Although no one was charged with her murder, most people believe poachers were responsible. Her efforts to conserve and protect mountain gorillas are continued by The Dian Fossey Gorilla Fund. (*See also* **Leakeys, The.**)

Rosalind Elsie
FRANKLIN

1920–1958

PHYSICAL CHEMISTRY,
MOLECULAR BIOLOGY

Rosalind Elsie Franklin won international recognition for her work in industrial chemistry. She is best remembered, however, for her essential contribution to one of the great scientific triumphs of the 1950s: the understanding of the structure of deoxyribonucleic acid (DNA), the molecular carrier of the genetic* information in all living organisms.

An Expert with X rays. Franklin was born in London into a family that was connected with banking and the arts rather than with science. However,

Franklin, Rosalind Elsie

Rosalind Franklin's greatest strength as a scientist was her skilled and precise use of X-ray techniques to examine the structure of molecules. Using her skills she made significant contributions to the study of three very different substances—coal, human DNA, and a plant virus.

she did well in the sciences as a scholarship student at St. Paul's Girls School, one of the few London schools that taught physics and chemistry to female students. Although she was encouraged by her father to consider a career in social work, Franklin decided that she wanted to study science. Subsequently, when she entered Newnham College at Cambridge University, she studied physical chemistry. She graduated in 1941 and accepted a research scholarship to work in the laboratory of future Nobel Prize winner Ronald Norrish.

The following year, Franklin went to work for the British Coal Utilisation Research Association. Together with other researchers, she formed a theory about the molecular structure of coal to explain the way coal absorbs liquids and gases and the way it expands when heated. Between 1947 and 1950, she worked at the Laboratoire Central des Services Chimiques de l'État in Paris, France, where she continued her work on coals and related carbon materials. She also studied X-ray diffraction, a method of using X rays to produce images of molecular structures. She developed a procedure for making detailed interpretations of X-ray diagrams of carbons. Using this tool, she was able to describe carbon structures more precisely than ever before. She focused on examining the changes that occur in carbons when they are heated to high temperatures to form graphite. Franklin showed that there are two broad classes of carbons, those that form graphite when heated to high temperatures and those that do not.

DNA and TMV. In 1951 Franklin received a fellowship to join the Medical Research Council Biophysics Unit at King's College in London. At the time, this group was working to solve the structure of DNA. Franklin was brought in to use her X-ray diffraction skills to produce clearer images of DNA. A few months later, she gave a talk on the results of the work that she had done with another scientist, Raymond Gosling. She showed that their data reflected that the basic shape of the DNA molecule was a helix (spiral- or coil-shaped) and noted that it could take one of two different forms, depending on the amount of water that surrounded the molecule.

Franklin conducted further investigations into the specific structure of the two forms of the DNA molecule. Although she refused to commit to the idea that the structure of the molecule was definitely a double helix, her interpretations of her results were leading her in this direction. However, she had not come to a firm conclusion when, in the spring of 1953, researchers James Watson and Francis Crick of Cambridge, England, announced that they had discovered that the structure of DNA was a double helix, with two parallel strands of material. This discovery earned them the 1962 Nobel Prize in physiology* or medicine. Ironically, Watson and Crick had received an important clue from one of Franklin's best pictures, which had not yet been published but which Maurice WILKINS, another member of Franklin's laboratory, had shown to Watson and Crick without her knowledge. In addition, her interpretations of the images provided Watson and Crick with the most compelling evidence to support their double helix model of DNA. On the eve of the announcement of Watson and Crick's discovery, Franklin was working on a paper in which she proposed

a double-chain helical structure for DNA, but her model departed from the correct double helix model in significant ways.

The same year, Franklin joined the Crystallography Laboratory of Birkbeck College in London, where she remained until her death five years later. She continued to publish her earlier work on coals and on DNA. She also applied her X-ray diffraction techniques to the study of the tobacco mosaic virus (TMV), which produces various diseases in the family of plants that includes tobacco. By 1956 she had greatly improved on the images of TMV compared to those done earlier, and eventually she was able to present a detailed structure of the virus. She contributed to studies of the molecular structure of TMV, demonstrating that the genetic material of the virus—its RNA*—takes the form of a single-strand helix, rather than the double strand found in DNA.

In 1956 Franklin fell ill and was operated on unsuccessfully for cancer. The following year she underwent a second operation, which was also unsuccessful. Neither operation disrupted her work, and just before her death she had begun studies of the structure of the poliovirus. She died in 1958 at the age of 37, internationally recognized as both an industrial chemist and a molecular biologist. (*See also* **Watson and Crick.**)

* **RNA** ribonucleic acid, a cellular molecule similar to DNA that is involved in the production of proteins in the cell

---

Sigmund
FREUD

1856–1939

PSYCHOLOGY

Sigmund Freud is sometimes called the founder of modern psychology, the scientific study of the mind and how it operates. During his long and influential career, Freud worked on understanding and relieving mental illnesses, developed a theory of the mind, and made psychology into a frame of reference for examining social and historical subjects. His major achievement was the creation of psychoanalysis, a method of analyzing and treating mental conditions. Although modern researchers have questioned and overturned some of Freud's ideas and conclusions, both supporters and critics of Freud agree that his exploration of the mind was one of the most significant scientific achievements of the twentieth century.

Life and Career

Throughout Freud's life, he placed a high value on the physical sciences. When he took up the study of medicine, his original goal was to become a researcher in biology, not a student of the mind.

Family Background. Freud was born in the city of Freiberg in Moravia, which was then a province of the Austrian empire. Today the city, known as Pribor, is in the Czech Republic. His father, Jakob Freud, was a wool merchant. His mother was Jakob's second wife, and she was 20 years younger than her husband.

Freud was the oldest child in his father's second family, although a much older half brother, who had a son about Freud's age, lived nearby. Freud later wrote that the confusion he felt at an early age about family relationships sharpened his intellect and his curiosity. He also described the effect of his mother's love and support: "A man who has been the indisputable

Freud, Sigmund

Sigmund Freud pioneered the exploration of the inner world of the human psyche (mind). His influential ideas about the mind and its workings made psychology one of the 20th century's most-used tools for examining not just the lives of individuals but society, history, and art as well.

favorite of his mother keeps for life the feeling of a conqueror, that confidence of success that often [brings] real success."

A collapse in Freiberg's wool trade forced the Freud family to move to Vienna in 1860. Freud's father was unemployed for much of the rest of his life, and at times the family was on the brink of poverty. Freud's parents encouraged him to be a good student, expecting him to have a distinguished career, and he shared this ambitious view of his future.

Education and Medical Training. Between the ages of 9 and 17, Freud attended the Sperl Gymnasium, a school in Vienna that emphasized the teaching of languages and mathematics and prepared students for university study. After graduating, he entered the University of Vienna, where he studied medicine, not because he wanted to practice as a physician but because he wanted to begin a scientific study of the human condition. Freud received his medical degree in 1881. He had taken three years longer than necessary to qualify for it because he spent much of his time conducting research under Ernst von Brücke, an expert in physiology*.

At Brücke's research institute, Freud studied the nerve cells of fish and crayfish and the anatomy of the human brain. Although he had made a successful start on a research career, he changed his plans in 1882 when he met and fell in love with Martha Bernays, the daughter of an intellectually distinguished German Jewish family. Freud's income as a researcher would not allow him to support a wife, so he decided to acquire the experience he would need to set himself up in medical practice.

In 1882 Freud joined the staff of the Vienna General Hospital and worked in various departments for short periods, but he spent 14 months

* **physiology** science that deals with the functions of living organisms and their parts

in the department of nervous diseases because he intended to specialize in neuropathology, the treatment of ailments of the nervous system. During this time, he continued his anatomical research on the human brain and began to study—and use—the drug cocaine, which he believed improved his mood and his ability to work. He published several articles on the medical benefits of cocaine, and in his letters to his fiancée he expressed his hope that this research would bring him fame. Within two years, however, reports of his cocaine addiction began to surface. The drug had not proved as beneficial as Freud had expected, and for a time his medical reputation suffered.

Professional and Personal Life. Freud left Vienna in late 1885 to spend four months in Paris, studying under Jean-Martin Charcot, France's leading neurologist*. Charcot focused his research on hysteria, a condition in which patients may suffer physical symptoms, such as paralysis, with no obvious physical cause. Freud also turned his attention to hysteria.

The following year Freud returned to Vienna and practiced as a neuropathologist, a specialist in the treatment of diseases of the nervous system. He married Martha and the couple had six children. One daughter, Anna, later became a colleague of her father and a noted psychologist.

Freud maintained his office next to his family's living quarters. He divided his time between his family, his practice, and extensive writing. In the early years of his practice, he also spent several days a week at a children's clinic, where he was head of the neurology department. Throughout his career, he lectured at the University of Vienna.

After his return from Paris, Freud had begun a friendship with Josef Breuer, a physician with experience in the study and treatment of nervous disorders, including hysteria. In 1895 Breuer and Freud published *Studies in Hysteria,* which described cases that helped Freud develop psychoanalysis*. Breuer, however, did not agree with some of Freud's ideas, and the friendship ended with bitter feelings on Freud's part.

Freud also befriended Wilhelm Fleiss, a doctor in Berlin with whom he corresponded between 1893 and 1900. In his letters to Fleiss, Freud discussed his developing theories of psychoanalysis. Fleiss provided a sounding board for Freud. Their friendship ended abruptly as well. Some modern psychoanalysts, using Freud's own ideas and methods, have interpreted these failed friendships as Freud's search for approval from an authoritative father figure. However, the search seems to have ended after Freud became the intellectual father figure of the psychoanalytic movement.

Freud remained in good health into his late 60s, but in 1923 he developed cancer of the jaw. He continued his practice, his correspondence, and his writing, but in spite of many surgeries, the disease eventually took his life. Freud died in London in 1939, a short time after the outbreak of World War II had driven him out of Vienna.

Ideas and Influence

Freud developed the theory and practice of psychoanalysis over many years, beginning with his treatment of hysteria. His private practice and

* **neurologist** scientist who specializes in neurology, the study of the structure, function, and disorders of the nervous system

* **psychoanalysis** method of treating emotional disorders in which the patient is encouraged to talk freely about personal experiences

his own rigorous self-analysis also contributed to what became an inclusive theory of human thought and behavior. Freud's followers made psychoanalysis an important part of psychological therapy, especially in the United States.

From the Brain to the Mind. In the early years, Freud made a significant contribution to traditional neuropathology. His first book, *Aphasia,* published in 1891, was a survey of the condition in which damage or injury to the brain leads to the loss or impairment of the power to use or understand words. His interest in aphasia might have been a reflection of his desire to understand how processes in the brain and nervous system relate to psychological, or mental, activities. In 1895 he published *Psychology for Neurologists,* which deals with this question. During the 1890s Freud also wrote three important works on cerebral paralysis in children.

The first phase of Freud's psychoanalytic thought was based on his experience with hysteria, which physicians believed had both physical and psychological causes. Hereditary weakness of the nervous system was blamed in most cases, and it was thought that a painful or stressful psychological event, acting on a weakened nervous system, produced the symptoms of hysteria, such as blindness, paralysis, or extreme excitability. Doctors usually tried to treat hysteria with physical therapies, such as bed rest or electric shock. Breuer, however, discovered that when he encouraged patients to talk in detail about their symptoms, the symptoms were relieved for a time. Breuer also found that if he hypnotized hysteric patients and told them that their symptoms would disappear, the symptoms did disappear, at least temporarily.

Freud's work with Charcot in Paris had already caused him to consider hysteria's psychological aspects as well as its physical ones. He adopted Breuer's methods of hypnotic suggestion and encouraged his patients to talk candidly about themselves. Freud doubted the value of electric stimulation and other physical therapies. From that point on, he directed his attention to the psychological rather than the physical causes of mental conditions.

Development of Psychoanalysis. After 1889 Freud expanded Breuer's "talking cure" into a technique he called free association. He encouraged the patient to say anything that came into his or her mind, without any conscious control. From what the patient said, Freud believed, a therapist could trace links to the patient's neurosis*.

* **neurosis** mental disorder with no obvious organic cause that involves anxiety, phobia, or other abnormal behavior; *pl.* neuroses

In developing the free association method, Freud formed several key concepts. One was the idea of the unconscious, a part of the mind that is not connected to conscious awareness, which he believed was a storehouse of hidden, forgotten, or forbidden thoughts, memories, and urges that had the power to influence behavior and to cause mental disturbance. He also believed that material unacceptable to conscious thought is buried or hidden in the unconscious by a mechanism that he called repression.

Freud also found that as he helped patients uncover and examine their repressed feelings, they often experienced feelings of love and desire for him. He called this process transference, because it meant that the patient was transferring buried feelings from their true object to the therapist. He believed transference was a regular and necessary part of psychoanalysis.

In 1896 Freud coined the term *psychoanalysis* to refer to the process of investigating the individual mind through free association and dream interpretation. He regarded psychoanalysis as a research tool and a means of developing theories about the human mind. At that time its usefulness in individual therapy was only secondary.

Mapping the Mind. Freud's experiences with female patients experiencing hysteria, together with his belief that the sexual organs produced nervous excitement or energy that affected the entire nervous system, convinced him that neuroses, or mental disturbances, were primarily sexual in origin. This principle remained one of the cornerstones of Freudian thought.

After the mid-1890s, Freud broadened the scope of his interest from hysteria to an overall theory of the mind. In a paper titled "Project for a Scientific Psychology" that was not published until 1954, he spelled out his ideas about how the structure and function of the nervous system affect thought and behavior. At the same time, Freud continued to develop and refine psychoanalysis by performing a long and detailed self-analysis. This was sparked, in part, by his father's death in 1897, an event that stirred up repressed emotions in Freud. His observations of his own mental states during this phase of the development of psychoanalysis were comparable in importance to all his case studies combined. Part of his self-analysis involved recording and examining his dreams.

Freud believed that dreams were a powerful tool for exploring the unconscious. He called them "the royal road to the unconscious" and believed that they were wish-fulfillment fantasies in which the unconscious expressed its desires. Sleep weakened the conscious mind's ability to censor and control the unconscious, allowing unconscious fantasies and urges to appear. However, because censorship did not disappear completely, these hidden feelings were often disguised in the form of symbols or images. For dreams to be useful in psychoanalysis, the analyst had to decode or interpret them. In 1901 Freud outlined methods of doing so in *The Interpretation of Dreams*, generally considered his most important work.

Four years later, Freud published *Three Essays on the Theory of Sexuality*, the second most important of his books. It summarized his ideas on the sexual basis of behavior that he had been developing for more than a decade. One of the most significant of these ideas was the concept of infantile sexuality, Freud's belief that sexual urges and desires are present even in the early stages of life. Freud used the term *libido* to describe the sexual impulse, and he believed that libido functioned as the sexual counterpart to hunger. He argued that libido, like hunger, is a greedy and demanding force that takes many forms.

In his book Freud claimed that from infancy to adulthood, people progress through a series of developmental stages, each with its own set of erotic or sexual feelings. For boys, one aspect of this development is a phase involving love of the mother and jealousy of the father. Freud linked this phenomenon to the Oedipus legend, after the character in Greek

Freud and the Nazis

Sigmund Freud knew the perils caused by anti-Jewish sentiments. After Adolf Hitler's Nazi party gained power in Germany, all Jews in German-controlled territory faced terrible discrimination and danger. When Germany threatened to invade Austria, Freud refused to flee to a foreign country, partly because he identified with Jews less fortunate than himself, those unable to flee. Finally, three months after Germany invaded Austria in 1938, Freud escaped to England. The Nazis burned his books and called psychoanalysis a "Jewish science," but they could not curb the spread of his ideas.

mythology that murdered his father and married his mother. Only after safely experiencing the various developmental stages do people achieve healthy sexual maturity. Sometimes, however, the psychological patterns and behaviors associated with early stages continue to dominate people during their adult lives, resulting in neuroses.

Freud's last major contribution to psychoanalytic theory was in 1923, when he published *The Ego and the Id,* which summarized his general theory of the mind, which he believed was divided into three parts. According to the book the first component of the mind, the id, sometimes seen as corresponding to the unconscious, consists of primitive urges—including libido—and desires for pleasure. Logic and reality have no effect on the id, which dominates in the infant mind. Over time, the unavoidable experience of frustration forces the infant to adjust to reality and to learn self-control. The second part of the mind, that which imposes controls and limits on the id, is called the ego. The third component of the mind, the superego, was Freud's version of the conscience, formed from the parents' commands and society's moral standards.

Psychology and the World. In the final phase of Freud's thought, he used his ideas about the structure and behavior of the mind as the starting point for an examination of culture, society, and history. *Totem and Taboo,* published in 1913, was Freud's most important work of social theory.

In *Totem and Taboo,* Freud drew on biologist Charles Darwin's theory that the first human societies were groups of brothers led by strong fathers. He also drew from anthropologist* James Frazer's influential book *The Golden Bough,* which points out that many societies have taboos* against incest (sexual intercourse between closely related persons) and against killing certain animals that are thought to be symbols, or totems, of groups or tribes. Freud expanded these ideas into the theory that in the distant past, sons had warred with fathers over control of their women. To overcome these violent tendencies, they had made rules against incest and against harming the father, who was identified with the totem animal. The totems that first represented ancestors eventually became the gods of organized religion.

Totem and Taboo dealt with the aggressive aspect of primitive society. In 1927 Freud wrote *Civilization and Its Discontents,* in which he described the hostile impulses that continue within developed societies. He claimed that social institutions that maintain order and justice represent the controlling superego, but that they can only *repress* aggression, not eliminate it. Discontent and turmoil are unavoidable in society because, beneath the orderly surface of civilized life, repressed primitive wishes and urges still produce guilt and anxiety.

Freud's Legacy. Freud's ideas were spread through Europe by the psychoanalytic movement that began with weekly meetings at Freud's home in Vienna. In 1910 the movement organized itself as the International Psychoanalytic Association. Leading members were Carl Jung of Switzerland and Alfred Adler and Sándor Ferenczi of Austria. Freud dominated the movement and said, "When the empire I founded is orphaned, no one but

* **anthropologist** scientist who specializes in the study of human beings, especially in relation to origins and cultural characteristics

* **taboo** prohibition imposed by social custom

The Fight over Freud

The controversy over Freud's place in the history of ideas made headlines in 1998, when the United States Library of Congress displayed part of its 80,000-piece Freud collection. A group of scholars opposed the exhibition, claiming that Freud's work is outdated and questionable. The exhibit's curator, however, pointed out that the important issue was not "whether the answers [Freud] gave were always correct but how his questions influenced the 20th century."

Jung must inherit the whole thing." However, Freud's insistence on controlling the movement drove away some of his closest European disciples. Adler disagreed with Freud about the importance of the Oedipus complex and left the group in 1911. Three years later, personal conflicts with Freud as well as differences over the importance of sexuality caused Jung to depart. Another disciple, Otto Rank, remained loyal to Freud until 1929, when he left the movement because Freud would not accept some of his ideas. Freud became convinced that Rank's move stemmed from his own neurosis. In fact, Freud and his followers often explained objections to Freud's ideas by claiming that those who disagreed with them were neurotic.

The authoritarian nature of the psychoanalytic movement was one reason for the relatively small influence of Freud's views in Europe. Another reason was its suppression by the Nazis after the early 1930s. The Nazis banned psychoanalysis and forced many of its practitioners, the majority of whom were Jewish, to leave Europe for England and the United States.

Freud's influence was strongest in the United States. Long before Freud received any similar honors in Europe, he was invited to give a series of lectures at Clark University in Worcester, Massachusetts. James Putnam, professor of neurology at Harvard University who became president of the newly formed American Psychoanalytic Society in 1910, welcomed Freud enthusiastically. American journals published articles by Freud and his followers.

Ironically, although Freud repeatedly said that medical training was of no value to psychoanalysts, in the United States physicians were the key element in the spread of his ideas. The American Psychoanalytic Association, which split from the international group in 1938, required psychoanalysts to be qualified as medical doctors. Traditionally, Americans respected the opinions of physicians. Because most psychoanalysts in the United States were physicians, and because even those physicians who were not psychoanalysts accepted parts of Freud's thought, the American population tended to view Freud and his ideas with respect.

Unlike Freud, who had valued psychoanalysis as a research method for developing the theory of the mind, American practitioners saw it primarily as a tool for treating patients. The peak of Freud's influence on American medicine came in the 1940s and 1950s, after World War II. The number of psychoanalysts increased. Psychiatry shared the flow of federal funds for medical research and education, and much of the money went to departments and institutions that strongly supported Freudian views. The increase in wealth in the United States also favored the growth of psychoanalysis, which was more costly than other forms of psychological therapy because it required more of a physician's time and lasted for longer periods. Only affluent people could bear the cost of psychoanalysis.

In later decades, new ideas, interpretations, and practices arose to challenge some of Freud's views. As far as the treatment of individual patients was concerned, traditional psychoanalysis began to give way to other methods, such as new drugs for controlling or altering mood and behavior, or short-term therapy with psychologists or counselors. In terms of theory, many psychologists began to consider Freud's ideas as outdated or wrong, and they began to investigate the degree to which he may have misinterpreted or misrepresented studies of patients to support his theories. Freud's emphasis on infantile sexual development as the main element that determined adult psychology gave way to more complex theories. Still, new views of psychological and sexual development continue to draw on his account of infantile sexuality, and his concept of the unconscious—the collection of invisible but powerful processes and ideas that drive thought and behavior—remains influential.

Freud, who opened the inner world to exploration, earned a lasting place in popular as well as scholarly culture. From the familiar image of the patient lying on a couch talking to a psychiatrist (a technique Freud developed) to the notion of the Freudian slip, an accidental mistake in speaking that reveals the speaker's true feelings, everyday life and language reflect Freud's influence.

Herbert Spencer GASSER

1888–1963

PHYSIOLOGY

Herbert Spencer Gasser made important contributions to the field of physiology, the science that deals with the functions of living organisms and their parts. In particular, he examined the way in which electrical signals are transmitted along neurons, the long, spindly nerve cells that connect the brain to the muscles and sense organs of the body.

Gasser was born in rural Wisconsin, the son of a doctor and a schoolteacher. The late 1800s were a time of exciting turmoil in science and culture, and Gasser's father had acquired books by such scientific thinkers as Charles Darwin and Thomas Henry Huxley, which the young Gasser read with great interest. He enrolled at the University of Wisconsin and majored in zoology before turning to medical studies, which he completed at Johns Hopkins University in 1915.

His early career was dominated by the events surrounding World War I. He studied the physical and mental shock suffered by soldiers, especially when they lost large quantities of blood. He also worked in the U.S. Chemical Warfare Service. After the war his career took him to Washington University, Cornell University Medical College, and finally to the Rockefeller Institute for Medical Research (now Rockefeller University), where he became director in 1935 and served in that position until his retirement in 1953. He continued active research until his death ten years later.

Gasser's pioneering research with neurons was done in collaboration with Joseph ERLANGER, whom he had met during his college years in Wisconsin. The two men found that they could record the electrical impulses of neurons using a cathode-ray oscilloscope—a common laboratory device that shows an electrical current as a waveform on a small screen. This technique was a major advance because it enabled scientists to measure and compare the different waveforms of various types of neurons.

When Gasser and Erlanger began their work, however, they encountered problems with the oscilloscope method because the instruments available at the time were not very sensitive. Because the electrical current generated by a neuron is very weak, it took many repetitions of the nerve impulse to draw a visible waveform on the screen. The repetitions, as well as the equipment, caused distortions, and the resulting images were not entirely reliable. This problem was not solved until more sensitive oscilloscopes became available, and Gasser was able to record single impulses of neuron activity.

Gasser studied many aspects of nerve impulses; he explored the relationship between the size of a neuron and the speed of the impulse; the activity of neurons that sense pain; the effects of myelin, a substance that coats some nerve cells; and the state of neurons after an electrical impulse had passed through them. In 1944 Gasser and Erlanger received the Nobel Prize in physiology or medicine for their work.

Gasser had clear ideas about the scientific work that guided his research. He believed that there are two opportune times for working on a problem—before anyone has thought of it and after everyone else has left it. He always liked to have either the first or the last word on a subject. Gasser also demanded that scientists use two different methods to approach a problem and consider the problem solved only when both methods yield the same results. He practiced this philosophy by studying nerve impulses not only with oscilloscopes but also with powerful electron microscopes. Gasser was often modest about his accomplishments, describing them in his papers with casual understatement. In addition to the Noble Prize, Gasser received many honors from universities in both the United States and Europe. He was also a member of the National Academy of Sciences, the American Philosophical Society, and a number of other professional societies.

Jane
GOODALL
born 1934
ANIMAL BEHAVIOR

* **paleoanthropologist** one who studies or practices paleoanthropology, the study of fossilized humans and their ancestral and related forms

Jane Goodall is the world's authority on chimpanzee behavior. She spent more than 25 years studying the behavior and social interactions of chimpanzees at Gombe Stream Reserve in Tanzania, Africa. Her sometimes-controversial methods have led to findings that contradict many widely held beliefs about chimpanzees. She also greatly extended knowledge of chimpanzee social behavior. Although no longer involved in primary research, Goodall continues to speak out about the ethical treatment of chimpanzees used in medical research and raises funds for their protection and continued study.

An Early Interest in Africa. Jane Goodall was born in 1934 in London, England. Her father was a businessman and her mother was a successful novelist. Early in her childhood, Goodall became fascinated with observing animal behavior. She read extensively about zoology and often sketched and made notes about the birds and animals in her neighborhood. Although neither of her parents had any special association with Africa, Goodall dreamed of traveling there to observe animals in their natural habitat.

After leaving school at age 18, Goodall worked as a secretary at Oxford University and took a second job with a documentary film company to save money to go to Africa. Her chance came when she was invited by a school friend to visit Kenya. There Goodall was introduced to the paleoanthropologist* Louis Leakey, who is best known for his discovery of early

Goodall, Jane

Jane Goodall began her career as an animal behaviorist in 1960, when she traveled to the Gombe Stream Research Center in Nigeria to study the behavioral patterns of chimpanzees. For more than 25 years, she spent nearly nine months each year in the region, observing and interacting with chimpanzees, as seen in this photograph.

* **evolution** historical development of a biological group such as a species

* **cannibalism** eating of the flesh of an animal by another animal of the same kind; also eating of human flesh by another human

* **ethnology** study of the division of humans into races and their origin, distribution, relations, and characteristics

human fossils at Olduvai Gorge in Tanzania. Goodall convinced Leakey to hire her as his secretary and as a participant in his anthropological dig in Tanzania.

In addition to studying early primate fossils, Leakey was interested in observing the behavior of living primates. He believed that the long-term study of the behavior of chimpanzees, gorillas, and other higher primates would provide information about primate evolution*. After getting to know Goodall, Leakey decided that she had the right temperament and personality to withstand the rigors of spending long periods alone in the jungle studying chimpanzees. Consequently, in 1960, Leakey funded Goodall's first expedition to study wild chimpanzees at Lake Tanganyika. However, some in the scientific community criticized his selection of Goodall as an observer because she did not have a college degree or formal training in the study of animal behavior.

Goodall's initial attempts to approach a band of chimpanzees met with failure. However, she soon found another nearby band that allowed her to approach and observe them. Day after day, Goodall followed the chimpanzees, taking care to behave in a nonthreatening way. She observed the chimpanzees' habits and social interactions, sometime imitating their behavior to gain acceptance. She also began feeding them bananas to encourage them to approach her. This activity was severely criticized by animal behaviorists. Her habit of giving the chimpanzees names and ascribing human emotions to their behavior also brought disapproval.

During the time she spent with the chimpanzees, Goodall noticed them hunting, eating small animals, and using natural materials as tools and weapons. She also observed cannibalism* among the chimpanzees, which shocked her romantic belief that chimpanzees are somehow morally better than humans. She also observed family bonding and social stratification within the group. Prior to her observations, chimpanzees were thought to be vegetarians, and scientists had believed that tool making and family bonding existed only among humans.

In 1962, while still in Africa, Goodall met Baron Hugo van Lawick, a Dutch wildlife photographer, and they were married two years later. (They were later divorced and she married Derek Bryceson, a former member of Parliament, in 1973.) In 1965 she returned to Cambridge to complete a Ph.D. in ethnology*, despite the fact that she had never attended college. Her thesis detailed her first five years of research in Africa.

Thereafter Goodall returned to Gombe Stream, where she continued her research and often supervised the work of many graduate students. She also wrote several books about her jungle experiences that serve as a bridge between scientific literature and popular writing. Her best-known books are *In the Shadow of Man, Through a Window: My Thirty Years with the Chimpanzees of Gombe,* and for children, *The Chimpanzee Family Book.*

Goodall is the recipient of many international conservation awards. Today she lectures about the ethical use of primates in medical research and raises money to rehabilitate chimpanzees and protect their habitat. The nonprofit Jane Goodall Institute for Wildlife Research, Education, and Conservation sponsors many of these activities. (*See also* **Fossey, Dian; Leakeys, The.**)

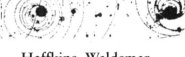

Waldemar
HAFFKINE

1860–1930

BACTERIOLOGY

* **inoculate** to introduce a disease agent into an animal or plant to produce a mild form of the disease and render the organism immune

* **physiology** science that deals with the functions of living organisms and their parts

* **virulent** extremely poisonous

Physician, Heal Thyself

During his first trip to India to fight cholera, Haffkine experienced a great deal of hostility from the local population. In one village, he and his team were stoned and some of their equipment was destroyed. To prevent a panic, Haffkine raised his shirt and had another doctor inject him with the vaccine in full view of the crowd. This drastic measure worked, settling the crowd and arousing their curiosity. Of the 200 people present, 116 received the vaccine. Only nine people in the village, who had not received the vaccine, died during the epidemic.

Waldemar Haffkine made important breakthroughs in the prevention of cholera and the bubonic plague, two of the most deadly diseases known. His efforts to inoculate* poor villagers in India exposed him to physical danger and scientific controversy. Nevertheless, his work brought major improvements in public health and he was rewarded with the acclaim of the scientific community.

Haffkine was one of six children of a Jewish family in Odessa, Russia. As a child he attended the Gymnasium in Berdyansk, where he became interested in books, science, and physical fitness and received the highest grades in his classes. He later enrolled in the University of Odessa, which offered him a teaching position in 1884 when he received his doctorate. To accept the position, however, Haffkine was required to convert to the Russian Orthodox faith. He refused and instead took a post as assistant at the Odessa Museum of Zoology.

Four years later, he went to Switzerland to teach physiology*, and the following year he became a librarian at the Pasteur Institute in Paris. After a year in Paris, he was named assistant to the director of the institute. While at the institute Haffkine began his research into preventive medicine. At the time the city of Paris was suffering from a cholera epidemic, and Haffkine worked to create a vaccine based on a very virulent* strain of the disease. He injected himself with an extremely strong dose and when he suffered no bad reaction, he determined that the vaccine was safe for humans.

After perfecting his vaccine, Haffkine wanted to test it on a wider population. When the epidemic in Paris was brought under control, Haffkine went to Calcutta, India. He traveled throughout the city and countryside with a small team of doctors and assistants, carrying inoculation equipment on horse-drawn carriages. Despite threats to their safety from distrustful villagers, Haffkine and his team inoculated nearly 45,000 people. The vaccine cut the death rate of the disease by nearly 70 percent. Still, there was no way to determine how much protection it offered or how long the immunity would last.

In late 1890 Haffkine contracted malaria and was forced to leave India. He returned to England to recover his health. The following year he went to Bombay, which was in the midst of an epidemic of the bubonic plague. Within a year he developed an antiplague vaccine that proved effective on animals. He injected himself with the vaccine, but few of his colleagues knew of this. Although he experienced fever and pain, he did not contract the plague. When he told his colleagues about the injection, hundreds volunteered to receive it themselves. Haffkine urged the Indian government to train medical officials to administer the vaccine, but his request was ignored. He then offered his vaccine and services to the Russians, who were also experiencing outbreaks of cholera and the plague. But Russian officials refused the offer as well. Despite these rebuffs, scientists from around the world visited Haffkine to learn his techniques, and he received several scientific honors for his work.

In 1902 when another plague epidemic broke out in Punjab, India, Haffkine requested that England send a dozen doctors and 30 soldiers to carry out an extensive inoculation campaign, but the government sent

* **tetanus** infectious disease marked by contractions of the voluntary muscles; also known as lockjaw

* **bacteriologist** specialist who studies microscopic organisms called bacteria that can cause infection and disease

only a small team. After he inoculated tens of thousands of people, 19 contracted tetanus* and died. All the deaths were traced to a single bottle of vaccine. Haffkine was accused of sending contaminated vaccine to India and was suspended without pay. A commission, none of whose members was a bacteriologist*, examined the matter during an eight-year investigation but failed to issue a report.

Finally, after public and private pressure, the commission released its findings. An important factor leading to release of the report was a letter to the London *Times* signed by ten prominent bacteriologists. The letter stated that the evidence showed that contamination had occurred when the bottle of vaccine was opened in the village where the deaths occurred. Those in charge of administering the program apparently ignored the instructions on how to handle the vaccine. In addition, the forceps used to open the bottle had been dropped and had not been properly sterilized.

Haffkine's reputation was restored, but the incident damaged his morale. He returned to India to continue his work, retiring from practice at age 75. He devoted the remainder of his life to Jewish affairs, including the creation of the Haffkine Foundation to promote religious, scientific, and vocational education in Jewish universities in Eastern Europe. Five years before his death, the Plague Research Institute that he founded in Bombay was renamed in his honor.

John Burdon Sanderson
HALDANE

1892–1964

PHYSIOLOGY, BIOCHEMISTRY, GENETICS

* **genetics** branch of biology that deals with heredity

* **physiologist** one who specializes in physiology, the science that deals with the functions of living organisms and their parts

Few scientists of the twentieth century are as popular as John Burdon Sanderson Haldane, who is best known for his brilliant contributions in the field of genetics*. He also authored dozens of books, essays, and articles in which he discussed science, politics, and society in ways that ordinary people could understand. He even wrote a book about genetics for children. With daring and humor, Haldane literally threw himself into his work, conducting experiments on his own body and putting his life at risk to test some of his ideas.

The Family Spirit. John Burdon was the son of John Scott HALDANE, himself an important physiologist* who taught at Oxford University. Haldane's father and mother were both members of distinguished Scottish families, and their son inherited their confidence that a Haldane could accomplish anything with the right spirit and effort.

The younger Haldane developed an early distrust of authority, although he apparently accepted his father's guidance. As a child he helped in his father's private laboratory. He also joined him on trips to investigate mining accidents and to offer advice on physiology to the British navy. His interest in genetics was kindled by a lecture on the work of the Austrian monk Gregor Mendel, who had experimented with crossbreeding plants in the 1860s and whose papers were rediscovered in 1900. Haldane pursued this early interest by studying his sister's guinea pigs—all 300 of them.

The Army and the Academy. In 1914 Britain was engulfed in the horrors of World War I. Haldane engaged in combat in Western Europe and

In writings that range from contributions to mathematics to the theory of natural selection to many essays explaining science to laypersons, John Haldane expressed his belief in the unity of science. He also stressed the social responsibilities of science and wrote more than 300 articles for a Marxist newspaper and a children's science book.

* **biochemist** person who specializes in the science that deals with chemical compounds and processes occurring in living organisms

* **enzyme** any of numerous complex proteins that are produced by living cells and catalyze specific biochemical reactions at body temperature

* **thermodynamics** physics of the relationship between heat and other forms of energy

* **chromosome** structure in the cell that contains the DNA (genes) that transmit unique genetic information

in the region that is present-day Iraq, suffering wounds in both campaigns. Later he joined his father and another scientist in France on an urgent assignment to design gas masks to protect the Allied troops from the poisonous gas attacks initiated by the Germans. This work began Haldane's lifelong interest in respiration and led to a book he wrote about gas warfare.

After the war Haldane took a position at Oxford, and soon he began teaching physiology, but respiration was the only part of the subject he knew anything about. In fact he knew so little about physiology that his father had to give him a crash course; as Haldane put it, he had "about six weeks' start on my future pupils."

From 1921 to 1933, Haldane taught at Cambridge University under the supervision of the great biochemist* Frederick HOPKINS and did important research on enzymes* and genetics. Haldane calculated the rate at which enzyme reactions occur and proved that enzyme reactions obey the laws of thermodynamics*.

Research in Genetics. Haldane's interest in genetics led to several studies at Cambridge. In particular he focused on gene linkage, the idea that if two genes responsible for different traits are located on the same chromosome*, they will be passed on and inherited together. Haldane also conducted experiments in crossbreeding animal species, observing how their offspring

Haldane, John Burdon Sanderson

* **natural selection** theory that within a given species, individuals best adapted to the environment live longer and produce more offspring than other individuals, resulting in changes in the species over time

* **evolution** historical development of a biological group such as a species

* **hemophilia** disease characterized by the delayed clotting of blood

* **Communist** referring to Communism, a social system in which land, goods, and the means of production are owned by the state or community rather than by individuals

The Human Experiment

Haldane literally gave himself to his work. When he first began teaching at Oxford, he and a young colleague investigated how carbon dioxide in the human bloodstream affected the body's regulation of breathing. To do so, they swallowed large amounts of baking soda and ammonium chloride in order to generate carbon dioxide in their blood. In other experiments, Haldane used various means to induce changes in his body's sugar and phosphate levels. He measured these changes by monitoring his blood and urine. Haldane described these experiments in an article titled "On Being One's Own Rabbit," which was published in 1927.

were either all of one sex or unable to produce further offspring. In 1932 Haldane published his work in genetics in his classic book, *The Causes of Evolution*. He emphasized the role of natural selection* rather than of genetic mutations (relatively permanent change) in driving evolution*.

The following year Haldane left Cambridge and took a position at University College in London. He continued his work in genetics, creating a partial map of the human X chromosome, the sex chromosome present in all humans. He identified the locations on the X chromosome of genes that cause color blindness, night blindness, sensitivity of skin to light, and two mutations of the eyes. With a colleague, Julia Bell, he studied the genetic linkage between color blindness and hemophilia*. He also produced the first estimate of how often genetic mutations occur in the human species.

Haldane suffered one setback in his career. While teaching at Cambridge and then at University College, he simultaneously held a part-time position at a botanical institute outside London. There he studied the genetics of the color of flowers. However, he was not an experienced botanist, and he lacked some of the skills necessary for conducting botanical experiments. These difficulties were worsened by his aggressive attitude at the institute, resulting in the cancellation of his appointment there in 1936.

The Return of War. The late 1930s were a time of military and political stress, as the European continent seemed headed toward another war. The British navy was urgently testing new submarines when one of them, the *Thetis,* sank during a trial run, killing 99 sailors. A union of engineers hired Haldane to represent them in the public inquiry that followed, and Haldane applied his expertise on the subject of respiration. He even sealed himself and four others in a chamber designed to simulate the conditions of the damaged submarine. Soon thereafter the navy hired Haldane to conduct further studies about escapes from submarines, designs for very small submarines, and many other questions of underwater science. Haldane and his colleagues regularly put their own lives at risk to investigate the navy's concerns. One of Haldane's colleagues was a biologist named Helen Spurway, who later became his second wife after he divorced his first wife, the journalist Charlotte Franken.

Haldane's expert knowledge was so valued that the British navy was willing to work with him even though he was a member of the Communist* Party, which he had joined in the late 1930s. He also served for several years as an editor of the country's Communist newspaper, the London *Daily Worker*. He spent much of his time outside the laboratory as a political activist. In Spain, during the civil war, he advised the government on precautions against gas warfare. In Britain, he joined a movement among scientists that demanded better defenses against the anticipated German air raids as the country headed toward war.

In 1957 Haldane left Britain and moved to India. He announced that he was doing so to protest the British and French invasion of the Suez Canal in Egypt, but he was also interested in India's fine research facilities. After living there for several years, Haldane was diagnosed with cancer. While seeking treatment, he displayed his typical humor and high spirits by publishing a short poem entitled "Cancer's a Funny Thing." The poem

brought Haldane both criticism and praise—criticism from some for his lack of feelings, and praise from others for his courage. He died in Bhubaneswar, India, at the age of 72.

John Scott HALDANE
1860–1936
PHYSIOLOGY

* **physiologist** one who specializes in physiology, the science that deals with the function of living organisms and their parts

The British physiologist* John Scott Haldane is known primarily for his work on the physiology of respiration. During a distinguished career, Haldane developed various procedures for studying the physiology of breathing and the blood, as well as for the analysis of different gas exchanges that occur in the body. He worked hard to apply the results of his physiological research to the solution of several social and industrial problems. Haldane was also a philosopher of science who tried to clarify the philosophical basis of biology and its relation to other sciences.

Early Life and Career. Born in Edinburgh, Scotland, Haldane was a descendant of an old Scottish family. His father, Robert Haldane, was a lawyer and writer. Haldane was educated at Edinburgh Academy and Edinburgh University and earned a degree in medicine in 1884.

Haldane's early research was on the composition of air in dwellings and schools. An account of this study was published in 1887. Soon afterward, Haldane joined his uncle, a professor of physiology, at Oxford University, which remained his base of operations until his death in 1936. Haldane also served on a number of royal commissions. Elected to the membership of the Royal Society in 1897, he was awarded two of the society's most distinguished medals—the Royal Medal in 1916 and the Copley Medal in 1934. For much of his later life, Haldane also served as director of a research laboratory established by the coal mining industry.

Haldane's most important work took place at Oxford. During his years at the university—much of it as a fellow at New College—he played a significant role in bringing the Oxford school of physiology into international prominence. A tireless worker and gifted scientist, he showed that a scientific investigator must sometimes look beyond the laboratory and examine practical situations to make progress. He also showed that an active and constructive relationship between theoretical and applied science could exist.

* **toxicity** degree of being toxic or poisonous

* **hemoglobin** protein in red blood cells that carries oxygen to the tissues of the body

* **clinical** related to the observation and treatment of disease in actual patients rather than in artificial experiments

Achievements. Studying the hazards faced by coal miners, Haldane produced a classic report on the causes of death in mine disasters. He particularly stressed the deadly effects of carbon monoxide gas on the respiratory system. This study inspired Haldane to find the reasons for the toxicity* of carbon monoxide. He found that carbon monoxide binds with hemoglobin* in the blood, preventing it from carrying oxygen throughout the body. In his experiments with laboratory rats, he discovered that placing the rats in an environment that uses greater than normal pressure could counteract this effect. However, the full clinical* implications of his work were not appreciated for more than half a century.

In 1898, realizing the need for better analytic methods in this type of work, Haldane devised an instrument for analyzing gases. A few years later, working with the Irish physiologist Joseph Barcroft, he also developed a method for determining the blood gas content from small amounts of blood. Both of these methods are still in use.

Haldane's best-known paper, written with the British scientist J.G. Priestley, set forth the idea that breathing is controlled by the partial pressure of carbon dioxide in blood reaching the respiratory center of the midbrain. Published in 1905, this work increased Haldane's interest in the physiology of respiration. In later research he showed that, except under extreme conditions, the respiratory reflex is triggered not by a deficiency of oxygen but by an excess of carbon dioxide in the arterial blood. Haldane also proceeded to unravel the basic mysteries of heatstroke and caisson disease, better known as the "bends," a sometimes fatal disorder that is caused by the release of nitrogen in body tissue following a rapid decrease in air pressure after a stay in a compressed atmosphere. He worked out a method for decompression that remains in use in deep-sea diving operations and in underwater construction.

Members of the engineering profession often turned to Haldane for advice because of his interest in problems that were unique to that field. He became very influential in planning safety measures for tunnel construction and mining and diving operations. He also solved ventilation problems in buildings, ships, and submarines.

Haldane summarized most of his work in a series of lectures given at Yale University in 1916 and published as *Respiration* in 1922. The work remained the standard textbook on respiratory physiology for many years. The book also demonstrated the extent to which Haldane's work laid the groundwork for the field of modern respiratory physiology.

Alice
HAMILTON
1869–1970
PUBLIC HEALTH

Alice Hamilton established the field of industrial medicine in the United States. She was the first American physician to study industrial diseases and industrial hygiene. She based her reports on personal examinations of the working conditions in several factories and mines. Her work led to voluntary and regulatory improvements in industrial working conditions, a decrease in workers' exposure to toxic (poisonous) chemicals, and the passage of worker's compensation laws. After her death, the National Institute of Occupational Safety and Health (NIOSH) named a major laboratory and a science award in Hamilton's honor. In 1995 she was chosen to be part of the United States Postal Service Great Americans stamp series.

Career over Marriage. Hamilton was born in New York City. She grew up in an extended family in Fort Wayne, Indiana, surrounded by many cousins close to her in age. She was homeschooled during her early years, and in 1886, was sent to a boarding school in Connecticut. Four years later, she enrolled at the Fort Wayne College of Medicine because she believed that becoming a doctor would give her the freedom to live life as she wished. She never married. She transferred to the University of Michigan in 1891 and earned her medical degree in 1893. Preferring research to the

* **pathology** study of diseases and their effects on organisms

practice of medicine, she continued her education in Europe. She returned to the United States in 1897 and became a professor of pathology* at Women's Medical College at Northwestern University in Chicago, Illinois.

Hamilton moved into Hull House, a settlement house on Chicago's south side founded by social reformer Jane Addams. It provided assistance and education to poor women and children. During the 22 years that Hamilton lived there, she saw firsthand the effects of industrial and urban diseases on the families that came to the well-baby clinic that she established at the house. Her experiences led to an interest in public health.

Into the Factories. In 1907 Hamilton read a book by Sir Thomas Oliver called *Dangerous Trades.* It examined working conditions and industrial diseases in Europe. The book influenced Hamilton to change her focus from public health to industrial medicine. A short time later, the governor of Illinois, having heard of Hamilton's work at Hull House, appointed her to survey the state's lead industry.

On the advice of social workers from Hull House, Hamilton insisted on visiting workplaces herself. She saw the actual working conditions and interviewed the workers, rather than relying on reports from factory managers. Her contemporaries considered it revolutionary for a woman to visit factories and mines, climb ladders, peer into vats of chemicals, and talk to the workers. Hamilton compiled a report that gave a complete picture of how workers' living and working conditions related to their disease symptoms. This rigorous firsthand approach gave her data credibility and moved politicians and the public to demand new protections for workers.

At the time of Hamilton's investigation, lead was used in many industrial applications. Freight car seals, coffin trim, cigar wrappers, pottery, tile, paint, and batteries were all made using lead. Most physicians thought that workers became ill because they neglected to wash their hands after handling lead. Hamilton proved that breathing lead fumes and dust caused their illnesses. Because of her findings, the state of Illinois was first to pass a law providing compensation to workers who suffered industrial diseases caused by breathing poisonous fumes. Other states gradually followed suit.

Blending her interests of science and social reform, Alice Hamilton's research concerning workplace hazards, industrial diseases, and industrial hygiene, helped bring about safer working conditions for many Americans.

Hamilton went on to investigate similar problems in many other industries, including mining and steel making. During World War I she examined chemicals used in the manufacture of explosives and discovered the toxic effects of trinitrotoluene (TNT), picric acid, and nitrous acid. Because she was not permitted inside the ammunition plants, Hamilton went to bars, union halls, and other places workers gathered. There she looked for people whose skin had turned yellow from exposure to the picric acid used in the manufacture of explosives. She followed the workers home to interview them about their working conditions.

In 1919 Hamilton became the first female faculty member at Harvard University. Later Hamilton joined the industrial hygiene department at the School of Public Health. The appointment of a woman to the Harvard faculty met with some disapproval. Officials instructed her to never enter the Harvard Club, ask for football tickets, or walk in the commencement procession. Hamilton lectured at Harvard for almost 30 years before the university accepted women as medical students.

At Harvard, Hamilton continued investigating the relationship between working conditions and disease. She wrote two books on the subject, *Industrial Poisons in the United States,* published in 1925, and *Industrial Toxicology,* published in 1934. She also gave many lectures, wrote many articles in scientific and popular journals, and traveled to Europe and Russia to continue her studies on industrial medicine. In 1935 she retired from Harvard and began to work as a consultant for the U.S. Department of Labor's Division of Labor Standards. She received awards in recognition for her contributions to industrial medicine, including an honorary doctoral degree from the University of Michigan, and was named New England Medical Woman of the Year in 1956. She continued to support the causes of social justice and workers' rights until her death at the age of 101.

Dorothy Crowfoot
HODGKIN
1910–1994
X-RAY CRYSTALLOGRAPHY

* **insulin** hormone produced by the pancreas that is used in the treatment of diabetes

The British scientist Dorothy Hodgkin used a technique known as X-ray crystallography to decipher the structure of complex biologically active molecules, such as vitamin B_{12}, insulin*, and penicillin. Her work proved the usefulness of the new technique of X-ray crystallography and had far-reaching consequences in the fields of medicine and molecular biology. In 1964 Dorothy Hodgkin was awarded the Nobel Prize in chemistry, primarily for determining the structure of vitamin B_{12}.

A Childhood Interest in Crystals. Hodgkin was born in Cairo, Egypt, where her father worked for the Egyptian Ministry of Education as an archaeologist. Her mother was an amateur botanist and an expert on early Egyptian weaving techniques. Around the age of ten, Hodgkin became interested in crystals and chemistry. At the start of World War I, Hodgkin and her two sisters moved to England. For many years, Hodgkin saw little of her parents because of the war, and because her father's career required that he live abroad. Still, they supported her educational interests.

In 1928 Hodgkin graduated from the Sir John Leman School in Beccles, England. She was one of only two girls permitted to study chemistry with a class of boys. After graduation she spent one season with her parents at an archaeological* dig in North Africa. She enjoyed archaeology, but she was determined to study chemistry. Later that year Hodgkin entered Somerville College for women at Oxford University. Early in her university career, Hodgkin began to attend a special course in crystallography because she was intrigued by the new technique of using X rays to determine the molecular structure of crystals.

* **archaeological** referring to the scientific study of material remains of past human cultures, usually by excavating ruins

How X-ray Crystallography Works. X-ray crystallography combines techniques from chemistry, physics, and mathematics to examine the three-dimensional structure of complex molecules. When crystals of purified material are bombarded with X rays, the crystals scatter the X rays in a pattern that is unique to that molecule. The resulting picture, called an X-ray diffraction pattern, consists of bright and dark spots on photographic film.

The bright spots are where the scattered X rays constructively interfere with or reinforce each other. The dark spots are where the X rays destructively interfere with each other or cancel each other out. This pattern is a visible representation of the mathematical relationship among the individual atoms in the molecule. By performing complex mathematical calculations, the three-dimensional molecular structure of the crystallized material can be determined. However, the more complex the molecule, the more involved the X ray patterns and the mathematical calculations become.

Deciphering Complex Molecules. In 1932, when Hodgkin graduated with honors from Oxford, she began to work at Cambridge University as an assistant to crystallographer John Desmond BERNAL. She made a significant contribution by determining the three-dimensional structure of the protein called pepsin*. The work proved difficult and tedious, because proteins consist of long, repeated, folded sequences of atoms called polymers.

Two years later Hodgkin returned to Oxford to teach, and she also continued the research necessary to complete a Ph.D. in 1937. Her laboratory at Oxford was poorly equipped and was located at the top of a staircase that Hodgkin found difficult to climb because she suffered from rheumatoid arthritis*. In addition, Hodgkin was excluded from the chemistry faculty research club because she was a woman. She persevered, however, and in 1934 she took the first X-ray photographs of the protein insulin. A few years later Hodgkin received research grants that enabled her to better equip her laboratory, and she gained the support of students

* **pepsin** one of the enzymes in gastric juice that breaks down proteins during digestion

* **rheumatoid arthritis** inherited condition that cripples the joints, especially in the hands and feet, often developing in early adulthood

Dorothy Hodgkin determined the molecular structure of penicillin, vitamin B$_{12}$, insulin, and many other compounds using X-ray analysis. She also pioneered the use of computers in biological research and was an advocate of world peace.

X-Ray Crystallography and Computers

The mathematical calculations involved in X-ray crystallography are complex and time-consuming. By applying computing power to solve a biochemical problem, Dorothy Hodgkin broke new ground. She worked with an analog IBM computer to complete the X-ray calculations for penicillin. When she tackled the structure of vitamin B_{12}, she used equipment at the University of California at Los Angeles. She telegraphed and mailed her data from England to the United States. Her work on the structure of insulin had to wait until advances in computer technology made the calculations possible.

* **pernicious anemia** severe form of anemia caused by the failure of the intestines to absorb vitamin B_{12}

* **Communist** referring to Communism, a social system in which land, goods, and the means of production are owned by the state or community rather than by individuals

and faculty. Hodgkin remained associated with Oxford for the rest of her professional life, becoming a full professor in 1957.

During World War II, Hodgkin and a graduate assistant determined the structure of penicillin. Hodgkin amazed some of the world's chemists by using X-ray crystallography to deduce the composition and structure of penicillin where traditional organic chemistry methods had failed.

Following the war, Hodgkin turned her attention to vitamin B_{12}, a complex molecule about four times larger than penicillin. Standard chemical techniques had revealed little about its structure. Hodgkin worked for nine years to determine the three-dimensional configuration of this molecule. Not only was this the most complex molecule analyzed by X-ray crystallography, it was medically significant in treating pernicious anemia*. As the result of this work, Hodgkin received the Nobel Prize in chemistry in 1964, only the third woman to have been selected for this award. (The other two were Marie Curie in 1911 and her daughter, Irene Joliet-Curie, in 1935.) The following year, Hodgkin became the first woman since Florence Nightingale to be awarded the British Order of Merit. As a testament to her persistence, she dedicated nearly 34 years to the study of the structure of insulin.

In addition to working in her laboratory, Hodgkin championed the cause of world peace. She helped found the International Union of Crystallography, served as its president for six years, and was a member of Science for Peace. Hodgkin insisted that crystallographers from Communist* nations be allowed to participate in conferences. She also traveled to Communist countries such as the Soviet Union and China to attend scientific meetings. After her retirement in 1977, she was active in the Pugwash Conference on Science and World Affairs. Because of her alleged association with Communists, for years the United States denied her a visa to attend conferences. In 1990, however, with the fall of Communism in the Soviet Union, the visa restriction was lifted. Hodgkin died in England in 1994.

Frederick Gowland
HOPKINS

1861–1947

BIOCHEMISTRY

* **biochemist** person who specializes in the science that deals with chemical compounds and processes occurring in living organisms

* **physiology** science that deals with the functions of living organisms and their parts

The British biochemist* Frederick Gowland Hopkins is best known for his pioneering work with vitamins. His discovery of vitamins earned him the Nobel Prize in physiology* or medicine in 1929. He shared the prize with Dutch physician Christiaan Eijkmann.

Early Life, Education, and Work. Hopkins was born in Eastbourne, England, the son of a bookseller. His father died when Hopkins was an infant, and he was raised by his mother and an unmarried uncle. He became interested in science when his mother gave him a microscope that had belonged to his father. He used it to study marine life. As a student Hopkins displayed little academic distinction, except in chemistry. He began working in the London office of an insurance company at age 17, a career chosen for him by his uncle.

He later worked as an analyst for a large railway company. While working for the railway, Hopkins enrolled in classes at the Institute of

Chemistry. His performance on an examination caught the attention of Thomas Stevenson, an expert medical analyst for the British government. Stevenson invited Hopkins to be his assistant, and in that capacity Hopkins became involved in the investigation of several celebrated murder cases. His skills played an important role in gaining convictions.

By his mid-20s Hopkins became aware of the importance of formal training and a university degree. He took courses at the University of London and earned a bachelor's degree. In 1888, at the age of 27, Hopkins received a small inheritance and decided to enter the medical school at Guy's Hospital in London. Six years later he received a medical degree. For many years after that, he worked in the medical school by day and in a privately owned clinical* research laboratory in the evenings. In 1898 Hopkins accepted a teaching post at Cambridge University at the invitation of Michael Foster, professor of physiology.

Foster hoped that Hopkins would teach what was then called chemical physiology, a course that included instruction in physiology and anatomy. Through his work, Hopkins helped establish the department of biochemistry at Cambridge, and he became the first professor of biochemistry at the university in 1914.

Discovery of Vitamins. Hopkins pursued research into uric acid, a chemical compound present in urine and a major component in kidney stones. His training as an analyst enabled him to develop an improved method of determining the presence of uric acid in urine.

The effects of diet on the excretion of uric acid sparked his interest in proteins and his efforts to obtain crystalline* forms of these substances. This work led Hopkins to the discovery and isolation of the amino acid* known as tryptophan. Hopkins showed that tryptophan and certain other amino acids are essential to life and must be present in the diets of humans and animals. His discovery of tryptophan ushered in far-reaching research projects in several biochemical laboratories.

Hopkins questioned the accuracy of nutritional studies conducted by other researchers. A classic set of experiments on mice led him to conclude that there must be something in food that was not present in a diet made up of pure protein, pure carbohydrate, fats, and salts. What that missing substance was, however, he did not yet know.

Hopkins observed that young mice fed a diet consisting mainly of pure protein, pure carbohydrates, fats, and salts failed to grow. They lost weight unless given small amounts of milk. He concluded that milk contains certain "accessory food factors" that are required in small amounts and are essential for normal growth and health in animals and humans. Hopkins later called these substances vitamins. In 1929 he received the Nobel Prize in physiology or medicine for his work on vitamins.

Research on Muscles. In the early 1900s Hopkins and a colleague, Walter Fletcher, conducted a series of investigations on muscles. At the time scientists believed that muscular contraction was associated with the formation of lactic acid. Hopkins and Fletcher were among the first to recognize that previous methods used to determine the amount of lactic acid in

* **clinical** related to the observation and treatment of disease in actual patients rather than in artificial experiments

* **crystalline** composed of tiny crystals
* **amino acid** class of compounds that function as the building blocks of proteins

Mysteries of Good Health

Although Frederick Hopkins discovered and identified vitamins, he was not the first to note the health benefits of certain foods. The ancient Greek philosopher Aristotle knew that eating raw liver helped cure night blindness. The English explorer and adventurer James Cook noted that lime juice prevented scurvy, a disease that plagued sailors. Aristotle, Cook, and others, however, did not know what mysterious substances in these foods contributed to better health. Hopkins discovered the answer and gave these substances their general name—vitamins.

muscles involved stimulation of the muscle. This meant that the muscles of control subjects and those of experimental subjects that were stimulated had similar amounts of lactic acid, making meaningful comparison impossible. What was needed was a method that extracted lactic acid without stimulating the muscles.

Hopkins and Fletcher achieved this by dropping thin, small muscles into cold alcohol and rapidly grinding them so that the activity of enzymes* was greatly reduced. This was perhaps the first time that any researcher recognized the need to stop enzyme activity as a precursor to chemical analysis of tissue. Their research laid the foundations for a modern understanding of the chemistry of muscle contractions. It served as a starting point for the study of the metabolism* of carbohydrates in muscles and paved the way for studies of fermentation* and similar processes in bacteria. Hopkins and Fletcher's work on muscles also emphasized the importance of enzyme activity in living tissues. One outcome of this was that Hopkins grew interested in the oxidation* of enzymes. He became especially intrigued by the importance of certain compounds in respiration.

Later Career. During World War I, Hopkins served on the Royal Society's Food Committee. The problems of food rationing and nutrition claimed much of his attention. After the war Hopkins focused on developing and improving the biochemistry department at Cambridge University.

During the latter part of his career, Hopkins received many awards. He was knighted in 1925, received the Copley Medal of the Royal Society the following year, and shared the Nobel Prize in physiology or medicine with Christiaan Eijkmann in 1929. Hopkins was elected president of the Royal Society in 1931 and received the Order of Merit—the most prized of all civil distinctions—in 1935. In addition, he was awarded numerous honorary degrees from universities throughout the world. In addition to his accomplishments as a researcher, Hopkins was an inspiring teacher. At the time of his death in 1947, about 75 of his former students were professors in colleges and universities around the world.

* **enzyme** any of numerous complex proteins that are produced by living cells and catalyze specific biochemical reactions at body temperature

* **metabolism** physical and chemical processes involved in maintaining life

* **fermentation** chemical reaction in which complex organic compounds are split into relatively simple substances

* **oxidation** chemical reaction in which oxygen combines with another substance

Bernardo Alberto
HOUSSAY
1887–1971
PHYSIOLOGY, PHARMACOLOGY, MEDICINE

* **pituitary gland** gland whose secretions control the actions of other glands and influence growth and metabolism

* **physiology** science that deals with the functions of living organisms and their parts

Bernardo Alberto Houssay was one of the most influential Latin American physicians and medical scientists of the 1900s. In addition to conducting important research on the pituitary gland*, he led intensive efforts to improve the training of his colleagues in Latin America. Many individuals who trained and worked under Houssay later assumed important positions in medical and scientific research and training institutions throughout South America.

The son of a lawyer, Houssay was a gifted student who received his bachelor's degree at age 13 from the Colegio Nacional de Buenos Aires, Argentina. Four years later in 1904, he graduated first in his class from the School of Pharmacy at the University of Buenos Aires, where he then began to study medicine. During this time he was named an assistant in the medical school's department of physiology* and was later appointed chair of physiology at the School of Veterinary Science.

After his graduation Houssay established a private practice and became chief of a hospital service. At the same time, he continued to serve as a professor in the School of Veterinary Science and as a part-time instructor in physiology at the medical school. At age 28 he was appointed head of the section of experimental pathology* at Argentina's National Public Health Laboratories. While there, he developed an antiserum* to protect against the effects of the bites of certain poisonous spiders. In 1915 he assumed the chair of the department of physiology at the University of Buenos Aires's School of Medicine. He transformed the department into a full Institute of Physiology and a center for experimental research. Houssay served for 25 years as the director of the institute and developed it into one of the world's leading centers of physiological research.

In 1943, following a revolution that established a military dictatorship in Argentina, Houssay was stripped of his university posts. He was reinstated two years later but again lost his position when the government of Juan Perón came to power. In 1955 he recovered his post at the Institute of Physiology. He continued to train scientists and to try to stop the flow of technically talented scientists out of Argentina. Houssay served as director of the Argentine National Council for Scientific and Technical Research until his death in 1971.

Houssay's most important research was his investigation into the action of the pituitary gland. This work identified the key role played by the anterior (frontal) lobe of the gland in the metabolism* of carbohydrates, which was previously thought to be influenced by the posterior (rear) lobe. For this research Houssay received the 1947 Nobel Prize in physiology and medicine, which he shared with Gerty and Carl Cori, a husband and wife team. Houssay's investigations opened up new areas of research in the field of endocrinology*. Other areas he studied include pancreatic secretion of insulin (the hormone* that is used in the treatment of diabetes), hormonal control of fat metabolism, and factors regulating arterial blood pressure.

Houssay was a long-time member of the Argentine Academy of Medicine and the founder of the Argentine Association for the Advancement of Science and the Argentine Biological Society. He received many honors, including degrees from Paris, Oxford, Cambridge, and Harvard. He was an associate foreign member of many scientific societies in the United States, Britain, Germany, France, Italy, and Spain. Houssay is remembered as one of the most powerful advocates for the promotion and training of scientific personnel in his country. (*See also* **Coris, The.**)

* **pathology** study of diseases and their effects on organisms

* **antiserum** serum containing antibodies; used to treat, or give temporary protection against, certain diseases

* **metabolism** physical and chemical processes involved in maintaining life

* **endocrinology** study of the physiology of the endocrine glands, which secrete hormones into the bloodstream

* **hormone** internally secreted substance transported by body fluids to stimulate the functions of organs or tissues

Percy Lavon
JULIAN
1899–1975
ORGANIC CHEMISTRY

* **synthesize** to create artificially

The African American research chemist Percy Lavon Julian is best known for developing the processes for extracting and synthesizing* many commercially valuable products from soybeans. He also was active in the National Association for the Advancement of Colored People (NAACP). He supported the Civil Rights movement by raising money to promote legal rights and educational opportunities for African Americans. Julian was elected to the National Academy of Sciences in 1973.

Julian, Percy Lavon

Denied a teaching position at DePauw University because of racism, Percy Julian became an industrial researcher. Several years later he started his own company, which was a great financial success. Julian was an active fundraiser for the National Association for the Advancement of Colored People (NAACP) and an advocate of the civil rights movement.

---

* **alkaloid** group of naturally occurring organic bases containing nitrogen, such as caffeine, morphine, and nicotine

* **steroid** class of organic compounds that form the building blocks for cholesterol and certain hormones and play an important role in the body's functions

* **hormone** internally secreted substance transported by body fluids to stimulate the functions of organs or tissues

Julian was born in Montgomery, Alabama, at a time when the educational opportunities for African American children there were limited. He was fortunate to be born to educated parents who had attended the State Normal School for Negroes in Montgomery. He too graduated from that school in 1916, after which he continued his education at DePauw University in Greencastle, Indiana, where he was at the top of his class. After teaching at Fisk University for several years, Julian enrolled at Harvard University and received his master's degree in chemistry in 1923. For the next three years, he remained at Harvard as a research fellow. Thereafter he worked at West Virginia State College for Negroes and at Howard University. In the late 1920s Julian received a fellowship from the Rockefeller Foundation to continue his graduate work at the University of Vienna in Austria. In 1931 he earned a doctoral degree from that university and returned to the United States, where he held several positions at American universities.

Julian's first commercial breakthrough came while he was employed at DePauw University as a research fellow and instructor. In 1935 he isolated an alkaloid* from the Calabar bean that was useful in treating glaucoma, a disease in which increasing pressure in the eye causes deterioration of vision. Despite his contributions as a researcher and instructor, racial prejudice against African Americans limited his academic career, and he was denied a professorship at the university.

The following year, Julian left academic life and became the director of research at the Soya Products Division of the Glidden Company in Chicago. He had an 18-year career at Glidden, becoming director of their Durkee Famous Foods Division and manager of the Fine Chemicals Division. It was at Glidden that Julian conducted his commercially important research. He focused his work on extracting useful compounds from soybeans and developed a method of extracting oil-free soybean meal, which had industrial uses in paint and paper manufacture. Julian then supervised building a plant to mechanize the process so that Glidden could produce tons of this material daily.

Next Julian successfully developed a soy protein that served as the base for the fire-fighting foam used by the United States military during World War II. Other soy products developed under Julian's supervision include soy proteins used in livestock feed and an edible oil that is used in margarine, salad dressings, and other food products.

Julian's most important breakthrough was the process that he developed to extract steroids* from soybeans in 1940. Before that time, steroids, which are used to treat medical conditions, were available only in very small quantities because they had to be extracted from the sex organs and spinal cords of slaughtered animals. Julian's process of extracting sterols (a type of steroid) from soybeans and converting them into several hormones* made these products available in large quantities to pharmaceutical companies. It also made possible the development of many new and valuable drugs.

In 1954 Julian left Glidden and formed his own company, Julian Laboratories, in Franklin Park, Illinois. He developed complex processes to extract steroid hormones from a Mexican plant commonly called wild yam. Although he later sold his laboratory to a major pharmaceutical company, Julian continued as director of the Julian Research Institute until his death in 1975.

Edward Calvin KENDALL

1886–1972

ENDOCRINOLOGY, BIOCHEMISTRY

* **hormone** internally secreted substance transported by body fluids to stimulate the functions of organs or tissues

* **steroid** class of organic compounds that form the building blocks for cholesterol and certain hormones and play an important role in the body's functions

* **extract** solution that contains the essential components of a more complex material

* **crystalline** composed of tiny crystals

* **clinical** related to the observation and treatment of disease in actual patients rather than in artificial experiments

* **rheumatoid arthritis** inherited condition that cripples the joints, especially in the hands and feet, often developing in early adulthood

* **physiology** science that deals with the functions of living organisms and their parts

Edward Calvin Kendall began his career in medical research by studying the endocrine system, which is responsible for the production and regulation of hormones* in the body. His most important accomplishment, however, was the discovery of the steroid* called cortisone.

After receiving his doctorate from Columbia University, Kendall joined the pharmaceutical firm Parke, Davis, and Company to work on extracts* from the thyroid gland. He later worked at the Mayo Clinic in Rochester, Minnesota, where he continued this research. At that time, several disorders of growth and mental development were being traced to the endocrine system, which includes the thyroid gland. Kendall was the first scientist to isolate the crystalline* form of thyroxine, the hormone produced by the thyroid. He began work on its chemical structure but was outstripped in this effort by a rival in England.

Kendall then began to search for hormones in the adrenal gland, which is located near the kidney, because extracts from that gland had been used to cure a fatal disorder called Addison's disease. After several years of work, he identified a substance that he believed to have the properties of these extracts. But the substance turned out to be a complex mixture of several hormones rather than a single steroid hormone. Kendall and others continued to seek clinical* uses for this mixture of steroids, now known as corticosteroids. In 1949 Kendall and a colleague, Philip S. Hench, discovered that one of these corticosteroids, cortisone, was effective in relieving the pain of rheumatoid arthritis*. For their discovery, they and a third researcher, Tadeus Reichstein, shared the 1950 Nobel Prize in physiology* or medicine. Kendall retired shortly thereafter, but he continued his research on adrenal extracts until he died in 1972.

Elizabeth KENNY

1886–1952

PHYSICAL THERAPY

Elizabeth Kenny was born into a rural Australian family and educated at home. As a child she tended livestock and helped with other farm chores. Her first contact with medicine occurred when she broke her wrist, and a doctor showed her textbooks on muscles and how they worked. She graduated from St. Ursula's College in 1902 and later served as a nurse in the remote bush country. Working alone with little or no formal scientific or medical training, she developed the first effective treatment for the crippling disease polio.

Kenny traveled across the countryside to treat rural patients who did not have access to professional medical care. Most of her patients were expectant mothers or farmers suffering from work-related injuries. But one day in 1911 she encountered a two-year-old girl with horribly deformed limbs, so she sent a telegram to a doctor to seek advice. He replied that the child suffered from incurable infantile paralysis (or polio) and told her to

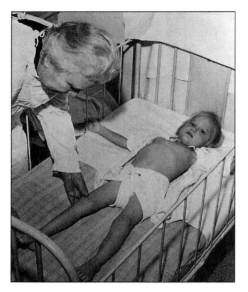

Elizabeth Kenny, who introduced the first successful treatment for polio, was voted the most admired woman in the United States in 1952. She is seen here attending to a young polio victim.

do what she thought was best. At the time the standard treatment for polio was to immobilize the patient's limbs with splints and casts. Kenny, however, decided to try a new treatment. She wrapped the girl's legs in strips of a wool blanket soaked in hot water and helped her exercise the affected muscles. The girl recovered fully, as did six other patients Kenny treated.

In 1931 a polio epidemic swept Australia. Interest in Kenny's alternative treatments increased and "Kenny Clinics" sprang up across the nation. Despite her successes the Australian medical community dismissed her methods. Kenny then traveled to the United States to try to convince American physicians of the value of her techniques. She met opposition there as well, but the University of Minnesota gave her a chance to demonstrate her treatment.

The success of her experiment changed the treatment of patients with polio worldwide and earned Kenny immediate fame. Recognition was fleeting, however, because the development of a polio vaccine by Jonas SALK virtually eliminated the threat of polio. When Salk's vaccine was first widely used in 1955, new polio cases fell by more than 80 percent. Kenny's methods were still employed to treat those who already suffered from the disease, but the dramatic drop in new cases due to Salk's vaccine ensured that his name, not Kenny's, would forever be linked to the defeat of polio.

Karl Martin Leonhard Albrecht
KOSSEL

1853–1927

PROTEIN CHEMISTRY

* **DNA** deoxyribonucleic acid, the material in chromosomes that carries genetic information from ancestor to offspring

* **nucleic acid** class of complex chemicals, including DNA and RNA, that is found in all living cells and viruses

Albrecht Kossel's major work was the study of nucleoproteins—the protein molecules that exist in the nucleus of each living cell. Nucleoproteins react with each other in ways that determine the structure of the living organism. Kossel's discovery that nucleoproteins are essential to the development of life made his work an important step toward the understanding of DNA*.

Kossel was born in the German city of Rostock, where his father was a merchant and civic official. As a youth Kossel had a great interest in botany. He later chose to go to Strasbourg to attend the lectures of Anton de Bary, an expert on mushrooms and other fungi. Kossel also studied medicine and became the pupil of Felix Hoppe-Seyler, at the time Germany's foremost professor of physiological chemistry—the chemistry of the body's functions. In 1883 Kossel received his medical degree and became director of a physiological institute in Berlin. Ten years later he directed a similar institute in the city of Marburg.

During his time in Berlin and Marburg, Kossel and his students investigated the structure of nucleoproteins, also known as nucleins. During their research they identified several important molecules, including adenine, thymine, and cytosine, and discovered that they came from the breakdown of nucleic acids*. Kossel and his group found that these molecules helped to distinguish between two types of nucleoproteins: true nucleins of the cell nucleus and what Kossel termed "paranucleins," which are found in milk and egg yolks. This distinction was invaluable because it enabled scientists to focus on those nucleoproteins directly responsible for reactions in the cell's nucleus. However, since Kossel was unable to identify correctly the carbohydrate component of nucleoproteins at that time, his discoveries were slow to be accepted by other scientists.

A thorough researcher, Kossel was not content merely to study the chemical reactions of proteins; he always wanted to know how they affected the actual physiology* of living things. This approach led him to his discovery that the function of nucleoproteins is not to store or provide energy for muscle movements; rather, their function is to help create new body tissues. Not surprisingly, he found that the tissues of embryos* are rich in nucleins.

Kossel knew that the building blocks of nucleoproteins were smaller molecules called amino acids; some were singles, known as monoamino acids, and others were compounds, known as diamino acids. In a further study Kossel showed that all nucleoproteins are structured around a core of diamino acids and that monoamino acids are added on as the embryo develops. By contrast, when an organism creates a sperm cell or egg cell, the monoamines are stripped away to leave only the diamino core in the nucleus of the sperm or egg. Kossel demonstrated this process by studying the sperm of salmon and other fish species.

In 1901 Kossel became chair of the department of physiology at the University of Heidelberg, where he remained until his retirement in 1924. He won the 1910 Nobel Prize in physiology or medicine for his work with nucleoproteins. At this stage in his work, he clearly saw that the structure of nucleoproteins had a direct effect on the reactions they were involved in, and that these reactions had a direct effect on the physiology of the living organism. These ideas were later incorporated into modern theories of genetics*.

After his retirement from the University of Heidelberg, Kossel worked at the Institute for Protein Chemistry at the new Heidelberg medical clinic. He received many awards and honorary degrees during his lifetime and was a member of several scientific academies. He was also the editor of Germany's *Journal of Physiological Chemistry* for more than 30 years. Kossel's colleagues knew him as a reserved and modest man who pursued his work conscientiously and produced careful results of high quality.

* **physiology** science that deals with the functions of living organisms and their parts

* **embryo** organism at the early stages of development before birth or hatching

* **genetics** branch of biology that deals with heredity

Hans Adolf
KREBS

1900–1981
BIOCHEMISTRY

* **physiology** science that deals with the functions of living organisms and their parts

* **biochemist** person who specializes in the science that deals with chemical compounds and processes occurring in living organisms

Hans Adolf Krebs is known for his investigations into metabolism, the process by which living organisms derive energy from food. His greatest contributions to science are the identification of several metabolic cycles and the discovery of the chemical compounds that act in those cycles to promote metabolism. In recognition of his achievements, Krebs received the 1953 Nobel Prize in physiology* or medicine, which he shared with Fritz Lipmann, a German biochemist*.

Life and Career

Krebs, the son of a Jewish doctor, grew up in comfortable surroundings in the German town of Hildesheim. As a boy he was exposed to art and culture in his home and to nature on Sunday hikes in the nearby hills.

However, he showed little interest in the sciences, except for a curiosity about collecting botanical specimens.

School and Early Career. Krebs performed at the top of his class in middle school, but his high school performance, while solid, was not remarkable. Although he studied little science, by age 15 he had decided to follow in his father's footsteps and enter the medical profession. But World War I began, and he was drafted into the army at age 18. When the war ended Krebs entered the University of Göttingen, where he studied medicine. He worked hard to make up for the time he had missed as a result of military service. He transferred to the University of Freiburg because of its highly regarded faculty. He became interested in research and participated in a tissue-staining project, which became the basis of his first published scientific paper. Krebs graduated with high marks and began studies at the University of Munich, which had an outstanding program in clinical* medicine. He passed his final medical examination at age 23, again with high scores. In 1925 he received his medical degree.

While in medical school, Krebs had decided to pursue a career in research, but his father and others warned him that it would be difficult to make a living on research alone. Nevertheless, he participated in research projects and found that he was a talented independent investigator. However, he realized that he needed to learn more about chemistry if he was to conduct basic research. He took a special course in chemistry to strengthen his knowledge. In 1926 he received a position as a research assistant with the famous biochemist Otto WARBURG. Warburg instilled in Krebs an appreciation for repeated experimentation and precise measurement in scientific research. Under Warburg's influence, Krebs became interested in exploring the processes of metabolism. But Warburg had no interest in metabolism, and he demanded that his assistants work only on problems that interested him.

In 1929 Warburg informed Krebs that his term as a research assistant would end soon. Krebs thought that Warburg did not consider him a capable scientist because he did not help Krebs find another research position. Krebs began to doubt his talents but looked for work in clinical medicine that would also enable him to do research.

Krebs left Warburg's laboratory after four years and took a position practicing clinical medicine at a hospital in the town of Altona, near Hamburg. At the time scientists believed that lactic acid production was responsible for muscle contractions. Krebs built on the discovery of another researcher whose work showed that muscle tissues poisoned with the compound iodoacetate continued to contract even though they could not produce lactic acid. Krebs demonstrated that when lactic acid was added to the poisoned tissues, the process of respiration in those tissues was resumed. Shortly after making this discovery, Krebs moved back to Freiburg to work with a specialist in metabolic diseases. While there, Krebs performed the research that led to his first important discoveries.

Later Life and Career. When Hitler took power in Germany in 1933, Krebs lost his university position, as did many other Jews. He sought a

* **clinical** related to the observation and treatment of disease in actual patients rather than in artificial experiments

Hans Krebs made fundamental contributions to the chemistry of body processes. He identified two important metabolic cycles—the orinithene cycle and the citric acid cycle—and discovered the chemical compounds that act in those cycles to promote metabolism.

Scientific Privilege

Hans Krebs enjoyed a long and distinguished scientific career. He had his greatest period of innovation early on, and in his later years he relied heavily on his students and fellow researchers to carry out the experiments he planned. Krebs could be challenging to work with: he was sparse with praise and imposed high standards of performance, and he rarely engaged in personal conversations with his colleagues. Never known to be falsely modest, Krebs insisted that younger scientists accord him the respect due a Nobel laureate and a founder of the field of biochemistry.

* **urea** compound found in urine and other body fluids that is synthesized from ammonia and carbon dioxide

* **amino acid** class of compounds that function as the building blocks of proteins

The Ornithine Cycle

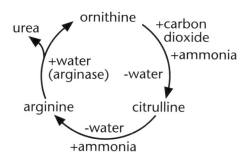

When Hans Krebs discovered the ornithine cycle in 1932, he began a new era in the study of metabolism. His later work on the citric acid cycle earned him a Nobel Prize.

post at Cambridge University, but the school had no funds to assist him. The Rockefeller Foundation, which had supported some of Krebs's earlier work, provided him with a research grant as they did for other refugee scientists. Krebs used the grant to fund his position at Cambridge, where he remained for two years before taking a job at the University of Sheffield. Although less prestigious than Cambridge, Sheffield offered him more laboratory space and the opportunity to assemble a team of student researchers. Krebs continued his work on metabolism, and he made the discoveries that resulted in his winning the 1953 Nobel Prize in physiology or medicine. He also met and married Margaret Fieldhouse, with whom he had three children.

Krebs left Sheffield shortly after receiving the Nobel Prize to join the faculty at Oxford University, where he supervised research teams and investigated the details of the metabolic cycles and pathways he had discovered in his earlier work. When he reached Oxford's mandatory retirement age of 67, he continued to do independent research at a separate facility until his death. After returning from a trip to Germany in 1981, he fell ill and died later that year.

Scientific Accomplishments

Krebs began his investigations of metabolism by studying how urea* is formed in the liver. During the course of these experiments, he discovered the ornithine cycle, the biochemical pathway by which most organisms obtain much of their energy by oxidizing molecules contained in food. His later discoveries, including his Nobel Prize–winning work, stemmed from these early efforts.

The Ornithine Cycle. At Altona, Krebs became interested in the process by which the body produces urea. At the time scientists assumed that amino acids* broke down to produce ammonia, which in turn was the source of the nitrogen found in urea. However, the process by which this occurred was still unknown. Krebs discovered that amino acids and ammonia produce urea only in liver tissue. He tested several amino acids and some chemicals produced during metabolism to see if any of them influenced the rate at which urea is produced. He found that an amino acid called ornithine increases the rate of urea production dramatically, and that ornithine itself can manufacture the nitrogen that is required for the formation of urea. Scientists knew that ornithine was produced by the breakdown of another amino acid known as arginine. Krebs wondered if that process was part of a larger cycle in which ornithine was converted back into arginine. He determined that when ornithine combines with carbon dioxide and ammonia, it loses a water molecule to produce another acid called citrulline. When citrulline combines with ammonia, it loses another water molecule to become arginine, which then combines with a water molecule to form urea and ornithine. Thus ornithine gives rise to arginine, which then produces both urea and ornithine, starting the process over again. Krebs's discovery of the ornithine cycle was his first major achievement in biochemistry.

oxidize to combine with oxygen

The Citric Acid Cycle

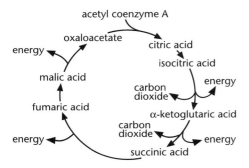

The citric acid cycle is a series of chemical reactions in which molecules are converted from food into carbon dioxide, water, and energy. In the beginning of the cycle, oxaloacetate (2 carbon molecule) combines with acetyl coenzyme A (4 carbon molecule) to form citric acid (6 carbon molecule). The remainder of the cycle involves the rearrangement of the citric acid molecule and the loss of its carbon atoms, which are released in the form of carbon dioxide (CO_2). Four electrons, in the form of energy, are also released. Finally, when the original molecule of oxaloacetate is regenerated, the cycle restarts. Krebs described this cycle in 1937, and it earned him the 1953 Nobel Prize in physiology or medicine.

The Citric Acid Cycle. Soon after arriving at Sheffield, Krebs studied the question of how organisms produce amino acids. In particular he looked at the formation of amino acids from other acids, called ketonic acids, and ammonia. He determined that the ketonic acids were potentially connected to the metabolism of carbohydrates. One of the ketonic acids, pyruvic acid, was seen as a substance that linked many of the intermediate pathways between the intake of food and its metabolism to produce energy. Many separate intermediate pathways had been found, but Krebs's work with pyruvic acid created the possibility of joining all these pathways into a single network. His work enabled scientists to trace the process of carbohydrate metabolism from beginning to end, as well as to link it to the metabolism of fatty acids.

Scientists knew that citric acid accelerated the respiration of tissues that was necessary for metabolism. However, citric acid had never been directly linked with other intermediate acids involved in the metabolic process. When Krebs and an assistant added pyruvic acid and oxaloacetic acid to pigeon breast muscle, they found that the muscle produced large quantities of citric acid. Later he read a paper in which other scientists had proposed that a metabolic pathway linked citric acid to the intermediate products of metabolism known as α-ketoglutaric acid and succinic acid. He performed experiments showing that when citric acid is added to pigeon breast muscle, under the right conditions, it generates both of these intermediate products. Krebs conceived of a cycle in which citric acid produces succinic acid, which in turn produces malic acid and oxaloacetic acid, which finally gives rise again to citric acid. During this cycle, two molecules of carbon dioxide and hydrogen are given up. The hydrogen is then oxidized* with the production of energy. Further experiments showed that some other unknown product of carbohydrate metabolism that Krebs called "triose" reacts with the oxaloacetic acid.

Following this lead, Krebs's assistant performed an experiment in which he added citric acid to pigeon breast muscle and noted that it absorbed more oxygen than was necessary to oxidize the citric acid. (The oxidation of chemicals such as citric acid is necessary to change them into other chemicals useful to the metabolic process.) Krebs felt that this meant the citric acid acted to speed up the reaction and was being regenerated to oxidize the "triose." Thus Krebs had discovered that citric acid formed the basis of a cycle by which important intermediate acids could act on carbohydrates to convert them into the energy necessary to sustain life.

Krebs continued to study metabolic cycles even after his work on citric acid won the 1953 Nobel Prize in physiology or medicine, a distinction he shared with Fritz Lipmann. He believed that "metabolic cycles seem to be a feature peculiar to life," and he encouraged researchers to look for cycles in their studies of metabolism and to try to determine why they arise.

Krebs's work with the metabolic process established his reputation as one of the founders and leading researchers in the field of biochemistry. He was elected a fellow of the Royal Society of London and received the society's Royal Medal. He also received awards from the Netherlands Society for Physics, Medical Science, and Surgery and was knighted in 1958.

Krebs was awarded honorary degrees from the Universities of Chicago, Freiburg-im-Breisgau, Paris, Glasgow, London, Sheffield, Leicester, Berlin (Humboldt University), and Jerusalem.

Schack August Steenberg
KROGH

1874–1949
ZOOLOGY, PHYSIOLOGY

* **physiology** science that deals with the functions of living organisms and their parts

Love and Science

August Krogh's best collaborator was his wife, the physician Marie Jørgensen. They married in 1905 and had three daughters and one son. She assisted him in nearly all his work. In fact, the couple coauthored a study of the diet of the Eskimos who lived on icy Greenland. In the early 1920s, Krogh devoted himself to studying, manufacturing, and selling the drug insulin at no profit because his wife suffered from diabetes.

August Steenberg Krogh inspired his students and colleagues with his lively and curious mind, which took him across the fields of zoology and physiology*. His main interest was the exchange of gases during respiration, and he approached the problem as a physicist might, by studying the physical properties of the gases and constructing many brilliant new devices to test his ideas.

His talents as a scientist were matched by the kindness and sympathy he extended to his students. He was a superb lecturer and writer who wrote not only technical papers but also popular books about science for general readers and schoolchildren. He even contributed entries in the *Oxford English Dictionary*. Though Krogh was sometimes given to arguing a point too long or too often, he was his own best critic. He once said: "We may fondly imagine that we are impartial seekers after truth, but with a few exceptions, to which I know that I do not belong, we are influenced—and sometimes strongly—by our personal bias; and we give our best thoughts to those ideas which we have to defend."

Inspired to Experiment. Krogh grew up in the southern part of Jutland, a long peninsula in northern Europe that includes the mainland of Denmark. His family had lived there for more than 300 years, and he never lost his affection for the area. Krogh's father was a brewer who had once studied to design naval ships, and as a young man Krogh volunteered for training as a naval officer. Later a family friend encouraged him to study zoology and physiology with the professor Christian Bohr, who served as a mentor and inspiration for the rest of Krogh's career. In 1899 Krogh graduated with a master's degree and then earned a doctoral degree in medicine from the University of Copenhagen in 1903.

Krogh began working with Bohr in the late 1890s, when the older scientist believed that the exchange of gases in the lungs occurred through secretions of chemicals, as though the lungs were a gland controlled by the nervous system. To investigate this question, Krogh turned his attention to the tiny bubbles of air breathed by the larvae of certain insects. He also studied frogs and demonstrated that the exchange of oxygen takes place through the thin walls of their lungs, while carbon dioxide passes through their skin. Krogh won international fame for a paper on the exchange of nitrogen gas as well.

To measure the exchange of gases, Krogh devised a series of ingenious instruments. He was so skilled at visualizing devices that he often was able to build them without sketching them first. One such invention was the tonometer, an instrument with which he could measure the pressure of tiny amounts of gases, either in small bubbles or dissolved in blood. Krogh also took great care in designing and evaluating his experiments, especially when they yielded results that were different from those that

Krogh, Schack August Steenberg

A brilliant designer and inventor, August Krogh made many of the research instruments that he used his laboratory. He even built a small merry-go-round to study the movements of 32 grasshoppers as they revolved on the circular platform.

previous scientists had found. As he explained: "Disagreement with former results should never be taken easily, but every effort should be made to find a true explanation. This can be done in many more cases than it actually is . . . [but] it may require a great deal of imagination, and very often it will require supplementary experiments."

New Theories and New Problems. Krogh pursued these experiments until 1908, when he left Bohr's laboratory to take a teaching position at the University of Copenhagen. Two years later Krogh published his findings in seven articles that are famous today. In his publications, he rejected his mentor's theory that the lungs were like glands. Rather, he showed that the exchange of gases occurs through the process of diffusion of gases, whereby molecules of gas move from an area where they are more concentrated to an area where they are less concentrated. For example, when oxygen is inhaled into the tiny air sacs of the lungs, the oxygen there is more concentrated than in the tiny blood vessels, called capillaries, that surround them. The oxygen therefore diffuses from the sacs into the bloodstream, which carries the dissolved oxygen to the body's cells.

A few years later Krogh wrote a book about the respiratory exchange of gases in animals and humans. Although it was a fairly dry reference text, it opened the way for new medical treatments. For instance, doctors began to try inflating the lungs by forcing air down the windpipe. They also attempted to lower the body temperature during heart surgery because the lower temperature slowed down the exchange of gases.

In 1910 Krogh acquired a new laboratory of his own, and he and his family lived in the small rooms above it. There he continued to invent new instruments to evaluate the functions of blood flow and respiration. He shifted his focus from the lungs to the blood vessels that move the gases throughout the body. Krogh began to work with Johannes Lindhard, who specialized in studying the gymnastic movements of the body. Together they analyzed the relationship between blood flow and muscle work.

From these studies Krogh concluded that the capillaries in the muscles are partially closed during rest and mostly open during work. With precise experiments and instruments, he conclusively demonstrated his theory. In 1920 he received the Nobel Prize in physiology or medicine.

Krogh's growing fame brought scientists from many other countries to his laboratory. With his new colleagues, he demonstrated how capillaries are influenced by both nerves and hormones*. In 1922 he published a book titled *The Anatomy and Physiology of the Capillaries*. Unlike his previous book about the respiratory exchange of gas, this work was extremely well written and informative; it went through several editions and translations.

Late Interests and Dangers. That same year, the Rockefeller Foundation awarded Krogh a grant to build new facilities. Krogh involved himself closely in planning the new building, even considering whether trees outside would cast their shadows into the laboratory rooms. He also hoped to create special dustless rooms, but the building materials available at the time made this goal impossible. The new Rockefeller Institute opened in 1928 with six university laboratories, and Krogh returned to work.

Krogh continued to improve his methods for measuring the pressure of gases in the blood. But he never lost his longtime interest in animal physiology. He devoted much time to the study of fish—how they absorbed oxygen and whether they could feed on food dissolved in water.

Unfortunately Krogh's scientific career was interrupted during World War II, when the Germans invaded and occupied Denmark. With his life in danger, Krogh fled to Sweden and lived in hiding there until the war ended. When peace returned Krogh retired from the Rockefeller Institute, but in his private laboratory he pursued the interests of his youth, including the flight of insects and birds and the budding of trees. He died in 1949, having earned much praise and many honors, including membership in scientific and medical societies, honorary degrees, and medals.

Karl
LANDSTEINER
1868–1943
MEDICINE, SEROLOGY, IMMUNOLOGY

* **hormone** internally secreted substance transported by body fluids to stimulate the functions of organs or tissues

* **immunology** science that deals with the immune system, which protects the body from foreign substances, cells, and tissue by causing an immune response

Sometimes called the father of immunology*, Karl Landsteiner made great advances in understanding how the body's immune system responds to the invasion of foreign substances. Landsteiner was the first to describe human blood groups and explain why some of these blood groups were incompatible with one another. This was a key step in the development of blood transfusion technology. Landsteiner also discovered the Rh factor* in blood and contributed to the understanding of such diseases as poliomyelitis* (polio), syphilis (a sexually transmitted disease), and typhus*.

The only son of a newspaper publisher, Karl Landsteiner was born near Vienna, Austria. He studied both organic chemistry and medicine, but his main interest was in medicine, and he received his medical degree

Landsteiner, Karl

* **Rh factor** genetically determined protein in the blood of humans and some animals; named for the rhesus monkey, in which the protein was first detected

* **poliomyelitis** viral disease that causes paralysis and deterioration of muscle tissue, often resulting in permanent disability or death; also called infantile paralysis

* **typhus** bacterial disease transmitted by body lice that causes severe fever, headache, and delirium

* **physiology** science that deals with the functions of living organisms and their parts

* **serology** study of the properties and reactions of serums, clear watery fluids in animal bodies

* **pathology** study of diseases and their effects on organisms

* **serum** clear liquid that separates from the blood after the blood cells clot

* **antibody** protein produced by the immune system to neutralize the presence of a foreign protein in the body

in 1891. Thereafter, Landsteiner began his career working in a series of research laboratories. In 1922 he moved from Europe to the United States to accept a post at the Rockefeller Institute. He became an American citizen seven years later. Landsteiner was a modest, timid, and self-critical person who did not seek the spotlight. His colleagues knew him as an avid reader and an excellent pianist.

Landsteiner was awarded the Nobel Prize in physiology* or medicine in 1930 for discovering the human blood groups and for developing the system of distinguishing blood types that enables people to receive blood transfusions. He was the recipient of many awards, including honorary doctorates from the University of Chicago, the Free University of Brussels, and Harvard and Cambridge Universities. He continued to study blood groups and immunological chemistry for the rest of his life. In 1943 he had a heart attack in his laboratory and died two days later in the hospital of Rockefeller Institute.

Discovering Human Blood Groups. After receiving his medical degree, Landsteiner spent three years working in chemistry laboratories in Austria, Germany, and Switzerland. In 1896 he joined the department of hygiene at the University of Vienna, where he became interested in serology* and immunology. While he was pursuing these interests, he worked as the assistant to the director at the Pathological-Anatomical Institute of the university. He conducted 3,639 postmortem examinations there, which gave him a comprehensive view of medicine and a strong background in anatomy and pathology*.

In 1900 Landsteiner published a paper with footnotes that contained information on one of his most important discoveries—the agglutination (clumping) that occurs between the blood serum* and cells of different humans. The following year, Landsteiner divided human blood into three groups that he called A, B, and C (later changed to O). Other scientists working with him soon found a fourth blood group that was later named AB. The differences in these blood groups were demonstrated by the fact that when the blood of two different people is mixed, it agglutinates, causing death. In the same paper, Landsteiner explained that agglutination occurs because blood is composed of serum and blood cells; the red blood cells contain proteins called agglutinogens that make the cells susceptible to clumping in the presence of different blood types. It is this presence or absence of certain agglutinogens that determines blood type. Type A blood has A agglutinogens. Type B blood has B agglutinogens; AB has both; and O has neither.

Blood serum also contains antibody* proteins called agglutinins. Landsteiner found that people make agglutinins that are *different* from their blood type. For example, a person with type A blood makes anti-B agglutinins, and one with type B blood makes anti-A agglutinins. People with type O blood make both anti-A and anti-B agglutinins, and people with AB blood make neither.

He explained that agglutination occurs when blood containing A agglutinogens is mixed with blood that contains anti-A agglutinins or when blood with B agglutinogens is mixed with blood that contains anti-B agglutinins.

Landsteiner went on to develop a simple method to test the blood of different people for compatibility. The pattern of blood types he found was inherited. His discoveries made possible the safer transfusion of blood from one person to another because the correct blood type could be identified and used. However, several years passed before his findings were put to practical use.

A New Kind of Fingerprint

Karl Landsteiner believed correctly that an individual's blood could serve as identification based on the presence or absence of different inherited blood proteins. Today scientists can test for dozens of other blood factors. Using DNA techniques, blood found at the scene of a crime can be matched with blood from a suspect or a victim, yielding results that are as accurate as traditional fingerprint matches. Because blood factors are inherited, blood matching using the same techniques used in criminal work can be employed with a high degree of accuracy to settle disputes about the paternity of a child.

Other Discoveries in Immunology. In addition to explaining A-B-O blood types, Landsteiner identified another element in human blood—the Rh factor. He discovered that a person whose blood is Rh-positive, or contains the inherited protein that he called the Rh factor, cannot safely donate blood to anyone whose blood lacks that factor. A transfusion across blood types would stimulate the immune system to produce antibodies, which can cause death during prolonged exposure to Rh-positive blood. Working with colleagues at Rockefeller Institute in New York, Landsteiner also demonstrated the presence of other blood factors (proteins), including a set that he called M, N, and P.

In addition to working with blood proteins, Landsteiner studied polio, syphilis, and typhus. He discovered that polio is caused by a virus and developed a procedure that used serum to diagnose the disease. He was able to demonstrate that syphilis is caused by a bacterium and was successful in growing the bacteria that caused typhus in the laboratory.

Landsteiner's work with blood proteins, however, has had the most far-reaching effects. Along with the work of Richard Lewisohn, who developed a way to keep stored blood from clotting, Landsteiner's simple tests for blood incompatibilities made possible modern blood banks and safe blood transfusions.

The LEAKEYS

Louis Seymour Bazett Leakey
1903–1972
PALEOANTHROPOLOGY

Mary Douglas Leakey
1913–1996
PALEOANTHROPOLOGY

Richard Leakey
born 1944
PALEOANTHROPOLOGY

For many decades in the mid-1900s, one family dominated paleoanthropology, the study of early humans and the traces they left behind in the form of fossil bones and stone tools. With a series of stunning fossil discoveries, Louis and Mary Leakey and their son Richard opened new vistas into the origins of the human species.

Although not all of the Leakeys' theories have stood the test of time, modern paleoanthropologists continue to build on the Leakeys' most important contributions. The Leakeys made Africa the focus of their searches for fossils of human ancestors. They also were the first to realize that human origins date further back and are more complicated than scientists had previously thought.

Louis Leakey Becomes an Anthropologist. Louis Seymour Bazett Leakey was born in Kabete, a village near Nairobi, Kenya. His English parents were Anglican missionaries among the East African Kikuyu people. Leakey grew up surrounded by African culture and participated in many tribal rituals. One Kikuyu chief called him "the black man with a white face." Leakey's later career reflected his love for Africa as well as his desire to probe into its past and to share his discoveries about Africa with the world.

Leakeys, The

During their archaeological expeditions in Africa, Louis and Mary Leakey excavated many bones and tools used by prehistoric peoples and their ancestors. The Leakeys' fossil discoveries changed the way scientists thought about human origins and evolution. With their son Richard, the Leakeys are known as "the first family of anthropology."

* **archaeology** scientific study of material remains of past human cultures, usually by excavating ruins

* **anthropology** study of human beings, especially in relation to origins and cultural characteristics

* **evolution** historical development of a biological group such as a species

Leakey developed an early interest in birds and made bird-watching expeditions into the African countryside. During such trips, he came across prehistoric stone tools, which turned his thoughts toward the human past. When he began his higher education at Cambridge University in England, he studied archaeology* and anthropology* and received his B.A. in 1926.

At the age of 21, Leakey took a year away from his college work. He joined a British Museum archaeological expedition to present-day Tanzania in East Africa. His experiences on the expedition left Leakey with the firm belief that Africa was the place of origin of the human species. This was a striking claim from a young scientist in training. Although Charles Darwin, the nineteenth century biologist whose work was central to the concept of the evolution* of species, had suggested Africa as the source of human origins, most paleoanthropologists of the early 1900s thought that the human race had originated in Asia. Leakey set out to prove them wrong.

Throughout the late 1920s and early 1930s, Leakey divided his time between advanced study at Cambridge and fieldwork in East Africa. In 1929 he excavated a 200,000-year-old stone ax, convincing him that Africa did indeed have something to tell about early humans. Two years later, he made his first trip to Olduvai Gorge, a canyon in northern Tanzania. Twenty miles long and 800 feet deep, the gorge is a dry channel that runs through an ancient lake bed. On his first day at the gorge, Leakey found stone tools and human fossils, leaving him determined to investigate the place thoroughly.

By the early 1930s, Leakey had married and started a family. However, while spending time in England in 1933, Leakey met the woman who became his second wife and his partner in his paleoanthropological finds, Mary Nicol.

Archaeologist Mary Nicol.

Mary Douglas Nicol was born in London into a family with an interest in the past. Her mother's great-grandfather had found prehistoric stone tools in England, and her father, a painter, was fascinated by archaeology. During her childhood, the family traveled often to southern France, the site of many cave paintings created by prehistoric artists. While in France, Mary accompanied the curator of a local museum to digs, or excavations, at prehistoric sites. She also studied the museum's large collection of ancient stone tools. Such artifacts became the first focus of her professional career.

During her late teens, Mary learned something about English prehistory during visits to such sites as Stonehenge. She also became acquainted with an archaeologist named Dorothy Liddell. Their meeting helped Mary realize that a woman could make a career in archaeology. Thereafter, she took courses in archaeology and geology at the University of London and began to assist Liddell at a dig at Henbury in southern England. Mary's specialty was in making accurate drawings of stone tools.

Mary met Louis Leakey in 1933, when he commissioned her to draw some illustrations for his book *Adam's Ancestors*, a survey of the current knowledge about human origins. While working together in England, the two formed a close personal and professional relationship. She accompanied Leakey to Olduvai Gorge in 1935, and the following year, after Leakey had obtained a divorce, the two were married in England. The couple promptly returned to Africa to resume their paleoanthropological work.

Searching for Human Origins.

The Leakeys spent the next few years digging for fossils and artifacts at various sites in East Africa. During World War II, while Louis worked with the British military in Nairobi, Mary continued to excavate. She discovered a number of stone axes.

After the war Louis became director of Nairobi's Coryndon Museum. Despite shortages of both funds and time, the Leakeys continued to make expeditions into the field whenever possible. In 1948 Mary made a major discovery on Rusinga Island in Kenya's Lake Victoria, unearthing nearly all of the fossilized skull of an apelike creature dating from 18 to 25 million years ago. She gave it the scientific name *Proconsul africanus*.

The *Proconsul,* the first fossil ape skull ever located, was a landmark find in paleontology*. The discovery also seemed to be a great boost to Louis's theory that humans had evolved in Africa. *Proconsul* appeared to combine qualities of both apes and humans. Scientists believe that it stood upright and walked on two legs rather than four. Its jaw lacked a feature known the "simian shelf" that appears in the jaws of modern apes. The Leakeys and some paleontologists believed that *Proconsul* was an ancestral hominid, a common ancestor of both apes and humans. Today, however, scientists believe that it was more closely related to apes.

* **paleontology** study of extinct or prehistoric life, usually through the examination of fossils

Mary Leakey's Laetoli Footprints

In 1978 Mary Leakey led a team to what she considered her greatest discovery. They were investigating fossil beds at a place called Laetoli, not far from Olduvai Gorge in Tanzania. The fossil beds had been covered with a layer of volcanic lava known to be 2.4 million years old, which meant that the hominid fossils she found at the site were even older. However, the most exciting find at Laetoli was not a fossil bone but a trail of several sets of hominid footprints left by beings who walked upright, on two legs, across a bed of soft volcanic ash about 3.5 million years ago. The footprints, which had been covered and fully preserved until her excavation, were clear evidence that hominids walked upright far earlier than scientists had previously thought.

The *Proconsul* find drew the attention of scientists. The Leakeys' next major find brought them worldwide fame even among nonscientists. In 1952 they returned to Olduvai Gorge and began a systematic excavation of the site that lasted many years. Mary unearthed several stone tools. Although it was impossible to date these artifacts, the finds encouraged Louis to think that tool-making hominids had inhabited the site at a very early date.

In 1959 the Leakeys were again excavating at Olduvai. One afternoon Mary cast her glance over a small slope and saw some fossilized teeth sticking out of the ground. She spent the following days carefully picking and brushing the earth away from her find, which proved to be the complete skull of a hominid she called *Zinjanthropus*, which means "East African man." Using a new archaeological technique called potassium-argon dating, scientists were able to calculate the approximate age of the *Zinjanthropus* fossil. At 1.75 million years old, it was the oldest truly humanlike fossil that had yet been found.

Other archaeologists had already discovered the remains of the *Australopithecus*, a more apelike ancient hominid, in Africa. Louis believed that the *Zinjanthropus* was the "missing link" between *Australopithecus* and the ancestors of modern humans. However, this idea has not held up, and most modern experts consider the *Zinjanthropus* a type of *Australopithecus*. Mary's find remains of vital importance, however, because of its great age.

The discovery of *Zinjanthropus* made the Leakeys known to the world. The National Geographic Society publicized their findings and awarded them grants that enabled them to continue their work on a full-time basis at Olduvai Gorge. People in many countries followed the story of the Leakeys through newspaper and magazine articles, and scientists made pilgrimages to Olduvai in the hope of working with the famous paleoanthropologists.

During the early 1960s the Leakey team uncovered more hominid remains at Olduvai—among these was a skull found by Jonathan Leakey, one of Louis and Mary's sons. Louis believed that these fossils represented a new species, closer to modern humans than *Zinjanthropus*, although of about the same age. He named them *Homo habilis*, or "handy man," because he linked them with the stone tools found at the site. The term *Homo* indicates that they belong to the same general category of living beings as modern humans, *Homo sapiens*.

The Olduvai fossils, which proved that the ancestors of modern humans had existed in Africa far earlier than anyone had thought, were the basis for Louis's theory about human origins, with which he rocked the scientific world in the mid-1960s. He suggested that more than one kind of hominid—*Homo habilis*, one or more types of *Australopithecus*, and several strains of *Homo sapiens*—could have lived in the same part of Africa at the same time. Although later research failed to support his theory in its entirety, modern paleontologists agree that different species of hominids undoubtedly did overlap. Human evolution was more like a bush with many branches than like a straight line from one hominid to the next, and Louis Leakey was the first to recognize this complexity.

Richard Leakey's Career in Anthropology.

None of the Leakeys' three sons, Jonathan, Richard, or Philip, showed any early interest in paleoanthropology. Although Richard had always been interested in the subject, he did not want to compete with or be professionally dominated by his father. He dropped out of school and became a safari guide. However, when he found an *Australopithecus* skull in 1963, Richard reconsidered and decided to make paleoanthropology his profession.

In 1967 Richard visited a region on the shore of Lake Turkana, in northern Kenya, that he felt looked like good fossil-hunting terrain. He obtained funds from the National Geographic Society to begin an excavation there at a site called Koobi Fora. The site proved to be an even richer source of material than Olduvai Gorge. Within ten years, Richard Leakey and his team discovered the fossil remains of approximately 230 individual hominids, both *Australopithecus* and *Homo habilis.* One of the most dramatic and significant finds was a *Homo habilis* skull nearly 1.9 million years old. In 1975 he found the skull of another hominid, *Homo erectus,* in a layer of earth that also contained *Australopithecus* fossils.

Richard's finds are proof that various branches of the human family tree lived in East Africa at about the same time. His theory that at least one large-brained genus had occupied East Africa by 2.5 or even 3.5 million years ago is outlined in his books *Origins, People of the Lake,* and *The Making of Mankind,* the first two of which were coauthored by Roger Lewin, a science writer.

Wildlife and Politics

In 1989 Richard Leakey turned from fossil hunting to preserving living animals. Kenya's president appointed Leakey head of the country's Wildlife Service (he had already served for 20 years as director of national museums). Leakey launched an ambitious program to protect animals from poachers. His decision that poachers could be shot on sight caused controversy, and his refusal to allow commercial development on land inside wildlife sanctuaries drew the anger of political opponents. In 1994, frustrated by the obstacles placed in his way, Leakey resigned his position. The following year he helped form a new Kenyan political party, called Safina, to push for democratic reforms.

Later Years.

After the mid-1960s, Mary Leakey remained at Olduvai Gorge for many years, continuing her careful, patient, and scientifically strict work at the site. She received an honorary doctoral degree from the University of Witwatersrand in South Africa, but she refused to accept the degree until university officials spoke publicly against apartheid, the policy of racial separation that was then in force in South Africa. In 1979 she published a work describing the decades that she spent in the field, *Olduvai Gorge: My Search for Early Man.*

Louis Leakey spent more and more time traveling around the world, raising funds for research, promoting his ideas, writing books—*Olduvai Gorge, 1951–61,* published in 1965, and *Unveiling Man's Origins,* cowritten with Jane GOODALL and published in 1969—and working to get the general public and young scientists interested in paleoanthropology. He also encouraged young biologists to study modern primates, the closest relatives of humans. He inspired Goodall's research on chimpanzees, Dian FOSSEY's on gorillas, and Birute Galdikas's on orangutans.

Personal and professional disagreements led to a rift between Richard Leakey and his famous father. In 1972, however, Louis visited Richard's Lake Turkana site and admired his son's work. He died soon afterward in London. In her autobiography, *Disclosing the Past* (1984), Mary revealed that she too had grown apart from her husband in the years before his death. She felt that he was too quick to base startling new theories on scanty evidence. She preferred a more cautious approach and was content to focus on gathering material for others to interpret. Mary continued to lecture, raise research funds, and conduct fieldwork until shortly before her death in Nairobi in 1996.

Joshua
LEDERBERG

born 1925

GENETICS

* **geneticist** scientist who specializes in genetics, the science of heredity

* **physiology** science that deals with the functions of living organisms and their parts

The American geneticist* Joshua Lederberg is best known for his work that demonstrated that bacteria, like more advanced forms of life, reproduce sexually and share genetic material. The discovery of this sharing process, called recombination, became one of the foundations on which modern genetic engineering was built. In recognition of this achievement, Lederberg shared the 1958 Nobel Prize in physiology* or medicine with George BEADLE and Edward TATUM.

Life and Career. Lederberg was the son of immigrants from Israel who came to the United States in 1924. His father, a rabbi, wanted Joshua to follow in his footsteps and pursue a religious career. However, the young Lederberg had no interest in becoming a rabbi, and he developed an early fascination for science. Lederberg recalls that his father eventually gave in to his son's interest, saying: "I guess there are many ways to follow the *Torah,* and if you want to seek the truth through science, that's alright too." Lederberg was academically advanced as a child, scoring very high on standardized achievement tests and consistently reading five to six grade levels ahead of his age. Consequently, he was often bored by his courses in school. Lederberg's elementary school teachers recognized his superior ability and made allowances for it. They agreed to let him sit in the back of the room and pursue his own work as long as he did not disrupt the class. Occasionally he assisted the teacher in instructing the other students. By the time he was 12, he had begun to read medical textbooks, an indication of the course of study he would pursue in college.

Lederberg enrolled in Columbia College at the age of 16 and after three years, received a degree in zoology. He then entered the College of Physicians and Surgeons at the Columbia University Medical School. After two years, he transferred to Yale University as a research fellow in

Although Joshua Lederberg is best known for his work that made bacteria a useful tool in genetic research, he is also involved with space programs seeking life on Mars, advocating the control of chemical and biological weapons, and in artificial intelligence research.

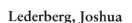

* **microbiology** study of microscopic organisms

microbiology* and botany. Lederberg received his Ph.D. in zoology in 1948 from Yale but never finished his medical studies, choosing instead to pursue a career in research.

In 1947 he accepted an assistant professorship of genetics at the University of Wisconsin, despite the fact that members of the administration made insulting comments about his religion. While at Wisconsin he organized the school's Department of Medical Genetics and served as its first chairman. In 1959 he accepted an offer to organize another department of genetics, this time at Stanford University. Three years later he became director of Stanford's Kennedy Laboratory for Molecular Medicine. In 1978 Lederberg became president of Rockefeller University and served in that position until 1990. He continues his research as professor emeritus, an honorary position.

In addition to his genetic research, Lederberg has served on a number of governmental and extragovernmental agencies. For many years, he was a member of the World Health Organization's Advisory Health Research Council. He is also past chair of the President's Cancer Panel and Congress's Technology Assessment Advisory Council. He served on several committees that advocated arms control and worked as an adviser to the Biological Weapons Convention. Today, Lederberg chairs a United Nations committee dedicated to improving global Internet communications for science and to helping people in less developed countries get access to computer networks.

Lederberg is also involved in research into artificial intelligence and has worked with the National Aeronautics and Space Administration (NASA) to investigate the possibility of life on Mars. In the early years of the U.S. space program, Lederberg served as the main proponent of measures to ensure that biological contamination did not occur on other planets when spaceships from earth landed there. He recommended procedures to safeguard life on earth from the danger of alien viruses or bacteria.

In addition to the Nobel Prize, he has received many other honors, including the Eli Lilly Award for outstanding young scientists and the prestigious National Medal of Science. Although he switched from medical studies and did not earn an M.D., Lederberg has been awarded honorary medical degrees by two universities. He is a member of both the National Academy of Sciences and the Royal Society of London.

Lederberg credits his accomplishments to several influences: parents who understood his desire to explore new ideas, teachers who motivated him to follow his interests, and luck. But he notes, quoting the eminent French scientist Louis Pasteur, "Chance favors the prepared mind." Lederberg also notes that he was fortunate to make his great discovery at an early age—he was just 33 when he won the Nobel Prize, for work he performed when he was in his early 20s. "Being successful at a very young age gave me the confidence and the capability to try out other things. I was very lucky, and I had the capacity to try a lot of other stuff."

Scientific Accomplishments. Lederberg did his most important work during the mid-1940s at Yale, working with Professor Edward Tatum and fellow graduate student George Beadle. At that time, scientists were just beginning to unlock the secrets of DNA*. Researchers had shown that certain organisms, such as mold, reproduced sexually by exchanging DNA, but no one was sure that bacteria could do so as well.

By crossing strains of different bacteria, Lederberg and his colleagues produced a new strain that contained genes from the parent bacteria. Scientists had previously thought that bacteria only reproduced asexually, when the cells split in two. Lederberg and Tatum showed that bacteria reproduced sexually as well, and that the genetic systems of bacteria resemble those of more complex multicellular organisms. This discovery expanded the type of genetic research that could be performed with bacteria, and they became one of the central organisms used in genetics research.

Lederberg and other colleagues later showed that the recombination of genetic material was the result of the presence or absence of a transmissible factor, named the F factor, which was passed on from parent to offspring. However, two cells with different F factors (F^+ and F^-) had to be in contact with one another for this to take place. This discovery proved that the reproductive process was sexual in nature.

Lederberg's work also demonstrated that bacteria might exchange genetic material by several methods. The process of conjugation, or the one-way transfer of DNA between bacteria, was shown to be especially important because genes that are resistant to antibiotics* may also be exchanged among bacteria.

Lederberg went on to make another important discovery concerning bacterial reproduction. While working with the bacterium known as *Salmonella*, he observed that a bacterial virus could carry genes from one bacterium to another. The gene then became part of the genetic makeup of the cell into which it was introduced. Lederberg named this process transduction. The discovery of genetic recombination and transduction showed researchers that bacteria could be important tools in genetic research. It also showed that scientists could actually place genes directly into cells, which was one of the first steps on the road to genetic engineering.

Rita LEVI-MONTALCINI

born 1909

DEVELOPMENTAL BIOLOGY

Rita Levi-Montalcini spent her professional life investigating the growth of nerve cells. She discovered a protein in the nervous system that is essential for nerve growth. She also demonstrated that the movement of neurons* during development is determined genetically* and that it is predictable for individuals of the same species. However, once these neurons reach their final position, their growth is determined by the presence of a nerve growth factor produced by the tissue that the neurons are intended to grow into. Levi-Montalcini isolated the first growth factors from animal tissues.

From Proper Young Lady to Medical Doctor. Levi-Montalcini was born in Turin, Italy, in 1909. Her father, Adamo Levi, was an engineer and managed a factory. Over the course of Levi-Montalcini's childhood, her father gradually turned away from Jewish traditions and became a liberal free thinker. Adele Montalcini, her mother, encouraged the children to continue to practice their religion.

Rita Levi-Montalcini was not allowed to pursue studies that would open the way to a professional career because her father believed it would interfere with the duties of a wife and mother. Around age 20, however, she realized she could not fulfill this role as conceived by her father and, with his permission, began to pursue a career in science that led to her winning a Nobel Prize.

* **histologist** scientist who studies the structure of tissues at the microscopic level

* **embryologist** scientist who studies the development of an egg and sperm into an embryo, an organism at the early stages of development before birth or hatching

* **neurology** study of the structure, function, and disorders of the nervous system

Levi-Montalcini, her two sisters, and her brother were educated at the local public elementary school. Her brother went to a university preparatory school and later became a prominent architect. The girls, however, attended a finishing school where they prepared for upper-class domestic life. Although she was an excellent student, Levi-Montalcini received no training in mathematics, science, Latin, or Greek. When she graduated, she was unqualified to continue her education at any university.

For several years Levi-Montalcini lived at home and followed the domestic path envisioned by her father. During this time her beloved governess developed stomach cancer and died. This exposure to illness and death convinced Levi-Montalcini that she wanted to study medicine. She convinced her father of her seriousness and studied with tutors to prepare for the university entrance examinations. She passed with excellent scores and entered Turin Medical School in 1930.

In medical school, Levi-Montalcini worked in the laboratory of Giuseppe Levi, a histologist* and embryologist* known for his rigorous and demanding approach to research. She began her research on the development of the nervous system. Her professional relationship with Levi lasted until his death 35 years later.

The War Interferes. In 1936 Levi-Montalcini earned a doctorate in medicine with specialization in neurology* and psychiatry from the University of Turin. She practiced medicine at the Turin Clinic for Nervous and Mental Disorders while continuing to do research at the university. Two years later, however, she and her Jewish colleagues lost their jobs when Italy passed laws banning Jews from practicing medicine. Levi-Montalcini continued her research at the Neurology Institute of Brussels until the Nazi invasion of Belgium forced her to return to Italy.

As World War II progressed, conditions in Italy worsened. Levi-Montalcini set up a small laboratory in her bedroom and studied the development of the nervous system in chicken embryos. Giuseppe Levi joined her to work in her homemade laboratory. Shortly thereafter Levi and the Levi-Montalcini family fled Turin because of heavy bombing by Allied forces. They moved to a farmhouse in the country where they reassembled their home laboratory.

By 1943 Italy was in chaos. German forces invaded from the north while Allied forces attacked from the south. Harsh Nazi administrative laws controlled the activities of Jews. Levi-Montalcini's entire household traveled south using forged identity papers. They hoped to find safety behind the Allied lines but failed to reach them. With the help of a friend, the family spent the remainder of the war living in Florence under false identities. When the British occupied Florence and made it safe for Jews to go about in public, Levi-Montalcini practiced medicine in the refugee camps set up by the Red Cross. However, she returned to research because she was discouraged by her inability to help many of the sick and injured.

Discovering Nerve Growth Factor. Based on their research during the war, Levi-Montalcini and Levi published a paper suggesting that the neuron and the tissue it supplied with nerves were mutually dependent. They believed that peripheral tissues supplied what they called a trophic factor,

Science, Jews, and World War II

The Nazis and their allies disrupted the work of many scholars during World War II. The Nazis blamed the Jews for many of the social and economic problems that developed between the world wars. In Italy anti-Semitic laws prohibited Jews from holding government positions, practicing medicine, teaching, or publishing. Similar restrictions affected German-occupied countries. Many scholars died or saw their lifework destroyed. Others fled to the United States or Great Britain. A few, like Levi-Montalcini, went into hiding and continued their work in secret.

* **culture** microorganisms, such as bacteria or tissue, grown in a specially prepared nutrient substance for scientific study

* **antibody** protein produced by the immune system to neutralize the presence of a foreign protein in the body

* **physiology** science that deals with the functions of living organisms and their parts

or growth factor, without which neurons could not function. On the strength of this paper, Levi-Montalcini was invited to fill a temporary research position at Washington University in St. Louis, Missouri. The temporary job lasted for more than 30 years. Although she lived in the United States during that time, she often returned to Italy.

After months of tedious research, Levi-Montalcini recognized that the migration of neurons during embryonic development was genetically controlled. She realized that the neurons' ability to make functional connections after migration was completely dependent on a chemical produced in the tissues. But chicken embryos grew too slowly to determine the relative contribution of environmental factors and genetic programming.

Levi-Montalcini turned to a simpler system. She used cultured* tissue to clarify the role of the substance that she and her colleague at Washington University, Stanley Cohen, isolated and purified. They called it nerve growth factor (NGF). Cohen confirmed their findings by performing additional experiments using antibodies* to neutralize the effects of NGF and observed that the nerve cells failed to develop. For these discoveries, Cohen and Levi-Montalcini shared the Nobel Prize in physiology* or medicine in 1986. The following year Levi-Montalcini received the National Medal of Science, the highest American award for scientists.

Levi-Montalcini established the Center for Neurobiology in Rome (later renamed the Institute for Cell Biology). She divided her time between that institution and Washington University until she retired in 1977. Thereafter, with her twin sister, an artist, Levi-Montalcini began a counseling program to help youth interested in the arts and sciences. She has served as president of the Italian Multiple Sclerosis Association and was the first woman appointed to the Pontifical Academy of Sciences in Rome.

Following the discovery of NGF, scientists identified many other growth factors affecting the development, repair, and maintenance of cells. Today, the interplay of genetic programming and tissue-specific environmental factors is recognized as having implications in the treatment of cancers and the regeneration of the nervous system. Growth factors also are essential to the understanding of conditions such as Alzheimer's disease and the treatment of developmental defects through genetic engineering. The topics that Levi-Montalcini spent her life exploring continue to be the subject of active research.

Jacques LOEB

1859–1924

BIOLOGY, PHYSIOLOGY

Jacques Loeb was interested in explaining behavioral and biological events in terms of physical and chemical reactions. In the late 1880s, when Loeb began his research, this was a substantially different way of looking at living organisms. His desire to find a physical basis for a variety of biological events led him to study animal instincts, the development of the fertilized egg, and the behavior of proteins in solutions. Although his critics often proved Loeb's research results to be incorrect, his attempts to explain biological events in terms of physical reactions were part of a fundamental change in the direction of biological research. In fact, elements of his physical-mechanical outlook are evident today.

From Philosopher to Scientist. Loeb never intended to become a biological researcher. Born into a prosperous Jewish family in Mayen, Rhine Province, Prussia, his first academic love was philosophy. In 1880, when he entered the University of Berlin, however, he became bitterly disillusioned with his professors of philosophy. After leaving Berlin he spent five years studying the physical functions of the brain at a university in Strasbourg and earned an M.D.

Two years later Loeb became the assistant to Adolph Fick, a professor of physiology in Wurzburg who was interested in applying the principles of physics to biology and medicine. During this time Loeb became friends with Julius von Sachs, a botanist who introduced him to the concept of plant tropisms (involuntary movements in response to a physical stimulus such as light or gravity). For example, the roots of plants always grow down into the earth, even when the seed is planted upside down. This is a tropic response to gravity and is caused by a chemical reaction in the plant cells. The way plants bend toward the light is another example of a tropic response. Introduction to this field of study proved to be a life-changing event for Loeb.

Loeb set out to establish that animals could also be irresistibly driven by external stimulation, rather than by their own willpower. Naturalists* knew from observation that certain types of caterpillars, shortly after they had hatched, always climbed toward the tips of branches to feed on leaf buds. Contemporaries of Loeb believed that this behavior was an example of the instinct for survival. However, Loeb showed that if the only source of light were located in the opposite direction, the caterpillars would move toward the light and starve. What scientists had attributed to instinct was essentially the organism's tropic response to a physical stimulus, light.

Loeb conducted other experiments with animal tropisms and believed that he had proved that tropic responses were widespread. Later, however, his critics showed that, although some animals did respond to tropisms, other behaviors that Loeb had considered tropic were really either avoidance responses or the result of trial-and-error learning.

New Country, New Research. In 1891 Loeb moved to the United States, where he taught at several universities. His research also changed direction. Loeb believed that physical and chemical reactions caused a fertilized egg to begin dividing. By exposing fertilized sea urchin eggs to seawater with a higher-than-normal concentration of salt, he believed that he could force them to divide. Quickly his critics proved that the same response could be obtained with unfertilized eggs. Loeb, however, was then able to use this finding to become the first biologist to grow sea urchin larvae by parthenogenesis, the process by which an organism develops from an unfertilized egg. This process occurs naturally in some plants and animals such as bees or can be artificially engineered using environmental shock. Larvae that were developed in this manner became an important research tool for embryologists*.

From 1918 until his death six years later, Loeb continued his goal of finding chemical and mechanical explanations for biological phenomena. In a series of experiments, he investigated the behavior of proteins. He

* **naturalist** one who studies objects in their natural settings

* **embryologist** scientist who studies the development of an egg and sperm into an embryo, an organism at the early stages of development before birth or hatching

109

demonstrated that proteins could react chemically as either an acid or as a base. He also unified concepts in physical chemistry and biology by showing how the complex distribution of proteins on either side of a semipermeable membrane* caused an equilibrium that accounted for many of the properties of proteins.

Loeb's principal statement of his basic philosophy was his famous speech "The Mechanistic Conception of Life," which was published as the title piece of his most widely read book in 1912. In this work, he argued that the mechanistic conception had made large strides in the first decade of the twentieth century, largely through his own research. Loeb believed that life and biological events, including behavior, could be explained by rational, reproducible physical and chemical events, which could in turn be understood through experimentation and objective analysis. This went against the spiritual and philosophical explanations of life and behavior that were popular in Loeb's lifetime. Although many of Loeb's specific findings were later proved incorrect, his approach to understanding behaviors and biological events moved science into a new era of experimentation and rational analysis, which remains a fundamental aspect of modern research methodology.

Otto LOEWI

1873–1961

PHARMACOLOGY, PHYSIOLOGY

Otto Loewi, a German-born scientist who became an American citizen, conducted basic physiological* research in two main areas: the metabolism* of proteins and carbohydrates, and the nervous system, particularly the nerves of the heart. In 1936 he and British scientist Henry Dale won the Nobel Prize in physiology or medicine for discovering how chemicals carry impulses, or messages, from nerve cells.

Background and Education. Loewi was born in Frankfurt am Main, Germany, the son of a wealthy wine merchant. At school his record was better in the humanities than in mathematics or physics, and he hoped to become an art historian. Loewi's family, however, wanted him to study medicine, which offered more promising career prospects than art history. In 1891 Loewi entered the University of Strasbourg, in northeastern France, as a medical student. The study of medicine, however, failed to capture Loewi's interest. During his first two years of medical school, he preferred lectures by the philosophy professors to his own studies. He barely passed his first medical examination.

When it was time for Loewi to write his dissertation, the research paper that candidates for doctoral degrees must present, he chose an area in which he was not well prepared: pharmacology, the scientific study of drugs and their medicinal properties. He studied and described the effects of various drugs on frog hearts that were kept alive outside the animals' bodies for research purposes. This work made him familiar with techniques that he later used to make his discovery about the nervous system, which was based on an experiment involving a frog's heart.

Beginning an Academic Career. Loewi received his medical degree from Strasbourg in 1896, then spent months studying various types of chemistry. He returned to Frankfurt to serve as an assistant in internal medicine at a hospital there and was assigned to wards for patients suffering from advanced tuberculosis and epidemic pneumonia. He became discouraged by the lack of effective treatments for these diseases and the high death rates they caused. He later said that the experience encouraged him to dedicate himself to basic research rather than to medical practice because he hoped that through research he ultimately could do more to help people.

For ten years beginning in 1898, Loewi moved from place to place, working and learning from his colleagues. He served as an assistant in a pharmacological institute at Germany's University of Marburg, where he wrote a research paper on human metabolism. He also spent several months in England, which he believed had replaced Germany as the center of physiological studies. He met and exchanged ideas with the leading English physiologists of the day.

After rising to the rank of assistant professor at Marburg, Loewi served for a short time as the director of the pharmacological institute there. He then moved to the University of Vienna in Austria, where he held the post of assistant professor. In 1909 he accepted a post as professor and head of pharmacology at the University of Graz, also in Austria. Although Loewi received offers from more famous universities, he remained at Graz for nearly 30 years, until he was expelled from his position by the Nazis. Like other male Jewish citizens of Graz, Loewi was imprisoned, but he was released two months later.

Metabolism Research. As early as his student days, Loewi had been interested in the problems of metabolism. Scientists were just beginning to explore these problems by examining the link between metabolic processes and disease. Loewi said that a paper about the relationship between the pancreas and diabetes was one of the five papers that inspired his own career. He was also influenced by a series of papers on the metabolism of salmon, which he called his "scientific bible."

Loewi's first publications on metabolism focused on urine, one of the products of metabolism. He argued that of all the components of urine, only uric acid depended on diet. In a later series of papers, Loewi examined whether a dog's metabolism could convert fat into sugar, concluding that it could not.

His major contribution to metabolic studies involved the formation of proteins in animal bodies. Scientists believed that animals could not synthesize, or create, proteins from basic materials. Loewi speculated that animals might be able to synthesize proteins if their diets consisted of the products of a whole organ rather than of isolated proteins, so he undertook a series of nutritional experiments to test the idea. Although the dogs Loewi used found the diet disagreeable at first, he eventually showed that they were capable of synthesizing proteins from elementary materials, such as amino acids*. This work established Loewi's early reputation and laid the basis for work in nutrition by other scientists.

Between 1902 and 1905, Loewi worked with three researchers on a series of five papers dealing with the function of the kidney and the actions

A Dream Experiment?

Otto Loewi liked to tell the story of how he devised the experiment that brought him fame. One night he woke from sleep and made some notes. The next morning he could not read them, although he was sure they concerned something important. When he returned to sleep the following night, the idea—the design of an experiment to test for chemical transmission of nerve impulses—returned to him. This time Loewi got out of bed, went to the lab, and performed his famous experiment on frog hearts. Loewi believed that his sleeping mind had recalled an experimental technique that he had used in earlier studies.

* **amino acid** class of compounds that function as the building blocks of proteins

111

* **diuretic** substance that increases the flow of urine

* **insulin** hormone produced by the pancreas that is used in the treatment of diabetes

* **hormone** internally secreted substance transported by body fluids to stimulate the functions of organs or tissues

* **vagus nerve** either of a pair of nerves that arise in the brain and supply the organs with nerve fibers

* **acetylcholine (ACh)** substance that transmits nerve impulses and forms salts that lower blood pressure

of diuretics*. Between 1907 and 1918 he published six more studies on metabolism, mostly dealing with the function of the pancreas and the metabolism of sugar in cases of diabetes. Later he studied the effects of insulin* on metabolism.

Nervous System Research. Another area that captured Loewi's interest was the autonomic nervous system, the part of the nervous system that governs such involuntary actions as salivation, digestion, and heartbeat. He claimed that his encounters with British physiologists had awakened this interest. His first papers on the topic dealt with subjects that were under investigation in England during the time of his visit there, such as the secretion of saliva and adrenaline. Loewi's first original contribution to nervous system research was his demonstration that drugs such as cocaine made organs governed by the autonomic nervous system more sensitive to adrenaline, a hormone* that the body secretes to raise blood pressure.

Beginning in 1912 Loewi turned his attention to the vagus nerve* and its action on the heart muscle. Using frog hearts, he studied the effects of various drugs and chemical solutions on the vagus nerve. Much of this work dealt with drugs whose main component was digitalis. Digitalis is a compound from the dried leaf of the purple foxglove plant that acts as a powerful stimulant to the heart. He determined that these drugs affect the heart by making it sensitive to calcium.

For some time Loewi had studied the physiology and pharmacology of the frog's heart and its nerves. None of this research, however, led directly to the work for which he won the Nobel Prize. That work focused on the idea that chemical substances were involved in transmitting nerve impulses, or sending signals through the nervous system. Although Loewi and others had suggested this possibility as early as 1903, none had been able to prove it through experimentation until much later.

In 1921 Loewi devised and conducted an experiment by which he proved the involvement of chemicals in the transmission of nerve impulses. He placed the living hearts of two frogs in a solution and stimulated the vagus nerve of one heart, which caused its beating to slow. He then transferred the solution around that heart to the second heart, and the beating of the second heart slowed. This proved that some property in the solution had affected the vagus nerve of the second heart. He concluded that the first heart had secreted a chemical substance that carried the nerve impulse, which was then transmitted to the second heart. The chemicals released by the stimulation of the nerves, not the nerves themselves, acted directly on the heart. Several years later Loewi and his colleagues identified one of the key chemicals as acetylcholine (ACh)*. He called it a neurotransmitter—a chemical that transmits nerve impulses.

Loewi described his experiment with frog hearts, which became a classic of physiological experimentation, in a four-part article. He followed this with more than a dozen additional articles about chemical transmission. Some scientists were slow to accept Loewi's conclusion, however, because they did not always get the same results he had obtained from the experiment. Loewi claimed that successful duplication of his results required using the hearts of frogs from the same species that he had used.

Other species were less responsive, he said, and even the season of the year could affect the experiment. In 1926 Loewi successfully performed the experiment before the International Congress of Physiology at Stockholm, Sweden, and before long his results were universally accepted. For this work, he received the Nobel Prize in physiology or medicine, together with Henry Dale, who also researched chemical transmission and worked with Loewi.

In later work, again in collaboration with Dale and others, Loewi attempted to identify the specific chemical substances released by nerves in the body when they were stimulated. He determined that when the vagus nerve was stimulated, it secreted acetylcholine, which acted as a chemical signal to the heart's accelerator nerve (which causes the heartbeat to speed up) to produce adrenaline. His work led to a better understanding of the action of certain drugs, called alkaloids*. Alkaloids interacted with the enzymes* that degraded acetylcholine. Loewi and his colleagues had originally used alkaloids to help them determine the identity and function of acetylcholine. Thereafter, they also used alkaloids to detect acetylcholine in tissues where it was present in very low concentrations or degraded rapidly. As a result, they were able to prove that nerve impulses were transmitted chemically in warm-blooded vertebrates*, and that this process occurred in parts of the nervous system where they had not thought it possible.

Later Career. Loewi's research career ended in 1936. Thereafter, he became a critic, reviewer, and guide for other researchers who explored the new lines of research that he had opened with his discovery of the chemical transmission of nervous impulses. His discovery launched a revolution in neurophysiology, the study of how the nervous system functions.

After Nazi Germany took control of Austria, Loewi—like all Jews in Nazi territory—faced considerable peril. In 1938 the Nazis imprisoned him and two of his four children. Months later they allowed him to leave for London, but only after he had turned over his Nobel Prize money to a Nazi-controlled bank as ransom for his life. Loewi left Austria, stripped of all property and funds. He found work in research institutes in Brussels and Oxford, and from 1940 until his death, he was research professor of pharmacology at New York University's College of Medicine. His wife, whom the Nazis had refused to release, joined him in 1941. Five years later the Loewis became American citizens. Loewi died 15 years later in New York and was buried in Woods Hole, Massachusetts, where he had spent summers at the Marine Biological Laboratory.

* **alkaloid** group of naturally occurring organic bases containing nitrogen, such as caffeine, morphine, and nicotine

* **enzyme** any of numerous complex proteins that are produced by living cells and catalyze specific biochemical reactions at body temperature

* **vertebrate** animal with a backbone

Barbara
McCLINTOCK
1902–1992
GENETICS

* **genetics** branch of biology that deals with heredity

Barbara McClintock devoted her life to studying the genetics* of Indian corn (maize). In doing so she discovered that genetic material, once thought to be fixed in place, can move along chromosomes* or from one chromosome to another. Because of this newfound mobility, these genes were given the name jumping genes. She also showed that these moving genes could act as on-off switches that affect the behavior of other nearby genes. While her work focused primarily on corn plants, it influenced understanding of how tumors grow and how cells become specialized in the embryo*.

McClintock, Barbara

* **chromosome** structure in the cell that contains the DNA (genes) that transmit unique genetic information

* **embryo** organism at the early stages of development before birth or hatching

* **physiology** science that deals with the functions of living organisms and their parts

At the age of 81, Barbara McClintock, shown here holding an ear of corn, became the first sole, female winner of the Nobel Prize in physiology or medicine. Other female winners—Cori (1947), Yalow (1977), Levi-Montalcini (1986), Elion (1988), and Nüsslein-Volhard (1995)—received the prize jointly with their male colleagues.

For years McClintock's colleagues ridiculed or ignored her work on jumping genes. Decades after she reported her findings, other researchers began reporting the presence of this phenomenon in other species. McClintock's work was given a second look and belatedly received the recognition that she deserved. In 1983 she was awarded the Nobel Prize in physiology* or medicine.

Unconventional from the Start. McClintock was born in 1902 in Hartford, Connecticut, the third of four children. Her father was a medical doctor who struggled to establish a profitable practice. Her mother's family background left her unprepared to raise children without the help of a large household staff, and she suffered emotionally under the strain. As a result, McClintock, who always had a difficult relationship with her mother, spent long periods of her childhood living with an aunt and uncle in Massachusetts.

From the start, McClintock showed an independent and solitary personality, preferring sports and outdoor activities to domestic pursuits, which at the time were considered more appropriate for girls. She also spent a lot of time reading on her own. Her parents insisted that their children only go to school when they wanted to, and they forbade the children's teachers from giving them any homework.

McClintock enrolled at Cornell University in 1919. At first she led a normal social life, dating and becoming president of the women's freshman class. However, at the end of two years of college life, she decided that she did not need close personal contacts, including family, and that she would defy convention by remaining single and devoting herself to science. She withdrew from several organizations because they practiced discrimination against women or minorities. McClintock received her bachelor's degree in 1923 and a Ph.D. in botany and genetics four years later, both from Cornell University.

During her time at Cornell, McClintock developed a new staining technique to make plant chromosomes more visible under a light microscope, the main tool for studying chromosomes at that time. Studying chromosomes in this manner was extremely tedious, precise, demanding work, but McClintock soon became an expert.

Genes That Move. During the seven years after she received her Ph.D., McClintock led a professionally precarious existence. Although she was recognized as an expert in her field, she could not obtain a faculty position at a university. Because most universities would not offer appointments to women, she worked as a laboratory assistant and part-time instructor. Her research was supported primarily by short-term grants. Most of this time she worked at Cornell University, except for a brief, unsuccessful visit to a laboratory in Germany. She arrived there just as the Nazis came to power, and the discrimination against Jews disturbed her.

During this unsettled time, McClintock and her graduate student at Cornell, Harriet Creighton, published a landmark study proving that some genes are not fixed in position and that genetic material and information can be exchanged between chromosomes during cell division, or

* meiosis special method of cell division to produce reproductive cells that contain half the number of chromosomes found in all other cells of the body

* mutation relatively permanent change in the structure of a material

Deciphering Jumping Genes

Kernels of Indian corn come in many colors. Some kernels are multicolored, and this pattern cannot be explained by simple genetic inheritance patterns. Barbara McClintock won the Nobel Prize for discovering transposons (genes that move from one location to another), which switch off the pigment-producing function of the gene next to them. The longer the transposons stay in position, the longer this gene is turned off, and the more white appears in the kernel. Although her work was based on plant genetics, this method of gene regulation was found to be important to understanding tumor growth and the specialization of embryo cells.

meiosis*. In 1936 McClintock finally received a faculty appointment at the University of Missouri. But she stayed there only five years because the university terminated the position. She then worked at the Cold Spring Harbor Laboratory on Long Island in New York. This laboratory was not associated with a university and was funded by the Carnegie Institute in Washington. She remained there for the rest of her career.

The Cold Spring Harbor Years. Cold Spring Harbor provided a stable environment where McClintock could pursue her research, most of which she performed alone. She was free to grow corn, breed specific strains, and investigate the genetics involved in its patterns of coloration, with no teaching or household responsibilities to distract her.

She noticed that some corn plants had colored spots that would not normally belong on the green or yellow leaves of that particular species of plant. She assumed that mutations* earlier in the plant's life had caused the discoloration and that the larger the spot, the earlier the mutation had occurred. Out of this observation emerged her interest in exploring the factors that regulate and control the transfer of genetic information. Her studies of the coloration pattern in individual kernels of corn led to the discovery that some genes act as controlling elements or switches. These genes could move either along the chromosome or between chromosomes. She called this process transposition, and she named the moving gene a jumping gene, or transposon. Further research showed that two factors controlled the appearance of pigment patterns in corn. A gene called a dissociator enables the genetic material to break and express a new pattern. The dissociator gene also allows the release of an activator gene, which can then be transposed to a different site. This jumping gene made it possible for plant offspring to have an unexpected pigment pattern. Throughout these experiments McClintock relied on a light microscope to examine the chromosomes and compare their changes to the color patterns of individual plants.

In 1951 McClintock presented her work on jumping genes to her colleagues at Cold Spring Harbor, but the concept went against the accepted theories of the time. Her work was difficult to understand, and she herself was inclined to be short-tempered with others who did not quickly grasp her ideas. Her professional peers ridiculed or ignored her findings because, at the time, most scientists involved in genetic research had turned away from studies that depended on observation to research involving the physiology of chromosomes and later the structure of DNA. McClintock, however, continued to rely on her microscope and corn plants, and she persisted with her breeding experiments.

Recognition at Last. In 1961, ten years after McClintock reported her findings, the French geneticist François Jacob and the biologist Jacques Monod (both of whom won the Nobel Prize in 1965) reported a system of operator and regulator genes in the chromosomes of bacteria that closely resembled the activator and dissociator genes that McClintock had found three decades earlier. As time passed, other scientists reported similar systems in other species. McClintock's work, which had been poorly received when it was presented, was then hailed as visionary.

Finally in 1983 McClintock was awarded the Nobel Prize and her pioneering work of the 1950s was recognized as pivotal in changing the way scientists thought about genetic inheritance and the expression of genetic traits.

Otto Fritz MEYERHOF

1884–1951

BIOCHEMISTRY

* **biochemist** person who specializes in the science that deals with chemical compounds and processes occurring in living organisms

* **physiology** science that deals with the functions of living organisms and their parts

* **enzyme** any of numerous complex proteins that are produced by living cells and catalyze specific biochemical reactions at body temperature

* **fermentation** chemical reaction in which complex organic compounds are split into relatively simple substances

The German biochemist* Otto Fritz Meyerhof discovered some of the basic chemical reactions in muscles that convert carbohydrates into lactic acid and energy. His work enabled other scientists to evaluate the efficiency of muscles as machines that run on chemical fuel. He was also devoted to the idea that biological processes can be fully described in terms of chemistry and physics.

Meyerhof was born in Hannover, Germany, the son of a merchant. He received his medical degree in 1909 and was interested at first in psychology and philosophy. After graduation he worked at a medical clinic where the well-known scientist Otto WARBURG turned his attention to the workings of living cells. Between 1919 and 1938, Meyerhof conducted his research at institutes in Keil, Berlin-Dahlem, and Heidelberg.

Early in his career, Meyerhof showed that when muscles contract in the absence of oxygen, the carbohydrate glycogen is converted to lactic acid. However, if enough oxygen reaches the muscles, about one-fifth of the lactic acid reacts with the oxygen to form carbon dioxide and water. This reaction also generates energy, which turns the rest of the lactic acid back into glycogen. In 1922 Meyerhof shared the Nobel Prize in physiology* or medicine with Sir Archibald Vivan Hill for this work.

Some years later Meyerhof isolated the enzymes* needed for converting glycogen to lactic acid. Earlier scientists had shown that the process was very similar to the way in which enzymes in yeast convert sugars to alcohol and carbon dioxide during fermentation*.

The career of this distinguished scientist was interrupted when the Nazis rose to power in Germany. Because Meyerhof was Jewish, he fled to Paris and then the United States. He spent the last part of his career at the University of Pennsylvania. Meyerhof's influence in the development of biochemistry was profound. It continued past the mid-1900s through the work of his former students. Noteworthy among them were the German Fritz Lipmann and the Spaniard Severo Ochoa, both Nobel laureates.

George Richards MINOT

1885–1950

MEDICINE

* **hematology** study of the formation, structure, and diseases of the blood

George Richards Minot made many advances in hematology*, but his best-known contribution was the discovery of a successful treatment for a fatal form of anemia*. Minot received his medical degree from Harvard Medical School in 1912. He was professor of medicine at Harvard University and director of the Harvard Medical Unit and Boston City Hospital.

Later, while working at Massachusetts General Hospital, Minot questioned the diets given to patients who were suffering from a severe form of anemia. George Whipple, a pathologist* and medical researcher at the

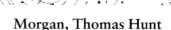

* **anemia** disease marked by the reduction of oxygen-carrying material in the blood

* **pathologist** specialist in the study of diseases and their effects on organisms

* **physiology** science that deals with the functions of living organisms and their parts

* **clinical** related to the observation and treatment of disease in actual patients rather than in artificial experiments

* **coagulation** transformation of a liquid into a semisolid or solid mass; clotting

* **platelet** minute particle in blood that assists in clotting

University of Rochester, had reported that feeding raw liver was effective in preventing anemia in dogs whose blood was periodically removed during experimental trials. Minot applied the therapy to human patients and noted a distinct improvement in their condition. This work won Minot, Whipple, and another scientist named William P. Murphy the 1934 Nobel Prize in physiology* or medicine.

Minot's later work ushered in a new era of quantitative measurement in clinical* hematology. Along with his colleagues, he did important early work on blood transfusion and coagulation* and studied blood platelets*, the effects of radiation on leukemia (cancer of the blood), and tumors of the lymph glands.

Minot was elected to the National Academy of Sciences in 1897 and served as president of the American Society of Naturalists, the American Association of Anatomists, and the American Association for the Advancement of Science. He also received honorary degrees from universities in the United States, England, and Canada.

Thomas Hunt
MORGAN
1866–1945
EMBRYOLOGY, GENETICS

* **genetics** branch of biology that deals with heredity

* **embryology** branch of biology that deals with embryos, organisms at the early stages of development before birth or hatching, and their development

* **cytology** branch of biology that deals with the structure, function, and life history of cells

* **evolution** historical development of a biological group such as a species

* **chromosome** structure in the cell that contains the DNA (genes) that transmit unique genetic information

* **physiology** science that deals with the functions of living organisms and their parts

Thomas Hunt Morgan was one of the most important experimental zoologists of the twentieth century. His contributions to science ranged over a variety of fields, including genetics*, embryology*, cytology*, and the theories of evolution*. However, he is best known for his pioneering work in genetics with the fruit fly, *Drosophila melanogaster.*

Morgan's experiments with *Drosophila* established experimentally the chromosome* theory of heredity, for which he received the 1933 Nobel Prize in physiology* or medicine. He showed that genes are arranged in a linear fashion on chromosomes, and that they play a central role in transmitting inherited traits from parents to offspring.

Life and Career

Because Morgan never restricted himself to a single field of inquiry, his investigations in one field typically provided ideas and information that suggested new questions for other areas of research. He had strong views about many subjects, such as the mechanisms of heredity and evolution, but he was open-minded and was ready to change his mind when presented with convincing evidence that ran contrary to his own views. These traits of intellectual curiosity and flexibility were key ingredients in his success.

Life and Career. Morgan was born in Kentucky to parents whose families played important roles in American history. He was the great-grandson of Francis Scott Key, the composer of the "Star Spangled Banner." His uncle, John Hunt Morgan, served as an officer in the Confederate Army and was the leader of the famous guerrilla band known as Morgan's Raiders during the Civil War. His father served as American consul to Sicily in the 1860s and assisted the rebel leader Giuseppe Garibaldi in his attempt to unify Italy.

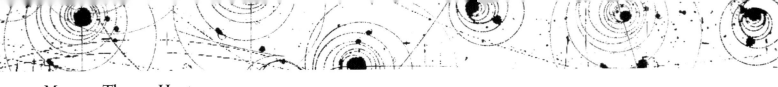

Morgan grew up in rural Kentucky but spent time in western Maryland when he visited his mother's family. In both places, he roamed the countryside collecting fossils and gaining an appreciation for natural history. During two summers, he worked for the United States Geological Survey in the mountains of Kentucky, an experience that reinforced his interest in natural history and the outdoors.

At age 16, Morgan entered the State College of Kentucky (now the University of Kentucky), studied zoology, and graduated in 1886 with honors. He spent the summer following graduation working at a marine biological station maintained by the Boston Society of Natural History. This marked his first experience working with sea life, an interest he maintained throughout his life.

Morgan pursued graduate study at Johns Hopkins University in Baltimore, Maryland, where he worked with William Keith Brooks. Brooks's ideas greatly influenced the course of Morgan's early career, although Morgan later turned away from Brooks's emphasis on morphology* in favor of more experimental fields of research. Following his studies at Johns Hopkins, Morgan accepted a position at Bryn Mawr College in Pennsylvania, where he remained for 13 years. In 1904 he accepted the position of chair of experimental zoology at Columbia University, a post offered to him by the well-known biologist Edmund B. WILSON. In 1928 Morgan resigned his position at Columbia to accept an offer to found the division of biological sciences at the California Institute of Technology. He served as an administrator and researcher there until his death in 1945.

*** morphology** branch of anatomy that deals with the form and structure of animals and plants

*** embryo** organism at the early stages of development before birth or hatching

Early Work and Changing Orientations.

Morgan's early work focused on morphology. Morphologists examined organisms and compared their anatomy, the development of their embryos*, their cellular structure and function, and their physiology to determine how they might be related. Morgan's mentor William Brooks was particularly interested in the study of marine organisms, which he believed represented the most ancient—and therefore the most fundamental—types of animals.

These considerations were the inspiration behind Morgan's early work, such as his doctoral dissertation on sea spiders (Pycnogonida). The purpose of his research was to determine whether Pycnogonida belonged to the Arachnida family (including spiders and scorpions) or to the Crustacea group (including crabs and lobsters). He studied large-scale anatomical changes and small cellular changes during the development of the embryo and determined that the development of sea spiders more closely resembled that of Arachnida than that of Crustacea.

Morgan subsequently investigated the embryology of other life-forms but grew increasingly dissatisfied with the morphological approach. On one hand, he believed that embryology and other disciplines should stand on their own and investigate their own problems rather than merely serve as a tool to explore evolutionary relationships. On the other hand, he felt that the methods used in morphology, such as the frequent use of comparisons to draw conclusions and the reliance on subjective descriptions, was speculative and unscientific. Consequently, he advocated an experimental approach to provide firm answers to specific scientific questions.

Democracy in the "Fly Room"

In his laboratory, known as the "fly room," Morgan promoted a very democratic atmosphere. Although he was older than most of his coworkers, he drew few distinctions between teacher and students. Ideas were shared freely, and rarely did anyone worry about who received credit for particular ideas. As one of his colleagues recalled, "As each new result or new idea came along, it was discussed freely by the group. The published accounts do not always indicate the source of ideas. It was often not only impossible to say but was felt to be unimportant, who first had an idea."

* **differentiation** process whereby cells, tissues, and structures are specialized to perform certain functions

Influences on Morgan's Outlook. Morgan's association with the physiologist H. Newell Martin and the biologist Jacques LOEB played a role in his rejection of morphology in favor of an experimental approach to biology. Martin, the chair of the biology department during Morgan's time as a graduate student at Johns Hopkins, supported the method and introduced experimental teaching laboratories at the university. Martin felt that physiology was the most important of the sciences, and that morphology was just one tool that could help unlock its secrets.

Loeb exposed Morgan to the mechanistic outlook on life, arguing that because all organisms operate according to the laws of physics and chemistry, one must approach the study of life from the viewpoint of physical chemistry. A proponent of experimental and quantitative methods of investigation, Loeb believed that only through such methods would biologists understand the physical and chemical processes underlying life.

The year that Morgan spent at the marine zoological station in Naples, Italy, further influenced his acceptance of the experimental approach. At the time, Naples was a meeting place for some of the most outstanding minds in the biological sciences, and the give-and-take of ideas stimulated Morgan to think and approach science in new ways.

Scientific Accomplishments

The focus of Morgan's earliest professional work was the effect of various influences on the development of embryos. These studies led him to question how sex is determined in developing organisms, which drew him into the controversy between supporters and opponents of an approach to heredity recently discovered by the Austrian geneticist Gregor Mendel. Scientists were divided on the question of whether internal factors (heredity) or external influences (environment) determined the differentiation* of embryonic cells. At first, Morgan was skeptical of Mendel's notion that genes were responsible for transmitting inherited traits from one generation to the next. However, Morgan's later work with *Drosophila* convinced him of the correctness of Mendel's ideas. This work also convinced him that genes are physical structures located on chromosomes and that they are the main mechanisms of heredity.

Experimental Embryology. Several years after joining the faculty at Bryn Mawr, Morgan began a series of experiments to study the effects of heredity and environment on the developing embryo. He did so by altering the environmental conditions under which the embryos developed. For example, in one experiment he injured the yolks of frog's eggs as well as the frog embryos and observed the course of their development afterward. In each of these experiments, he noted that, despite the environmental changes he introduced, the embryo still showed a tendency to develop along normal lines. These studies convinced him that environment might play some part in development, but that heredity was more important.

Morgan also expressed interest at this time in regenerating destroyed organs or tissues in various species of adult animals. The process of regeneration, he soon realized, was practically the reverse of embryonic development.

Morgan, Thomas Hunt

Thomas Hunt Morgan studied the laws and mechanisms of heredity. His work and influence helped transform biology from a descriptive, speculative discipline to a science based on quantification, measurement, and analysis.

* **cytoplasm** organic and inorganic substances outside the cell's nuclear membrane

In the embryo, generalized cells eventually differentiate into specialized tissues and organs that make up the adult organism. In regeneration, however, specialized cells regroup in the area of the injury, become generalized, and then redifferentiate into the type of cell needed to replace the lost tissue.

Morgan realized that the processes of embryonic development and regeneration both depended on the activation or deactivation of hereditary information within the cell. He knew that these processes were related in some way, but with the limited information at hand, he refused to speculate on the mechanism underlying them. Some scientists attempted to explain differentiation in the embryo by claiming that the cytoplasm* of the fertilized egg had a pre-existing organization that was expressed during development. However, Morgan argued that this did not offer an explanation for the underlying mechanism behind differentiation and that it merely pushed the process back one stage in the organism's life history. Morgan believed that to understand hereditary and developmental processes, one had to uncover the basic physical laws that governed those processes.

Sex Determination. A controversy between the rival promoters of heredity and environment as influences on development fueled Morgan's studies of sex determination. One school held that the sex of an organism is determined by environmental factors such as temperature or the amount

of food available to the embryo. The other claimed that sex is determined at or before fertilization of the egg and is controlled by factors inside the egg or sperm or both. Morgan published a review of the literature in this area that criticized both sides, claiming that neither had amassed enough evidence to support its claims. Both theories tried to explain the fact that males and females are found in generally even ratios among most species. But neither could account for other phenomena such as parthenogenesis—reproduction by the development of an unfertilized mature cell—or gynadromorphism, in which a single organism has some male characteristics and some female characteristics.

At first Morgan refused to accept arguments that were based purely on heredity because he believed that sex determination occurred during the course of embryonic development. At the same time, he found that the experiments of the environmentalists did not adequately support their arguments. By this time, a number of scientists were beginning to point to chromosomes and Mendelian factors as the determinants of sex. However, Morgan felt that the chromosomes were merely indicators of some unknown underlying processes that were the actual determinant of sex.

To explore this area, Morgan undertook studies on the movement and disposition of chromosomes during egg formation. He concentrated on those species in which parthenogenesis occurs naturally. His work proved that parthenogenic males were produced when a chromosome was lost during the development of eggs that have two full sets of chromosomes.

Earlier studies by other scientists suggested that sex could be determined by the disposition of the X chromosome. However, Morgan did not immediately relate sex determination to the X chromosome. He argued that sex was determined before the loss of the chromosome, which was simply an indication that the process had occurred. Other studies conducted at that time, however, changed Morgan's thinking about the role of chromosomes in sex determination. His colleague and close friend Edmund B. Wilson, as well as Nettie Stevens at Bryn Mawr, had compiled persuasive evidence that the X chromosome was responsible for sex determination. Although Morgan did not accept these views without reservation, the results and the rigorous experimental methods by which they were obtained impressed him.

Evolution and Heredity

Morgan was a supporter of Darwin's theory of evolution, but he questioned the idea that natural selection*, which Darwin considered essential, was the main mechanism of evolution. In 1903 Morgan published a book titled *Evolution and Adaptation,* in which he took issue with the theory of natural selection as contemporary followers of Darwin had interpreted it.

Morgan believed that natural selection operated mainly to remove unfavorable variations of organisms that had developed, but did not actually create new variations in an organism's germ plasm (cytoplasm of a reproductive cell). Darwin's followers felt that natural selection acts on only slight individual variations, which pass from one generation to another. However, contemporary evidence had suggested that such variations are

* **natural selection** theory that within a given species, individuals best adapted to the environment live longer and produce more offspring than other individuals, resulting in changes in the species over time

not heritable. Morgan believed that important evolutionary variations were large-scale because these were the only ones that seemed to be inherited. Moreover, he believed that the existing concepts of heredity did not adequately explain the mechanism behind variation and other developmental processes.

Sex Determination. Mendel's theory of factors could not explain the generally equal distribution of the sexes in most species. Nor could it account for the appearance of offspring that showed a blending of parental traits rather than the dominant or recessive traits possessed by one or the other parent. In addition, Mendel's theory outlined specific sets of categories into which any offspring should fall, but such categories rarely appeared in nature. Philosophically Morgan felt that neither Mendel's theory nor the related chromosome theory explained the basic processes of heredity, and both were based on too little experimental evidence.

One theory that captured Morgan's attention was the theory of mutation* proposed by the Dutch botanist Hugo de Vries, who was one of the scientists who had rediscovered Mendel's theories in 1900. He suggested that large-scale variations in one generation could produce offspring of a different species from their parents. Scientists later realized that the mutations that de Vries observed were not changes in genetic material but chromosome arrangements peculiar to that species. Although these arrangements did not produce new species in a single generation, de Vries's theory offered an explanation for the origin of large-scale variations that had evolutionary significance. His work was especially convincing for Morgan because it was based on controlled experimental studies that produced repeatable results.

Drosophila. Sometime in 1908 Morgan began breeding the fruit fly *Drosophila* to test de Vries's mutation theory in animals. He exposed *Drosophila* cultures* to radiation to create new mutations but never achieved the significant mutations that de Vries had obtained in his work with plants. However, about a year after he began this work, Morgan noticed that one male fly had white eyes rather the red eyes characteristic of the species. He bred the fly with its red-eyed sisters and produced offspring that all had red eyes. Breeding the brothers and sisters of this new generation produced some white-eyed flies, all of which were male.

Morgan continued to breed subsequent generations and noted that almost all the white-eyed offspring were males. He also observed that the trait of eye color behaved according to Mendel's laws, with the factor for red eyes being dominant over the factor for white eyes. The only explanation Morgan could find for this phenomenon was that eye color was determined by Mendelian factors, which were somehow associated with sex determination.

The work with fruit flies, along with additional studies by Wilson and others, convinced Morgan that chromosomes could be the carriers of Mendelian factors. He called the white-eyed condition sex-limited (later called sex-linked), which means that the genes determining eye color were carried on the X chromosome. In females, which have two X chromosomes,

* **mutation** relatively permanent change in the structure of a material

* **culture** microorganisms, such as bacteria or tissue, grown in a specially prepared nutrient substance for scientific study

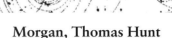

dominant genes on the second X chromosome mask or hide recessive genes on the other X chromosome that produce sex-linked traits (such as red eyes in *Drosophila*). Since males have only one X chromosome, recessive traits will almost always appear there. Morgan showed for the first time that one or more hereditary factors could be associated with a specific chromosome.

Friend or Foe?

Some scientists who worked with Morgan claimed that at times he was confused about fundamental issues involved in the research. Others thought he had a tendency to use the ideas of students without giving them full credit. But to most of his colleagues, Morgan was a clever, talented, and generous man. He often paid laboratory workers out of his own pocket, and he shared his Nobel Prize money with two longtime assistants to provide for the education of their children.

Experimental Proof. Morgan's findings on eye color were convincing, but they were inferred from his observations and had not yet been proven by experimental methods. The means of testing this idea was provided by the Belgian cytologist F.A. Janssens, who studied chiasma, the intertwining of chromosomes during cell division. He showed that chromosomes containing the same genes occasionally exchange parts during chiasma.

Morgan applied this information to the idea of genes as parts of chromosomes and concluded that strongly related genetic factors would be spaced closer together on the chromosome than factors that were more loosely related. The farther apart genes were on the chromosome, the more likely that a break would occur between them and disturb their linking relationship.

Many other major ideas came out of Morgan's work with fruit flies, including the concept of position effect, which suggests that that the expression of any gene is affected by its position on the chromosome and by the surrounding genes. Some scientists claimed that this concept was incompatible with Mendel's ideas and that it was an admission that the Mendelian and chromosome theories of heredity were incompatible. However, studies in the 1930s showed that position effect was merely an amendment of Mendel's ideas, not a contradiction of them.

Another important notion stemming from Morgan's *Drosophila* work was the balance concept of sex, according to which sex is determined by the ratio of X chromosomes to autosomes (non-sex chromosomes) in the nucleus of the cell. He found that genes for both male and female characteristics are found in both sexes and are located throughout the genome*, not just on the sex chromosomes. Thus, the expression of sex results from a complex relationship between sex chromosomes and autosomes, not simply from the presence or absence of certain genes.

* **genome** set of chromosomes that contains the genetic information of an organism

Work with *Drosophila* changed Morgan's ideas about Darwinian selection. Mendel's laws provided a mechanism for Darwin's theory of evolution, because they showed that variations were inherited in a definite pattern and were subject to the effects of selection. However, Morgan still could not fully relate heredity to developmental processes, such as cell differentiation and regeneration. The next generation of geneticists, many of whom were trained in Morgan's lab, later discovered the action of genetics at the level of the chromosome.

Later Work. Morgan's work eventually shifted away from *Drosophila* and toward efforts to summarize his genetic studies. He also returned to the problems of development and regeneration that had occupied his attention early in his career. In the mid-1920s, he began to spend his summers at the Marine Biological Laboratory at Woods Hole, Massachusetts, studying embryonic development. In 1928 he accepted an invitation to establish the

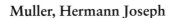

first division of biological sciences at the California Institute of Technology, where he continued his latest work in experimental embryology.

As he had done at Columbia, Morgan assembled a staff of skilled researchers at Cal Tech and based the department on the experimental approach to biology. The research staff at Cal Tech followed leads that Morgan provided during his work on *Drosophila,* particularly questions relating to gene functions. Those who worked under Morgan at Cal Tech were among the pioneers of the movement to molecular genetics that transformed the study of heredity in the 1950s and 1960s.

Morgan's Methodology and Legacy. Although trained in morphology, Morgan's experiences made him a confirmed believer in the experimental approach to science. He felt that speculation was harmful to the advancement of science. He did not object to the formation of hypotheses as long as they could be tested experimentally. However, Morgan did not accept conclusions simply because experiments had produced large amounts of similar kinds of evidence. He was more impressed when data from different types of research pointed to the same conclusions.

For example, his conversion to a belief in Mendelian principles arose from the combination of de Vries's data from plant breeding and the cytological work on chromosomes undertaken by Wilson and Stevens. Morgan urged his colleagues in biology to employ the same rigid standards of methodology that characterized the physical sciences: quantitative measurement, experimentation, and rigorous analysis. His insistence on this approach and his willingness to change his beliefs in the face of solid empirical evidence made a great impact on the field of biology. These qualities, along with his groundbreaking work on heredity and his important contributions to embryology, mark Morgan as one of the outstanding scientific figures of his time.

Morgan received many awards and honors during his career, and he belonged to several professional societies. He served as the president of the American Association for the Advancement of Science, the American Morphological Society, the American Society of Naturalists, the Society for Experimental Biology and Medicine, and the National Academy of Sciences. He was a member of the American Philosophical Society and the Genetics Society of America. In addition to the 1933 Nobel Prize, he received the Darwin Medal and the Copley Medal of the Royal Society of London.

Hermann Joseph
MULLER
1890–1967
GENETICS, EVOLUTION, EUGENICS

* **chromosome** structure in the cell that contains the DNA (genes) that transmit unique genetic information

Hermann Joseph Muller was an important figure in early research into the role of genes and chromosomes* as the basis of genetics*. His greatest discoveries involved his conviction that genes were responsible for producing all the physical components of the cell. His classic experiments on the effects of radiation in causing genetic mutations* won him the 1946 Nobel Prize in physiology* or medicine.

Early Life and Career. Muller was born in New York City to German immigrants. His father, who died when Muller was just nine years old, ran

* **genetics** branch of biology that deals with heredity

* **mutation** relatively permanent change in the structure of a material

* **physiology** science that deals with the functions of living organisms and their parts

* **evolution** historical development of a biological group such as a species

* **cytogenetics** study of heredity based on techniques used to examine the formation, structure, and function of cells

the family business of manufacturing bronze artworks. Even as a child Muller was interested in evolution* and the sciences, and he formed a science club in his high school. He received his undergraduate degree from Columbia University and attended Columbia and Cornell University medical schools in New York City. At Columbia he studied under Edmund B. WILSON, one of the pioneers of the chromosome theory of heredity, who influenced Muller's genetic view of biological problems. He also worked under the leading genetic researcher Thomas Hunt MORGAN.

After receiving his doctorate from Columbia, Muller accepted a post at the Rice Institute (now Rice University) in Houston, Texas, where he studied the relationship between genes and character traits. He realized the importance of individual genes while mapping the genes that control the expression of inherited traits. Muller studied mutations and decided that they were caused by variations in individual genes. Because genes are the only parts of a cell that can reproduce changes that occur in the cell, Muller concluded that genes are responsible for producing all the other components that make up a cell. He reasoned that life probably began with "naked genes," self-duplicating molecules that were similar to viruses.

Muller later transferred to the University of Texas, where he studied the frequency of gene mutations and determined which lethal mutations occur most commonly. He created genetic mutations in fruit flies *(Drosophila)* by exposing them to X rays. This study won him wide acclaim and became the basis for the study of radiation genetics. Muller continued his research at Berlin's Brain Research Institute in 1932, studying the structure of the gene.

The following year, when Adolf Hitler came to power, Muller accepted an offer to work with the well-known Russian geneticist Nikolay VAVILOV. For the next four years he studied radiation genetics, gene structure, and cytogenetics* in the Soviet Union. He engaged in a dispute about the work of a Soviet colleague, Trofim Lysenko, and left the Soviet Union when that nation's leader, Josef Stalin, backed Vavilov's rival's theories. In 1938 Muller was appointed to a position at the University of Edinburgh in Scotland, but when World War II started he moved to the United States. As a Jew, Muller felt it was safer to be farther away from Germany. He continued his genetic studies at Amherst College in Massachusetts, and in 1945 he was appointed to a permanent post as a professor of zoology at Indiana University. He remained there until his death in 1967.

Controversial Ideas. Receiving the Nobel Prize in 1946 brought Muller sufficient fame to publicize his efforts to stop the careless use of radiation by the medical, industrial, and military establishments. He also campaigned to reform the way biology was taught in American high schools. He believed the curriculum should have a strong evolutionary and genetic orientation. Muller was also a strong proponent of eugenics—the belief that human heredity can be improved by means of genetic control. If human beings could be perfected, Muller believed it was the responsibility of scientists to do so.

Muller tempered his eugenics advocacy when the Nazis came to power in Germany in the 1930s. Because the Nazis based their program on notions of the superiority of particular groups of people, Muller did not want to appear to support them. However, he returned to the idea of perfecting humans in the years after World War II. One outcome of his interest in eugenics was an idea that he called germinal choice, whereby he proposed that the semen of unusually gifted and healthy men be collected and used to breed genetically superior children. This plan provoked considerable public controversy, but it grew out of Muller's genuine scientific concern. He felt that modern technology was undercutting the survival of the fittest.

Muller earned honors as a member of many scientific societies around the world. He was a fellow of the Royal Society of England, served as the president of several genetics organizations, and was elected to the National Academy of Sciences in the United States.

Paul
MÜLLER
1899–1965
CHEMISTRY

* **physiology** science that deals with the functions of living organisms and their parts

The Swiss industrial chemist Paul Müller discovered that a chemical called DDT was an extremely effective insecticide. He won the 1948 Nobel Prize in physiology* or medicine for this work. DDT, which was first prepared in 1873, had a dramatic effect in eliminating diseases carried by insects and in increasing food supplies by killing pests that would have destroyed the crops. Müller secured the Swiss patents for the insecticide. Shortly after Müller's death, however, it became clear that DDT was building up in the soil and causing adverse reactions in the food chain, with the potential for poisoning animals and humans and causing a widespread environmental catastrophe.

Müller was born and raised in Switzerland. His father worked for the Swiss Federal Railroads, and this job took the family to the major Swiss city of Basel. Müller developed an early interest in chemistry, and as a youth he held jobs as a laboratory assistant in two industrial chemical firms. He studied chemistry at the University of Basel and received his Ph.D. in 1925. That same year, the dye firm J.R. Geigy A.G. hired Müller as a research chemist, and he spent his entire career there, rising to the position of deputy head of pest control research.

Müller's initial efforts at J.R. Geigy focused on plant pigments and natural agents for treating leather. These studies led him to ask biological questions, and he soon turned his attention to pesticides. In 1935 he drafted a list of the ideal qualities of an insecticide, noting that the chemical should be highly toxic (poisonous) to insects and that its action should be rapid and long lasting. It should have no odor, be available at a low price, and have little or no toxicity for plants and warm-blooded animals. But he did not consider whether the insecticide would decompose easily or remain stable for long periods.

After testing many chemicals on flies and other types of insects, he settled on dichlorodiphenyltrichloroethane, abbreviated as DDT. The chemical was manufactured from chlorine, ethanol, benzene, and sulfuric acid. These materials were all readily available from heavy industry; consequently, DDT was cheap and easy to produce. The new insecticide was introduced into the commercial market in 1942 and it quickly proved to be extremely effective. The armies of World War II used great quantities in tropical battle zones, hoping to protect their troops from malaria and other diseases carried by insects. In peacetime, the United States, the United Nations, and many national governments promoted heavy use of DDT to defend agricultural crops and kill the mosquitoes that caused malaria. In India alone, the death rate from malaria fell over a decade from 1 million per year to less than 5,000, and the average lifetime of Indians rose from 32 to 47 years. There seemed to be no harm to humans, and Müller was celebrated worldwide. In 1948 he was awarded the Nobel Prize in physiology or medicine for his work.

In the 1960s scientists began to notice that DDT remained in the soil for years. As plants and animals absorbed nutrients from the soil or consumed products from it, DDT moved up the food chain, building up in animals and humans to levels that some considered unsafe. Some bird populations decreased dramatically because they began to lay sterile or deformed eggs. The American ecologist Rachel CARSON's famous book *Silent Spring* did much to raise such concerns, leading the United States government to ban the use of DDT in 1972. However, U.S. companies continued to produce it, and other countries continued to use it widely for many years.

Müller retired from J.R. Geigy in 1961. He set up a private laboratory in his home and continued with his research for the remainder of his life. He died in 1965 in Basel.

Charles Jules Henri
NICOLLE

1866–1936

MEDICINE

* **typhus** bacterial disease transmitted by body lice that causes severe fever, headache, and delirium

Charles Jules Henri Nicolle discovered how body lice spread the deadly disease typhus*. He studied the role of bacteria and their carriers in creating medical epidemics, and he worked throughout his life to combat epidemics around the Mediterranean region.

Nicolle was an enthusiastic man with great faith in human abilities. However, he could be stubborn when he felt that his principles were at stake. Moreover, his relations with others were made difficult by his nearly total deafness from the age of 18. Nicolle dreaded social gatherings because he could not take part in the conversation, but he found solace and inspiration in poetry and literature. He wrote several novels and collections of stories.

Nicolle grew up in Rouen, France, where his father was a doctor at the city's hospital and a professor of natural history. His older brother Maurice became a noted scientist who studied bacteria and diseases. Although Nicolle thought he was better suited for literature than science, he followed the path of his father and brother and enrolled in medical school. In 1893 he earned his degree with a study of soft chancre, a sexually transmitted disease caused by the *Bacillus* bacteria.

Nicolle joined the staff of the hospital in Rouen and lectured at the city's medical school. He ran a laboratory for bacteriology, the study of bacteria, but he failed to achieve his goal of making Rouen a major center for medical research. He felt frustrated by the bureaucracy around him and grew impatient and discouraged. When he had the chance to direct the Pasteur Institute in the North African city of Tunis, he took it.

Nicolle faced a difficult task because the Paris-based Pasteur Institute in Tunis was an organization that existed only on paper. With great energy and devotion, Nicolle transformed a run-down laboratory into a well-respected facility. His new institute conducted extensive research, trained young doctors, and produced large quantities of vaccines for several diseases.

A few years after his arrival, an epidemic of typhus struck Tunis. Although the disease raged through the city, Nicolle found that it did not spread through the wards of the local hospital. He realized that the cause of the disease must be on the outside of the patients—on their hair, skin, and clothes—because they were bathed and their belongings cleaned when they entered the hospital. Nicolle conducted experiments to find the carrier of the disease and found that only lice could transmit the disease. His work inspired programs to delouse people and their belongings, bringing under control typhus and other diseases that were spread the same way. For his work, Nicolle won the Nobel Prize in physiology* or medicine in 1928.

For the remainder of his career, Nicolle studied other infectious diseases in the Mediterranean region and in Mexico. In further experiments with typhus, he found that a person would not get typhus if injected with blood serum* from a patient recovering from that disease. Nicolle applied this method, a form of vaccination, to other diseases and had great success in creating a vaccine against measles. He also described how, in some cases, a person could host bacteria or a virus without ever showing symptoms of disease. Nicolle's discovery of the carrier state was a boon to the emerging science of immunology* because it suggested how epidemics occur.

In his last years, especially after his nomination to the chair of experimental medicine at the Collège de France in 1932, Nicolle increasingly began to ponder scientific methodology, the evolution* of disease, and human destiny. He delivered lectures on the moral responsibility of science and offered the view that scientific inspiration was closely related to poetic and artistic inspiration. His lectures were published in several volumes and were widely read by the French scientific community. Nicolle believed that his own experience as a doctor and author proved his point.

* **physiology** science that deals with the functions of living organisms and their parts

* **serum** clear liquid that separates from the blood after the blood cells clot

* **immunology** science that deals with the immune system, which protects the body from foreign substances, cells, and tissue by causing an immune response

* **evolution** historical development of a biological group such as a species

Hideyo NOGUCHI

1876–1928

MICROBIOLOGY

* **microbiology** study of microscopic organisms

The Japanese physician Hideyo Noguchi is best known for identifying one bacterium in the brains of individuals suffering from paralysis and another that causes Oroya fever and verruga peruana, two different phases of a South American disease transmitted by sandflies. However, his tendency to jump to unfounded conclusions caused him to incorrectly identify another bacterium as the cause of yellow fever, a disease transmitted by mosquitoes. Although Noguchi's career was marked by key triumphs as well as setbacks, he gained fame in the field of microbiology*.

Born in Honshu, Japan, Noguchi was the son of peasants. He had a quick intelligence that allowed him to graduate from secondary school with honors. A childhood accident left him with a badly burned hand that was partially cured by a local surgeon for whom he worked filling prescriptions. He also worked as a janitor at a dental college, and during both of these jobs he found time to study medicine from borrowed books.

Hideyo Noguchi was an ingenious researcher with remarkable energy. Many believe that he lived and worked by fulfilling the youthful motto, "Success or suicide." He died of yellow fever while researching the disease in Africa.

---

* **antiserum** serum containing antibodies; used to treat, or give temporary protection against, certain diseases

After receiving a diploma to practice medicine at age 21, Noguchi entered S. Kitasato's Institute for Infectious Diseases. Two years later, when a medical commission from Johns Hopkins University visited the institute, Noguchi expressed an interest in studying in the United States. The head of the commission encouraged these wishes, and the following year Noguchi arrived at the University of Pennsylvania, unannounced and without any money. Fortunately, Noguchi received support from a local patron, enabling him to investigate snake venom. Three years later, he received a fellowship from the Carnegie Institution in Washington, D.C., to attend the Statens Seruminstitut in Copenhagen, Denmark, where he continued his studies. In 1904 Noguchi began an assistantship at the Rockefeller Institute in New York, which sponsored his work for the next 25 years. It was there that he discovered the bacterium *Spirochaeta pallida* in the brains of paralytics. He was also able to devise a valuable diagnostic skin test for syphilis.

When Noguchi was 39 he returned to Japan, where he received two high awards, the Order of the Rising Sun and the Imperial Prize. He also became familiar with *Spirochaeta icterohaemorrhagiae*, a bacterium that had been identified as the cause of Weil's disease, which is characterized by jaundice, circulatory collapse, and a tendency to bleed heavily. Noguchi studied the bacterium extensively, renaming it *Leptospira*. Three years later, he accompanied a Rockefeller Foundation team to Ecuador to study yellow fever. There he isolated an organism similar to *Leptospira* from several patients suffering from yellow fever. Noguchi ran a number of studies on both humans and guinea pigs afflicted by this organism, which he named *Leptospira icteroides*. Between 1919 and 1922, he published several articles in which he identified *Leptospira icteroides* as the cause of yellow fever. Based on his findings, the Rockefeller Institute prepared and distributed a vaccine and antiserum* for yellow fever. Although Noguchi's findings were controversial, they were not effectively challenged until 1924 at a conference on tropical medicine in Jamaica. Scientists had discovered that yellow fever was actually caused by a virus and not by *Leptospira* or any other bacteria.

While the debate about yellow fever was raging, Noguchi succeeded in solving the mystery behind the relationship between the diseases Oroya fever and verruga peruana. In a series of experiments, he isolated a bacterium known as *Bartonella bacilliformis* in a patient with Oroya fever and in patients suffering from verruga. In a series of experiments that he conducted on macaque monkeys, Noguchi proved that both diseases were caused by the same bacterium.

In 1927 Noguchi traveled to West Africa, where he independently confirmed the findings that yellow fever was caused by a virus. Around the same time, he contracted yellow fever and died shortly thereafter. Noguchi left a mixed legacy as a scientist who, despite his accomplishments, suffered from unbounded ambition and occasionally faulty procedures and conclusions. Although he often corrected and added to the discoveries of others, he often mistakenly applied bacteriologic techniques to viral diseases. Nevertheless, his contributions to microbiology earned him fame and recognition.

Christiane NÜSSLEIN-VOLHARD

born 1942

GENETICS

* **physiology** science that deals with the functions of living organisms and their parts

* **embryo** organism at the early stages of development before birth or hatching

* **biochemistry** science that deals with chemical compounds and processes occurring in living organisms

* **DNA** deoxyribonucleic acid, the material in chromosomes that carries genetic information from ancestor to offspring

The German scientist Christiane Nüsslein-Volhard specializes in genetics, the study of how genes shape organisms. She and fellow scientist Eric Wieschaus shared the 1995 Nobel Prize in physiology* or medicine for their work showing how specific genes control the early development of embryos*.

Turning to Biology. Nüsslein-Volhard was born in Magdeburg, Germany, into the artistic Volhard family. Her father was an architect, and her mother was a painter and musician. Two of her siblings became architects, and all of the children pursued interests in music and art. At an early age, Nüsslein-Volhard knew that she would follow a different path. "I remember that already as a child I was often intensely interested in things, obsessed by ideas and projects in many areas, and in these topics I learned much on my own, reading books," she wrote. "Early on I was interested in plants and animals, and I think I knew at the age of twelve at the latest that I wanted to be a biologist." Although her parents did not share her passion for science, they supported her decision by giving her "the right books," as she recalls.

By the time Nüsslein-Volhard graduated from high school, she was determined to study biology, with the goal of conducting scientific research. She had considered a career in medicine, but after a one-month nursing course in a hospital, she was certain that a medical career was not her destiny. She earned degrees in biology, chemistry, and physics from Johann Wolfgang Goethe University in Frankfurt and followed them with a degree in biochemistry* in 1968 and a doctoral degree in genetics in 1973, both from Eberhard Karls University in Tübingen.

During her years of study, Nüsslein-Volhard (who was married briefly and continued to use her husband's last name) gained experience in conducting laboratory experiments on DNA*. She developed techniques for purifying and isolating the molecular elements she wished to observe through a microscope. These laboratory skills contributed greatly to her later achievements.

Linking Genes to Development. After receiving her doctoral degree, Nüsslein-Volhard worked on projects at biological research institutes in Basel, Switzerland, and Freiburg, Germany, and later joined the European Molecular Biology Laboratory in Heidelberg, Germany. Together with Eric Wieschaus, she began an experimental project with an ambitious goal: to determine which genes controlled specific elements of the developing embryos of the fruit fly, *Drosophila*.

One stage of their work involved creating mutations (changes in the genetic code) in organisms, knowing that mutated organism would produce offspring that differed from the normal representatives of their species in some way. Nüsslein-Volhard and Wieschaus fed male fruit flies a substance that damages DNA. Female flies that mated with those males often produced mutated embryos. Nüsslein-Volhard and Wieschaus spent more than a year studying thousands of such embryos through a special dual microscope that allowed both of them to examine the specimen at the same time. Soon they discovered that particular types of damage to the embryos' structure could be linked to mutations of specific genes.

In 1980 the two researchers published the results of their work in *Nature,* a leading scientific journal. They had discovered that although the fruit fly has nearly 20,000 genes, only about one-fourth of these are important in early embryonic development, and fewer than 200 are essential. They also described how different categories of genes control the embryo's head-to-tail structure, its segmentation into different body parts, and the formation within each of its segments.

Nüsslein-Volhard and Wieschaus received the 1991 Albert Lasker Medical Research Award and the 1995 Nobel Prize for this work. They shared the latter with Edward Lewis of the United States, who had worked independently on fruit fly mutations. Nüsslein-Volhard became a director of the Max Planck Institute for Developmental Biology in Tübingen, Germany, in 1985. As head of the genetics division she continues to oversee investigations into the development of fruit fly embryos. Her new line of research is aimed at observing how the embryos of zebra fish develop from fertilized eggs into complete organisms.

Ivan Petrovich
PAVLOV

1849–1936

PHYSIOLOGY, PSYCHOLOGY

* **physiology** science that deals with the functions of living organisms and their parts

Awarded the Nobel Prize in physiology* or medicine in 1904, Ivan Petrovich Pavlov is probably best known for developing the concept of the conditioned reflex—the idea that humans and animals can be conditioned to respond in a certain way to an external stimulus, or signal. In a classic experiment, Pavlov rang a bell each time a research dog was fed. As the dog ate, saliva flowed in its mouth. By repeating this feeding routine many times, Pavlov trained the dog to salivate at the sound of the bell, even when no food was offered. Pavlov also emphasized the importance of conditioning in pioneering studies related to human behavior and the nervous system.

Life and Career

The son of a Russian Orthodox priest, Pavlov was born in Ryazan, Russia. At the age of 11, he began attending a religious school in Ryazan and later entered a local seminary and studied natural science. In 1870 he enrolled at St. Petersburg University, where he became interested in physiology and carried out experimental research on the influence of nerves on the circulation of the blood. Five years later, when he graduated from the university, he was awarded a gold medal for his student work on nerves.

Education and Early Work. To broaden his knowledge of physiology, Pavlov enrolled at the Military Medical Academy in St. Petersburg. His studies there were directed toward theoretical medicine. He conducted research on blood circulation and digestion and learned about current ideas on the influence of the nervous system on organisms. From 1884 to 1886 Pavlov conducted research on the physiology of invertebrates* at laboratories in Germany.

In 1890 Pavlov became a professor in the department of pharmacology* at the Military Medical Academy. At the same time, he was appointed director of the physiology section of the Institute of Experimental Medicine,

* **invertebrate** animal without a backbone
* **pharmacology** science dealing with the preparation, uses, and effects of drugs

Artist with a Knife

Ivan Pavlov was a highly skilled surgeon. He could put a catheter—a small hollow tube for draining fluids from the body—into a research animal almost painlessly and without any anesthetic. His careful and precise surgical methods enabled him to investigate the function of organs under relatively normal conditions. This was in great contrast to the traditional research technique of vivisection, which greatly disrupted the normal functioning of bodily organs.

* **vivisection** practice of dissecting or cutting into the body of a living animal for the purpose of scientific investigation

where he conducted research on the physiology of digestion and initiated new surgical procedures for working with research animals. These new techniques enabled scientists to observe organs functioning under normal conditions. Before this advance, scientists had to rely solely on analysis because their research disrupted the normal interrelation between the organ and its environment.

From 1895 to the end of his life, Pavlov concentrated his activities at three institutes: the Institute of Physiology of the Academy of Sciences, the Institute of Experimental Medicine, and the biological station at Koltushy (present-day Pavlovo), near St. Petersburg. As Pavlov's scientific work progressed he received increasing worldwide attention. His fame reached its peak in 1904, when he received the Nobel Prize in physiology or medicine for his research on digestion. He was elected to the prestigious Russian Academy of Sciences and received the Order of the Legion of Honor from the French government. Pavlov remained active until his death, presiding over the Fifteenth International Physiological Congress in 1935, which was held in Russia at the cities of Leningrad (present-day St. Petersburg) and Moscow. He died the following year.

Scientific Accomplishments

Pavlov insisted on following specific scientific approaches in conducting experiments with animals. He believed that it was necessary to study the whole organism under conditions of normal activity. For Pavlov, the living organism was a complex system whose study demanded the use of methods that included both analysis—the separating of an organism into its various parts—and synthesis—the combining of the various parts of an organism. He considered the main problems of experimental research in physiology to be the study of interactions within an organism and the relation of the organism to its environment.

Scientific Method. During the 1800s a widely used method of physiological research was vivisection*. Vast amounts of data had been collected over the years using this method. Increasingly, however, it became apparent that new data could only be acquired by studying the entire organism in its natural conditions. Pavlov understood the limitations of vivisection and devised a new approach—the long-term experiment. He conceived the method as both a technique of experimental research and a new way of thinking. This novel method of research ushered in a new era in the physiology of digestion. For Pavlov the goal of the new research was to determine precisely the nature of various physiological phenomena in a whole and normal organism.

Pavlov's research focused on two elements: the organism as a system, and any of its separate organs that fulfilled a definite function. He was not concerned with the basic principles and foundations of life, which he believed were the responsibility of researchers in other branches of science. Pavlov distinguished four levels, or degrees, of experimental physiological research—organismic, organic, cellular, and molecular—all of which reflect the properties of a living organism.

Scientific Research. Pavlov devoted his research to three main areas of physiology: the circulation of blood; digestion; and the brain and higher nervous activity. His earliest research on blood circulation focused on the mechanisms of the body that regulate blood pressure. He described the role of the nervous system in the activity of the blood vessels, specifying the role of the vagus nerve* as a regulator of blood pressure. He showed that the four nerves that respectively inhibit, accelerate, weaken, and intensify the action of the heart also govern the function of the heart.

Pavlov studied the physiology of digestion primarily between 1879 and 1897. His research in this area required that he devise new techniques, marking a turning point in his work. Pavlov's method for studying the action of the digestive organs involved surgery, which enabled him to observe the normal activity of a particular digestive gland in a healthy animal. Pavlov was a skilled surgeon, which he believed was a necessity for anyone engaged in physiological research.

Pavlov's experiments on digestion proceeded from contemporary ideas about the digestive process and its regulation by the nerves and other bodily fluids. He showed that there is a close connection between the

* **vagus nerve** either of a pair of nerves that arise in the brain and supply the organs with nerve fibers

Ivan Pavlov developed the surgical method of experimentation using normal, healthy animals, which enabled him to continuously observe the functions of their organs under relatively normal conditions. Until that time, scientists used vivisection and determined the function of an organ through a process of analysis. With his method of research, Pavlov opened the way for new advances in theoretical and practical medicine.

OBSERVATION—AND AGAIN OBSERVATION

Pavlov, Ivan Petrovich

* **enzyme** any of numerous complex proteins that are produced by living cells and catalyze specific biochemical reactions at body temperature

* **psychic** of or relating to the psyche (mind or soul); phenomenon outside the realm of physical science or knowledge

The Scientist and the State

Pavlov lived through a time of upheaval as Russia endured a civil war, transformed itself into the Soviet Union, and became a Marxist nation. He never joined the new Communist regime and once said, "For the kind of social experiment that you are making, I would not sacrifice a frog's hind legs." When Vladimir Lenin, the first leader of the Soviet Union, refused Pavlov's request to relocate his laboratory abroad, Pavlov openly criticized the government. Later he wrote to Lenin's successor, Joseph Stalin, "I am ashamed to be called a Russian." Despite his criticism, the Soviets valued Pavlov's work and his reputation and awarded him several honors.

properties of saliva produced in the mouth and the kind of food consumed. Pavlov clarified and explained the role of enzymes* in digestion and discovered enterokinase—also known as the "enzyme of enzymes"—in the intestinal tract. His theories had broad significance in the area of biology as well as great value in further research studies on the stomach and intestines.

Physiology of Behavior. Following his work on digestion, Pavlov turned his attention to behavior, the most famous area of his research. By the early 1900s many scientists had begun experiments to study the function of the brain.

Pavlov investigated the activity of two parts of the brain—the cortex and the cerebral hemispheres—and based his work on fundamental facts and concepts of the physiology of the nervous system. He approached this research through the study of the salivary glands, which had attracted his attention because of their modest role in an organism and because their activity could be measured quite easily. The most famous of his experiments with the salivary glands were conducted on dogs.

In his experiments with digestion, Pavlov had already encountered the phenomenon of psychic* salivation—the idea that animals would salivate when they anticipated a morsel of food. He studied this phenomenon in an objective manner. He saw the psychic stimulation of the salivary glands as a phenomenon that resembled the normal digestive reflex.

Pavlov reasoned that both digestion and salivation were reflex actions and that only the external agents that triggered these reflexes were different. The digestive reflex was triggered by the basic mechanical and chemical properties of the food, while salivary action was triggered by nonphysiological signals, such as the form and odor of the food. Using the concept of the reflex as an elementary response of an organism to external stimulus, Pavlov called the normal digestive reaction an unconditioned reflex and the activity of the salivary glands a conditioned reflex.

Pavlov described the formation of the conditioned reflex, showing it to be based on the fundamental, inborn activity of the organism. He showed that any environmental factor could enter into a temporary relation with the natural activity of the organism through combination with the unconditional reflex. He noted that conditioned reflexes are developed throughout the life of an organism, so they are subject to change depending on the environment. He also noted that conditioned reflexes could be provoked by stimuli that act as signals. Pavlov saw in the conditioned reflex a mechanism by which an organism adapts to its environment. He also believed that this reflex existed throughout the entire animal kingdom.

Through his experiments, Pavlov located conditioned reflex activity in the cerebral hemispheres of the brain, and he demonstrated that the center for such activity is in the part of the brain known as the cortex. Pavlov also showed that the formation of conditioned reflexes is linked to changes in the functional state of nerve centers. From this, he concluded that the cells of the higher sections of the central nervous system must undergo subtle but definite structural and chemical changes.

134

Later Career

Accompanying Pavlov's experimental work was his belief that neuroses* occur when an organism is subjected to contradictory stimuli. Pavlov believed such neuroses were the result of disturbances to the balance of certain brain activities. Extending his work, other researchers showed that disturbance of brain activity passes through four stages. The inhibiting stage is characterized by the absence of all reflexes. The paradoxical stage occurs when strong stimuli produce little or no effect, while weak stimuli produce greater effects. In the equalizing stage all stimuli, regardless of their intensity, produce the same effect. In the final stage, called intermediate to the norm, stimuli of average intensity produce the greatest effect, and strong or weak stimuli cause little or no effect.

Other Work. In addition to studying animal behavior, Pavlov and his colleagues tried to provide a scientific basis for the ancient Greek idea of human temperaments. They established the existence of four basic types of behavior, which they classified according to the strength, mobility, and constancy of basic nerve processes.

Beginning in the 1930s, Pavlov took up the genetic* study of behavior, and he set up a biological research station. He identified two signal systems that characterize conditioned-reflex activity. The primary system is found in both animals and humans, while the second system is unique to humans. This second system makes possible such unique human activities as abstract thought and speech. According to Pavlov the brain brings together a vast range of conditioned reflexes to shape behavior based on the specific circumstances and needs of the organism.

Through much of his career, Pavlov served as a distinguished scientific administrator. He created a large research school that employed up to 300 physiologists and physicians. He also organized several major research centers in Russia, including the physiological section of the Institute of Experimental Medicine and the Institute of Physiology of the Soviet Academy of Sciences, which now bears his name.

* **neurosis** mental disorder with no obvious organic cause that involves anxiety, phobia, or other abnormal behavior; *pl.* neuroses

* **genetic** relating to genes, the basic units of heredity that carry traits from ancestors to offspring

Stanley Ben
PRUSINER

born 1942

BIOLOGY

* **physiology** science that deals with the functions of living organisms and their parts

Stanley Ben Prusiner's search for the cause of fatal brain diseases led to the discovery of an entirely new category of disease-causing proteins that he called prions. For his work in identifying prions and in proving that they, not viruses, cause certain serious illnesses, Prusiner received the 1997 Nobel Prize in physiology* or medicine.

Investigating Brain Diseases. Prusiner was born in Des Moines, Iowa, but he spent much of his childhood in Cincinnati, Ohio. He found little that interested him in high school, but he discovered a world of intellectual stimulation at the University of Pennsylvania in Philadelphia, where he attended medical school. During this time he spent a year working in a research laboratory in Sweden. He graduated with a medical degree in 1968 and moved to San Francisco for postdoctoral study and research at the

Prusiner, Stanley Ben

Stanley Prusiner discovered prions, a new class of proteins unlike any other known to biologists. His research into how prions affect the brains of animals and people could lead to new knowledge about such devastating neurodegenerative illnesses as Alzheimer's, Parkinson's, and Lou Gehrig's diseases.

---

* **DNA** deoxyribonucleic acid, the material in chromosomes that carries genetic information from ancestor to offspring

* **pathogen** agent that causes disease, such as a bacterium or virus

* **mutation** relatively permanent change in the structure of a material

* **genetic** relating to genes, the basic units of heredity that carry traits from ancestors to offspring

University of California. His work there was supported by the National Institutes of Health, an agency that is a part of the United States Public Health Service.

It was at this time that Prusiner considered becoming a biomedical researcher rather than a practicing physician. His thoughts turned even more strongly in that direction after he treated a patient who was dying of Creutzfeldt-Jakob disease (CJD), which causes loss of memory. At the time, scientists believed that the disease and certain similar ailments were caused by a type of virus called a slow virus. Prusiner became fascinated by this group of diseases, which are called spongiform encephalopathies and which cause loss of mental function and death in both animals and humans. He decided to search for their cause.

Mysteries of the Prion. Prusiner began by studying scrapie, a disease that kills nerve cells in the brains of sheep. With the help of fellow scientists, he examined samples of infected brains and isolated the agent that appeared to cause scrapie.

To Prusiner's surprise, the disease-causing agent was not a virus but a protein. In addition, it appeared to lack nucleic acid, the main substance in DNA*. All life-forms that reproduce themselves, including viruses and bacteria, contain DNA. Prusiner's newly discovered pathogen*, however, did not.

In 1982 Prusiner announced the results of his research, coining the term *prion* for the disease-causing proteins that he had identified. A large part of the scientific and medical community initially greeted his news with skepticism and criticism. In Prusiner's own words, his article about prions "set off a firestorm." Scientists who studied viruses searched energetically for nucleic acid in the agent, hoping to prove that Prusiner's so-called prions were really viruses after all. Others felt that suggesting the existence of an entirely new class of agents was simply too extreme. No one could understand how Prusiner's prions could reproduce themselves without DNA. To some critics the discovery of prions seemed to threaten the foundations of modern biology.

Eventually, biological scientists admitted the existence of prions. The controversy surrounding Prusiner's work died down as his team and other researchers around the world learned more about prions and their properties. Prusiner's group made an important contribution to this ongoing research in 1986 by discovering that prions develop from a normal protein found in all animals and humans. They discovered that a gene named PrP governs this protein. When the PrP gene undergoes a mutation*, the protein changes and can become a prion. Prusiner and his colleagues also proved the existence of a link between prions and spongiform encephalitis diseases by developing a strain of genetically* altered mice with PrP genes that were mutated in the same way as those in human victims. The brains of these mice degenerated much like the brains of people suffering from prion diseases. Prusiner further established that the structure of the disease-causing PrP is flat, while that of the normal PrP is corkscrew-shaped. The shape of a protein is very important because it determines the protein's activity.

More recently, scientists have come to believe that prions cause the rare human disease kuru and the cattle ailment called mad cow disease as well as scrapie and CJD. Based on his study of prions, Prusiner maintains that prion diseases can arise spontaneously in people with mutated PrP, can be caught through infection, and can be inherited from parents. The idea that a disease can be both infectious and hereditary is a revolutionary new insight in medicine and has paved the way for important new research into the biology of disorders of the central nervous system.

In addition to the Nobel Prize, Prusiner has received numerous awards from scientific organizations and research foundations around the world. These honors include the Albert Lasker Basic Medical Research Award and the Potamkin Prize for Alzheimer's Disease Research. He is a professor of neurology*, biochemistry*, and biophysics* at the University of California, San Francisco.

* **neurology** study of the structure, function, and disorders of the nervous system

* **biochemistry** science that deals with chemical compounds and processes occurring in living organisms

* **biophysics** study of the structures and processes of organisms using the methods of physics

Santiago
RAMÓN Y CAJAL
1852–1934
NEUROANATOMY, NEUROHISTOLOGY

* **histology** branch of anatomy that deals with the minute structure of animal and plant tissues, observable only through a microscope

* **physiology** science that deals with the functions of living organisms and their parts

* **cytologist** specialist in the branch of biology that deals with the structure, function, and life history of cells

* **microscopy** skilled scientific use of a microscope

* **pathological** of or relating to pathology, the study of diseases and their effects on organisms

The Spanish medical researcher Santiago Ramón y Cajal spent his career investigating the anatomy and histology* of the nervous system. In 1906 he shared the Nobel Prize in physiology* or medicine with the Italian cytologist* Camillo Golgi for their discovery that neurons, or nerve cells, are the basic, individual units of the nervous system.

Background and Education. Ramón y Cajal was born in a poverty-stricken village in the Spanish province of Navarre. His father, a barber, earned a medical degree through hard work and sacrifice. As a student Ramón y Cajal showed an interest in art, but this displeased his father, who insisted that the boy study medicine. Ramón y Cajal became rebellious, showing contempt for his teachers and for education.

Notwithstanding his resistance, Ramón y Cajal gained enough formal education to enter the University of Zaragoza, where he studied medicine. After graduating in 1873, he joined the army medical service, and the following year he went to Cuba. Within a year, however, he became ill with malaria. Discharged from the service, he returned to Spain, where he began to pursue an academic career in anatomy, the only part of his medical education in which he was interested. This enabled him to conduct research as well as teach. In 1875 he returned to the University of Zaragoza for two more years of study toward his doctoral degree. He also mastered microscopy* and histology and became a skilled amateur photographer.

Exploring the Nervous System. In 1878 Ramón y Cajal became a professor of anatomy at the university in Valencia, and nine years later he took a position as a histologist in Barcelona. Five years after that, he became professor of histology and pathological* anatomy at the University of Madrid, where he remained until his retirement in 1922.

Ramón y Cajal's most productive period was from 1886 to 1906, when he laid the histological foundations for modern knowledge of the nervous system. He studied the details of the nervous system partly because he had systematically learned the entire field of histology by himself.

A Scientist's Self-Portrait

Santiago Ramón y Cajal's writings paint a picture of a proud and dedicated scientist more interested in research than in people. He was almost obsessively devoted to neurohistology. During the early years of his family life, his wife and children endured hardship while he spent money on his laboratory and publications. He expressed pride in Spain's culture, but he felt ashamed of his country's scientific backwardness. He resented foreigners' ignorance of the Spanish language, and he thought that scientists from other countries had read only a small portion of his work.

* **vertebrate** animal with a backbone

He was also fascinated by the fine structure of the nervous system. To him it represented the physical basis of thought. He believed that greater knowledge of the structure of the nervous system would lead to a better understanding of human physiology as well as psychology.

At the time scientists had no clear notion of how nerve impulses travel from the brain to the muscles because histological techniques could not reveal how nerve cells were connected in the gray matter of the central nervous system. Ramón y Cajal adopted a tissue-staining technique developed by Camillo Golgi in 1873. This enabled him to see very fine structural details of the nervous system through his microscope.

Most scientists at this time believed that nerve cells throughout the body were physically joined together in a large network. Ramón y Cajal discovered that nerve cells are single units that never form a direct network with the ends of other cells, however close they might be. He proved that the nervous system was composed of a set of individual units, or neurons, and not a true network. Ramón y Cajal's neuron theory replaced the network theory as the model of how the nervous system is organized. Based on his discovery, other researchers later discovered how nerve impulses or signals travel across the synapses (gaps) between neurons.

Ramón y Cajal made an extensive study of nerve cells in the human brain. He described and classified different types of neurons and showed where nerve fibers from the sense organs enter the brain. These studies helped establish the basis for understanding how different physiological functions are located in specific parts of the brain.

In 1904 Ramón y Cajal published *Textura del sistema nervioso del hombre y de los vertebrados* (Textbook on the nervous system of man and the vertebrates*). In this three-volume study, he brought together the results of 15 years of research. It contains the histological and cytological basis of modern neurology, the science of the nervous system. In it, Ramón y Cajal presents structural detail as a starting point rather than as an end in itself. He was not satisfied with merely determining the physical structure of the nervous system. He constantly asked: How does this system work? How has it evolved to its present form? What do these patterns mean?

In later work Ramón y Cajal studied the restoration of function in damaged nervous system structures, such as cut fibers. His research confirmed the widely held theory that severed nerve fibers could sprout new ends. Around 1913 he published the results of these studies in what is still considered the most complete account of the subject.

Career Highlights. Ramón y Cajal received many prizes and honors, both Spanish and foreign. In 1894 the Royal Society, Great Britain's noted organization of scientists and scholars, invited him to deliver a lecture. Five years later he was a special lecturer at Clark University in Worcester, Massachusetts. In 1906 Ramón y Cajal and his colleague Golgi shared the Nobel Prize in physiology or medicine, and three years later the Royal Society elected Ramón y Cajal to its membership.

Living in Spain and writing mainly in Spanish, Ramón y Cajal felt isolated from the mainstream of science. World War I, which disrupted life across Europe, increased his sense of seclusion. Still, he continued to work and publish papers. Some of his work from this period laid the foundation for later studies of tumors of the brain and central nervous system by other scientists.

Intensely patriotic, Ramón y Cajal wanted Spain to have a place in the scientific and intellectual world. He took a step toward that goal by founding a Spanish school of histology, the Cajal Institute in Madrid, in 1920 with support from King Alfonso XIII. Ramón y Cajal worked and taught there until his death. A number of his pupils made significant scientific contributions of their own.

Charles Robert
RICHET

1850–1935
PHYSIOLOGY, PSYCHOLOGY

Charles Richet had many interests in addition to physiological research and writing. He was attracted to aviation, building one of the first planes to leave the ground under its own power. He was also interested in spiritualistic phenomena and was a dedicated pacifist.

* **physiology** science that deals with the functions of living organisms and their parts

* **psychic** of or relating to the psyche (mind or soul); phenomenon outside the realm of physical science or knowledge

Charles Robert Richet made significant contributions to understanding several biological phenomena including digestion, muscle contraction, and the production and regulation of heat in animals. However, his most original scientific accomplishments involved describing and explaining the body's reactions to toxins (poisons). In 1913 the scientific community recognized his work in this field by awarding him the Nobel Prize in physiology* or medicine. Richet's work led to a better understanding of resistance and immunity and established a new field of physiological research.

Life and Career

Richet's father, a highly respected surgeon, hoped that Charles might follow in his footsteps. In secondary school, Richet studied both literature and science, eventually choosing to enter medical school. Although he found classes in anatomy and surgery boring, he continued with his studies. He wrote poetry and drama for pleasure. At age 23 Richet became an intern and was placed in charge of a ward of female patients at a local hospital. There he witnessed a hypnotic experiment that stimulated his interest in psychic* phenomena. He began placing patients in hypnotic trances. Two years later he published a report of his results in which he observed that hypnotic trances progressed in a series of predictable stages, just like the course of a disease. He also noted that the more often a person was hypnotized, the more distinct the stages became. Because of his work with hypnotism, Richet became fascinated with the relationship between psychic and physiological phenomena. His later research often drew on the lessons he learned from these early experiences.

Although Germany had recently replaced Richet's native France as the center of physiological research, Richet still studied and worked with an impressive group of scientists. These included the noted surgeon Aristide Verneuil and Jules Marey, who had developed the most accurate devices for recording physiological phenomena. Verneuil encouraged Richet to begin his first investigations into muscle contraction and digestion.

At age 28 Richet graduated from medical school and began to work in the physiological laboratory of the College of France's medical school. For the next several years, he studied the phenomenon of muscle contraction before turning his attention to the problem of traumatic pain. Several years later he became interested in experiments performed by the great

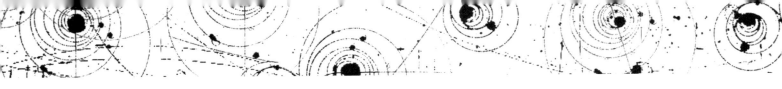

French scientist Louis Pasteur. Pasteur had discovered a way to protect chickens against a fatal form of cholera by injecting them with a weakened form of the disease. This stimulated Richet's greatest work, which resulted in breakthroughs in the understanding of the processes underlying resistance and immunity in animals.

Scientific Accomplishments

For the first 25 years of his professional career, Richet's investigations focused on conventional subjects in physiology. His research helped answer several outstanding questions in the field.

Digestion. While Richet was still enrolled in medical school, Verneuil convinced him to investigate gastric* digestion. Scientists did not completely understand the process of digestion at that time. One of the most important questions that remained unanswered concerned the composition of gastric juice. Some scientists thought it consisted of hydrochloric acid, some believed it was mainly lactic acid, and still others thought it contained some other type of acid. Researchers had collected gastric juice during the course of their experiments, but they discovered that it contained many types of acids, making it difficult to tell which acid was responsible for digestion. Using a process developed by scientists many years earlier, Richet mixed gastric juice with water and measured the amount of acid that dissolved in the solution. He then mixed the acid-water solution in ether (a flammable liquid used as a solvent) and measured the amount of acid that dissolved. He noted that more acid dissolved in the water than in the ether, suggesting that the main acid in gastric juice was a mineral acid and that it almost certainly consisted of hydrochloric acid.

Later, Richet confirmed his findings when working with fish, because the composition of their gastric juice was easier to study than the gastric juice of mammals. The juice contained more chloride than the salts extracted from the juice, supporting his argument that hydrochloric acid is the main acid involved in digestion. When he mixed sodium acetate with the juice, it produced acetic acid, just as he had predicted, although it was a smaller quantity than he had expected. Richet concluded that the hydrochloric acid in gastric juice also contained an organic substance. His report on the findings included a full review of the digestive process in mammals, fish, and invertebrates*. He also observed that the secretion of gastric juice is a nervous reflex that is unrelated to the presence of food in the stomach. He based this finding on his studies of a patient who had undergone an operation in which a hole between the stomach and abdomen was opened. The patient produced gastric juice when he chewed highly flavored foods, even though the food could not have entered his stomach.

Muscle Contraction. Many scientists had studied muscle contractions before Richet took up the subject in his late 30s. Using his recording equipment, Marey had measured and described the various phases of muscle contraction. He had also shown that a muscle that receives electrical stimulation experiences contractions, which are composed of a series of

* **gastric** of or relating to the stomach

* **invertebrate** animal without a backbone

small shocks. Repeating the stimulation at brief intervals produces shocks that fuse together to produce a prolonged contraction. Marey called this phenomenon, in which several small contractions combine after a short time to produce a prolonged contraction, latent summation.

Richet repeated these studies using the tail and claw of a crayfish. The tail produced brief, strong contractions but did not produce prolonged contractions unless the stimuli were repeated very frequently. The contractions of the claw, however, lasted much longer, and the claw muscle went into prolonged contractions much more easily than did the tail muscle. Examining the claw more closely, Richet found that the time between contractions (called the latent period) increased if the muscle was tired. However, if he stimulated the muscle while it was still contracted, he found that the second latent period was shorter than the first. This reminded him of his work with hypnosis, in which prior exposure to a stimulus affected the response of patients exposed to the same stimulus at a later time.

Animal Heat. Richet next turned to the study of animal heat. One of the key questions at the time was how warm-blooded animals maintain a constant body temperature. Was temperature regulation related to the loss of heat from the surface of the body? Was it regulated by some internal mechanism? Earlier studies had shown that when animals sustained particular types of injury to the central nervous system, the result was an increase in their internal temperature. Richet invented a special calorimeter (a device to precisely measure heat production) and used it to show that rabbits that suffered injuries to the cerebral cortex* always produced more heat. This experiment convinced him that internal production of heat was more important than the loss of heat at the body's surface in regulating temperature. Working with his calorimeter, Richet found that the amount of heat an animal produces is indirectly proportional to its size. The larger the animal, the less heat it produces per unit of weight. He showed that heat production is a function of the surface area of the animal's body.

In later work, Richet studied the differences in heat output between large and small animals. He knew that small animals are much more active and produce more heat per unit of weight than large animals, and he set out to discover the reason. In a series of experiments using his calorimeter, he found that anesthetized dogs did not produce heat in proportion to their surface area. This confirmed his suspicion that the central nervous system controls the amount of heat produced by an animal. Nevertheless, he believed that the difference in heat production among animals of different sizes was related to the activity of muscle tissue. That explained why large dogs tend to be slow, while smaller dogs are more active and shiver frequently. Richet showed that the internal temperature of an anesthetized dog decreases until it begins to shiver, at which point its temperature rises and returns closer to normal. He demonstrated that muscle activity is responsible for differences in heat output between animals of different sizes, and that shivering is a mechanism used to compensate for coldness.

Immunity and Resistance. Pasteur's experiments with cholera impressed Richet, who reasoned that cholera microbes* might produce a

* **cerebral cortex** outer layer of the gray tissue of the brain that is responsible for higher nervous functions

* **microbe** microscopic organism

* **inoculate** to introduce a disease agent into an animal or plant to produce a mild form of the disease and render the organism immune

* **culture** to grow microorganisms, such as bacteria or tissue, in a specially prepared nutrient substance for scientific study

* **abscess** localized collection of pus in the body surrounded by an inflamed area

* **toxicity** degree of being toxic or poisonous

* **extract** solution that contains the essential components of a more complex material

Cool Pants for Dogs

When Richet studied animal heat, he discovered that that when dogs pant (breathe rapidly), it acts as a cooling device. Because a dog's body is covered with fur, it is unable to sweat like humans to cool itself. However, when it pants, moisture evaporates from its tongue, cooling its body just as sweating does for humans. Richet also showed that this process had little to do with normal respiration and that it only occurs when the dog's blood contains enough oxygen that it does not need to breathe normally.

toxin that causes the disease. When chickens were inoculated* with the weakened microbes they became immune to cholera, suggesting that those animals produced a chemical substance that worked against the cholera toxin. Many years later, Richet discovered a new type of bacteria in the tumor of a dog. He cultured* the bacteria and injected it into dogs and rabbits. The rabbits died, but the dogs only developed a large abscess* that contained the bacterium. This was the same result that Pasteur had obtained for the pure cholera microbe—it killed chickens but created an abscess in guinea pigs. Richet grew a weakened form of the bacterium and inoculated rabbits with this strain; they became immune to the pure form.

To test his theory that the blood of resistant animals contains some substance that fights outside toxins, Richet injected rabbits with blood from dogs inoculated with the weakened bacteria. The rabbit died if the blood was introduced directly into a vein, but when the blood was injected into the abdominal cavity, the rabbit gradually absorbed the toxins and developed immunity to the bacteria. Richet called his procedure hemotherapy and sought to apply it in the treatment of tuberculosis. He first inoculated dogs with a form of avian (bird) tuberculosis to which they were resistant. This made the dogs immune to human tuberculosis, to which they were normally sensitive. When he transferred blood from the dogs into tubercular humans he was able to slow, and in some cases stop, the disease. However, he failed to develop an effective vaccine.

Richet later built on these findings in his study of the effects of poisons. On a scientific expedition, the prince of Monaco encouraged Richet to study the toxicity* of the tentacles of the Portuguese man-of-war (a large tropical sea creature). He isolated an extract* from the tentacles and found that it closely resembled the toxin of sea anemones. He injected dogs with varying amounts of the man-of-war toxin to determine the lethal dose. A short time later, he reinjected those animals that survived the first injections. He thought that the animals would have developed immunity because of the previous injection. However, Richet noted that the animals that had survived a large first dose of toxins suffered a fatal reaction to smaller doses. The immune systems of these animals, he reasoned, had become overly sensitive to further exposure to the toxin. He called this reaction anaphylactic, meaning "contrary to protection," because it was the opposite of immunization. Over the next several years, he found that other poisons produced the same reaction in different animals. Richet determined that a poison combines with some nontoxic substance in an animal to produce a toxic substance that makes the animal sick. Poisons, therefore, act just like microbial infections. Alternatively, as Richet put it, a disease is a form of slow intoxication. Disease microbes cause toxic substances to develop in the body, which in turn causes sickness.

Although the phenomenon of anaphylaxis was puzzling, Richet felt that it was a form of positive adaptation. He reasoned that if substances from one species were able to enter the blood and tissues of another species and remain there, the chemical identity of the second species would be threatened. He reasoned that anaphylaxis worked to preserve the chemical identity of each species. Richet's work uncovered the field of anaphylaxis, for which he was awarded the Nobel Prize in physiology or medicine in 1913.

When Richet served in World War I, he studied the problems concerning blood transfusions. His war experience was an unpleasant one for Richet, who was a committed pacifist. He wrote many history books that pointed out the destructive effects of war. After the war Richet resumed his medical research. He continued to write novels, poetry, and drama, and helped to design and build one of the first airplanes to achieve flight under its own power. Later in life he received the Cross of the Legion of Honor, one of France's highest honors. Richet died in Paris in 1935 at the age of 85.

Ronald
ROSS

1857–1932

MEDICINE

* **bacteriologist** specialist who studies microscopic organisms called bacteria that can cause infection and disease

* **parasite** organism that lives on or within another organism from whose body it obtains nutrients

* **gastrointestinal** relating to or affecting the stomach and intestines

* **parasitologist** one who specializes in parasitology, the branch of biology that deals with organisms that live on or within another organism from whose body they obtain nutrients

The British bacteriologist* Ronald Ross is famous for his work on the tropical disease malaria. Ross discovered the parasite* that causes malaria in the gastrointestinal* tract of the Anopheles mosquito and later proved that malaria is transmitted to humans by mosquito bites. His research laid the foundation for developing methods to combat the disease.

Early Life, Education, and Career. Born in Almora, Nepal, to a British army officer serving in India, Ross received his early education at English boarding schools. Although his greatest interest was in the arts, he followed his father's wishes and went on to study medicine. After earning his medical degree from St. Bartholomew's Hospital in 1879, Ross served in the Indian Medical Service for a number of years. While working in India, he became increasingly aware of tropical medical problems and felt that it was his duty as a physician to discover what caused them.

Research on Malaria. While on leave in London in 1888, Ross developed his interest in medical research. He took a course in bacteriology and earned a Diploma of Public Health. He returned to India the following year to study malaria. Initially he believed that toxic (poisonous) substances that formed within the human gastrointestinal tract caused the disease.

During a second leave of absence in England in 1894, Ross continued his successful and far-reaching research on malaria. His work was influenced in large part by the Scottish physician and medical researcher Patrick Manson. Manson introduced Ross to the pioneering work of the French parasitologist* Alphonse Laveran, who had observed parasites in the blood of malaria victims. Based on Laveran's observations, Manson believed that mosquitoes transmitted malaria, and he wrote a paper explaining this theory, which Ross's research later proved. Manson also entered into an extensive correspondence with Ross, constantly supporting him in overcoming the various problems that arose in his research.

Ross faced an enormous problem in trying to prove Manson's theory that mosquitoes transmitted malaria. Not only were there a great variety of mosquitoes to study, but there also were many types of parasites that might be responsible for the disease. He attacked the problem systematically. He demonstrated that volunteers who drank water contaminated with infected mosquitoes failed to contract malaria. This suggested that the disease was transmitted by some other means, possibly mosquito bites.

He also studied various types of parasites in mosquitoes and learned how to identify and dissect different species of mosquitoes.

From the beginning, Ross focused on parasites he found in the stomachs of mosquitoes. On August 20, 1897—a day that Ross later called "Mosquito day"—he observed a cyst in the stomach wall of the Anopheles mosquito, a species he had not encountered before. Ross immediately realized that he had found a promising lead, because the cyst was similar to ones formed by the parasites observed by Laveran. But because of his duties with the Indian Medical Service, he had to put aside his studies temporarily.

Several months later Ross resumed his study of the Anopheles mosquito and the malaria parasite. In a very important piece of research, he uncovered the parasite's life cycle and demonstrated that Anopheles mosquitoes could transmit malaria directly from infected birds to healthy ones. Around the same time, an identical demonstration of the life cycle of the human malarial parasite was accomplished by Italian scientists, giving rise to a dispute over who had first discovered the parasite's life cycle. The dispute was settled in 1902 when Ross was awarded the Nobel Prize in physiology* or medicine for his work on malaria, which laid the foundation for combating the disease.

* **physiology** science that deals with the functions of living organisms and their parts

Later Life. Ross's career in experimental research ended in 1899 when he retired from the Indian Medical Service. After his return to England, he became a lecturer at a new school for tropical medicine in Liverpool, where he played an influential role in pioneering tropical medicine education. In 1911 Ross was knighted, and the following year he moved to London and became a medical consultant.

Much of the remainder of Ross's life was concerned with organizing public health programs against malaria. In addition to giving lectures, he wrote a series of publications that contained information on such topics as how to avoid being bitten by mosquitoes and how to destroy them. He also traveled extensively to participate in malaria prevention campaigns.

In 1926 the Ross Institute of Tropical Hygiene was founded in London in honor of Ross's work. The purpose of this institute was to promote research and stimulate malarial control measures. Ross was the first director of this institution, which is still in existence. He remained in the position until his death in 1932.

Albert Bruce
SABIN
1906–1993
MEDICINE, MICROBIOLOGY

* **microbiologist** scientist who studies microscopic life-forms, such as bacteria and viruses

The Physician and microbiologist* Albert Bruce Sabin conducted research into cancer and viral diseases in humans. He is best known for developing an effective, live vaccine against the crippling disease poliomyelitis, or polio.

Background and Scientific Training. Sabin was born in Bialystok, Poland, which was part of Russia at the time of his birth. When he was 14, his family left Bialystok for the United States, in part to escape the persecution being suffered by Jews in the Russian empire. Although Sabin spoke no English when he arrived in the United States, two cousins taught him

Albert Sabin was one of two researchers in the 1950s who developed treatments to protect people against the devastating disease polio. In this photograph, he is seen with a child demonstrating how to "open wide" so that the sugar cube containing his oral polio vaccine could do its job.

enough of the language in six weeks so that he could enter high school in Paterson, New Jersey. An uncle agreed to pay for Sabin's college education if the young man agreed to become a dentist. Sabin dutifully entered dental school at New York University, but after reading a book called *Microbe Hunters* he became fascinated with the idea of medical research. He later said, "Melodramatic as it may sound, the book gave me a picture of what science meant to man."

Sabin switched to a course of medical study and, losing his uncle's financial support, went to work to earn money to complete his undergraduate degree and attend the university's medical school. It was during this period, in 1930, that Sabin became an American citizen. By the time he received his medical degree in 1931, Sabin had decided to become a researcher. He was particularly interested in infectious diseases of the central nervous system, such as polio. At this time polio was one of the most feared diseases and was especially contagious during the summer months. It struck thousands of people each year. Some victims died; others became crippled or paralyzed. Polio was also called infantile paralysis because it often attacked young children, although it could also affect adults. President Franklin D. Roosevelt, for example, developed polio as an adult. Roosevelt helped found the Infantile Paralysis Foundation, which launched a fundraising effort known as the March of Dimes to support research into the prevention and cure of polio.

The treatment of polio was generally limited to confining the afflicted child in cumbersome splints and braces. An Australian nurse named Elizabeth KENNY had success with a treatment that involved wrapping hot,

Sabin, Albert Bruce

moist blankets around patients' limbs. Kenny then put patients through a rigorous physical therapy program to stimulate their crippled muscles. She reported good results and "Kenny Clinics" opened in the United States and Australia, but many physicians remained skeptical of this mode of treatment. Some researchers, such as Sabin, hoped to treat the cause of the disease, not merely its symptoms.

The Polio Vaccine. After medical school Sabin held posts at Bellevue Hospital in New York and then at the Lister Institute of Preventive Medicine in London. In 1935 he returned to New York to work at the Rockefeller Institute for Medical Research, where he succeeded in growing the poliovirus in human tissue outside the body. The tissue cultures* were taken from the brain cells of human embryos*. After 1939 Sabin continued his work at the Children's Hospital Research Foundation of the University of Cincinnati. At the time most scientists believed that the virus entered the body through the nose and lungs. Sabin showed that this was not true, and he later proved that the virus works primarily in the digestive system.

Sabin's research was put on hold during World War II, when he became a medical officer in the army. He developed vaccines to protect troops against dengue fever and Japanese encephalitis, two infectious diseases encountered in combat zones. After the war he returned to Cincinnati and continued his investigation of polio.

Other researchers were also trying to find a vaccine for polio, and in 1955 one of them, Jonas SALK, announced that he had succeeded. His vaccine consisted of a killed form of the poliovirus, administered by injections. Salk was hailed as a hero, and governments launched large-scale public health programs in the United States and elsewhere to inoculate* children with his vaccine.

Sabin and some other scientists, however, had always believed that a vaccine using a killed virus was less effective than one using a live, weakened virus, which could offer longer lasting protection. By carefully breeding weaker and weaker strains of the poliovirus, Sabin finally produced one that he believed was safe enough to use but still strong enough to create a very mild case of polio, which would activate the body to produce natural disease-fighting agents called antibodies. It is these antibodies, not the vaccine itself, that protect the body in case of future exposure to the disease.

In 1954 Sabin tested his live-virus vaccine first on himself and his children and then on some prison volunteers. By the time his vaccine was ready for large-scale testing, however, Salk's vaccine was already in wide use in the United States, so Sabin's vaccine was tested on millions of people in Russia. The Sabin vaccine was much easier to administer than the Salk vaccine—it could be applied to a sugar cube and eaten. For this reason, it replaced the Salk vaccine in the United States and many other parts of the world after 1960. More than 100 million Americans were immunized with the Sabin oral vaccine. In time, however, scientists realized that the live-virus vaccine could cause polio in patients with immune system disorders. In such cases, they recommended that doctors administer the Salk vaccine. Nonetheless, Sabin's oral vaccine became the main defense against polio throughout the world.

* **culture** microorganisms, such as bacteria or tissue, grown in a specially prepared nutrient substance for scientific study

* **embryo** organism at the early stages of development before birth or hatching

* **inoculate** to introduce a disease agent into an animal or plant to produce a mild form of the disease and render the organism immune

Sabin Sundays

The first public use of Albert Sabin's polio vaccine in the United States occurred in Cincinnati, where Sabin lived and worked. One Sunday in April of 1960, more than 200,000 people made their way to schools, hospitals, and clinics where health workers handed out sugar cubes containing the vaccine. "Sabin Sundays" became a common feature across the country. By the end of the following year, more than 100 million Americans received the polio vaccine, and for the first time since the 1920s, the annual number of new polio cases fell below 1,000. By the early 1990s not a single case of polio was reported in the Western Hemisphere.

146

Later Career. Sabin remained at the University of Cincinnati until 1970, when he went to Israel to serve as president of the Weizmann Institute, a scientific research organization. He remained there for four years, after which he became a research professor at the University of South Carolina. From 1982 to 1986, despite ill health, he acted as a scientific adviser to the National Institutes of Health.

Among other honors, Sabin received the United States Presidential Medal of Freedom, the nation's highest civilian honor, and the National Medal of Science. The government of the Soviet Union awarded him the Medal of Liberty and Order of Friendship Among Peoples. It is estimated that, at the time of Sabin's death, his vaccine had prevented about 5,000,000 cases of polio and 500,000 deaths from the disease.

Florence Rena
SABIN

1871–1953

ANATOMY, IMMUNOLOGY

Florence Sabin was one of the first prominent women in medicine in the United States. She was the first female faculty member and first female professor at Johns Hopkins Medical School in Baltimore, Maryland; the first female president of the American Association of Anatomists; the first female elected to the National Academy of Sciences; and the first female to become a full member of the Rockefeller Institute (now Rockefeller University).

Sabin was the daughter of George Kimball Sabin, a mining engineer, and Serena Miner, a teacher. She received her early education at schools in Denver and Vermont. She then went on to earn a bachelor's degree from Smith College in Massachusetts, where she concentrated her studies on mathematics and science and decided to pursue a medical career. She graduated in 1893 and taught school for three years to earn money to pay for her medical education. In 1896 she entered the recently opened Johns Hopkins Medical School and began her career in medical research under the guidance of Franklin P. Mall, a professor of anatomy.

While a student at Johns Hopkins she constructed a three-dimensional model of the mid- and lower brain that was published as *An Atlas of the Medulla and Hindbrain* in 1901, a year after Sabin received her M.D. That year Sabin also received a fellowship in anatomy at the medical school. She was appointed assistant professor of anatomy in 1902 and professor of histology* in 1917.

In her research at Johns Hopkins, Sabin studied the origin of blood cells and the lymphatic system*. She proved that the lymphatic vessels arose from the veins instead of from the spaces between tissues. She traveled to Germany on research trips to learn and bring back new laboratory techniques, such as the staining of living cells. She used this technique to study cellular response in tuberculosis, as well as to research the site of antibody production.

In 1925 Sabin left Johns Hopkins and established a laboratory at the Rockefeller Institute in New York. Her research there was focused on the role of white blood cells in the body's immune response. Thirteen years later, she retired from the institute and moved to Denver. In 1944 she headed a subcommittee to examine public health in Colorado. The commission

* **histology** branch of anatomy that deals with the minute structure of animal and plant tissues, observable only through a microscope

* **lymphatic system** system of vessels that produces lymph, a fluid that removes bacteria and proteins from tissues and supplies white blood cells

found that, contrary to Colorado's image as a resort state, its public health record was among the worst in the nation. Sabin spent a great deal of time and energy drafting new state health laws. In 1947 she was appointed chair of Denver's Interim Board of Health and Hospitals, holding the post until 1951 when she was appointed chair of a new Board of Health and Hospitals. She resigned this position a year later. From that time, she was increasingly occupied with care of her ill sister. Sabin died of a heart attack in 1953.

Jonas Edward
SALK
1914–1995
MEDICINE, VIROLOGY

* **inoculate** to introduce a disease agent into an animal or plant to produce a mild form of the disease and render the organism immune

* **virologist** scientist who studies the microscopic disease-causing agents called viruses, their effects, and methods of controlling them

The American physician and medical researcher Jonas Edward Salk became a widely known scientific figure when he developed a vaccine to inoculate* children against the disease poliomyelitis, or polio, in the 1950s. Although Salk's vaccine was soon replaced by other preventive treatments, he remained a popular hero, sometimes called "The Man Who Saved the Children." As a virologist*, Salk also carried out research on vaccines against other diseases, including influenza and AIDS, and he founded a research institute.

Becoming a Medical Researcher. Salk was born in New York City, the son of Russian Jewish immigrants. His parents encouraged their children to study and take advantage of the educational and career opportunities available to them. When Salk entered the College of the City of New York (City College), he became the first member of either his mother's or his father's family to attend college.

At first Salk planned to become a lawyer. "I entered college enrolled as a pre-law student, but I changed to pre-med after I went through some soul searching as to what I would do other than the study of the law," he later said. "I was interested in science, and I began to think about the scientific aspect of medicine. My intention was to go to medical school, and then become a medical scientist." Salk aimed at a career in medical research rather than a physician's practice because he believed he might make a greater contribution than he could by treating individual patients.

After graduating from college in 1934, Salk attended medical school at New York University, receiving his medical degree five years later. By that time he had already focused on the area that would become his life's work: viruses and the vaccines that could protect people from them.

Viruses and Vaccines. During his final year of medical school, Salk had the opportunity to work with a laboratory group that was studying influenza, or the flu. Scientists had recently discovered the influenza virus, and they were looking for an effective way to use it in a vaccine.

To be effective, a vaccine must consist of the virus itself, but in a form that either has been deactivated, or killed, or is too weak to cause a serious or infectious case of the disease. A vaccine works by producing a reaction that is similar to a mild case of the disease. In response, the vaccinated person's body creates antibodies* to fight off the reaction. Those antibodies remain present in the system, and if the person is later exposed

* **antibody** protein produced by the immune system to neutralize the presence of a foreign protein in the body

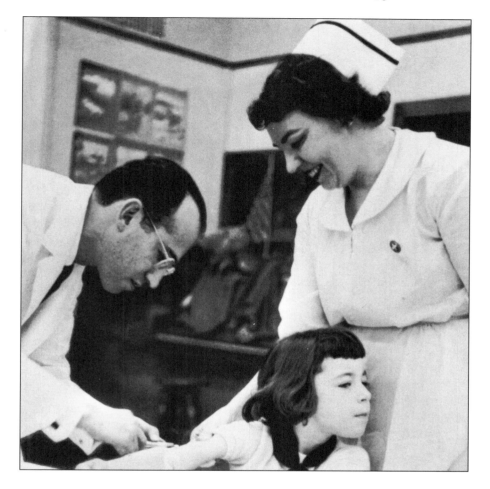

The polio vaccine developed by Jonas Salk in 1952 was ready for its first large-scale tests two years later. That year, nearly 2 million children were saved from the crippling condition. Salk is seen here inoculating a child with the polio vaccine.

to the active form of the disease-causing virus, the antibodies will make the body immune to the disease.

The influenza vaccine that Salk and his colleagues sought to develop needed to be strong enough to create antibodies and make an individual immune, but weak enough that it did no harm. Salk and his medical school colleagues succeeded in preparing a form of the influenza virus that had been killed. The virus could not reproduce and spread infection, but it was still strong enough to immunize.

After completing his medical internship in 1942, Sabin joined a team of researchers at the University of Michigan's School of Public Health, who were working to develop an influenza vaccine for use by the United States Army. World War II was under way, and some leaders feared that there might be another deadly worldwide outbreak of influenza like the one that had occurred in 1918, following World War I. Salk and other researchers successfully produced an effective vaccine that was used in the armed forces during the war. No epidemic ensued.

In 1947 Salk accepted an appointment to teach in the medical school of the University of Pittsburgh and to head a virology research lab there. He planned to continue working on the influenza vaccine and to begin work on one for poliomyelitis. At the time polio was a dreaded disease

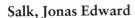

Salk, Jonas Edward

Competition, Awards, and Fame

Jonas Salk achieved great fame for developing a vaccine that conquered polio, but he did not win a Nobel Prize for the accomplishment. The Nobel Foundation also overlooked his rival, Albert Sabin, who developed a competing vaccine to prevent the disease. The only scientist to earn the prize for work linked to polio was John Enders of Harvard University. Enders and his fellow researchers devised a way to grow polio in test tubes, providing vaccine researchers everywhere with plenty of virus to use in their experiments.

throughout the world, and many medical scientists were determinedly searching for a cure or for a vaccine.

Salk had written several papers on the poliovirus that caught the attention of the Infantile Paralysis Foundation, an organization formed to raise money toward the prevention or cure of polio. The organization offered him generous funding for research to find a vaccine, and Salk set to work. He built on the advancements made by a Harvard University team led by John Enders, which discovered how to grow the poliovirus in test tubes. This finding provided Salk and other researchers with an unlimited supply of the virus for research and experimentation.

Because Salk felt that a killed virus vaccine was safer than one made from an attenuated (weakened) but live virus, he turned his research in that direction. From the work of other scientists, he adopted a method of using the chemical formaldehyde, long known as a preserving agent, to kill the virus. He developed killed virus vaccines for each of the three known strains of polio. When he injected these vaccines into monkeys, the monkeys developed antibodies but did not become sick.

By 1952 Salk was ready to test his vaccine on humans. He showed his confidence in his own work by inoculating himself, his wife, and their three children, along with other volunteers. All of them developed antibodies, but no one became ill with polio. The following year Salk published his findings in the *Journal of the American Medical Association,* and the year after that the first large-scale tests of the vaccine took place. In 1954, in the largest medical experiment that the United States had yet undertaken, almost 2 million schoolchildren rolled up their sleeves and received vaccinations in their arms. Some children were administered the vaccine, while others received a placebo (harmless and ineffective substance). Follow-up studies later determined that the vaccine had worked on those who had received it.

Success. Despite 260 tragic cases of polio, including 10 deaths, caused by batches of vaccine that had been incorrectly prepared in haste, the overall results were both positive and dramatic. By early 1955 Salk knew that his vaccine was a success. With great fanfare, the vaccine was put into use across the United States, and soon it was in use in other countries as well. Polio, it appeared, was on its way to being eradicated. This was rightly considered a major breakthrough in public health, and Salk rapidly became a world-famous hero.

However, not everyone saw Salk in this light. Many of his fellow scientists accused him of seeking publicity and neglecting professional courtesy. Even before the vaccine was perfected, researchers who had labored on the problem of polio for years resented the lavish funding and attention that Salk, a relative newcomer, received. After his success, many felt that he did not give sufficient credit to Enders's group at Harvard and to his colleagues at Pittsburgh for their contributions. They felt that he allowed the public to perceive the vaccine as a one-man triumph when in reality it was a group effort.

Some scientists continued to argue that a live virus vaccine was more effective than Salk's killed virus injection. Within a few years, despite Salk's argument that his killed virus vaccine was safer and more effective,

* **microbiologist** scientist who studies microscopic life-forms, such as bacteria and viruses

* **bacteriology** science that deals with bacteria, microscopic organisms that can cause infection and disease

the United States replaced his vaccine with an easier-to-use live virus vaccine, taken orally, developed by microbiologist* Albert Sabin. Salk and Sabin carried on an open rivalry over their work with the polio vaccine. The debate over the benefits and drawbacks of each type of virus continues, and both types remain in use.

Despite his new status as a highly recognized public figure, Salk continued his career as a teacher of bacteriology*, preventive medicine, and experimental medicine at the University of Pittsburgh until 1963. That year he became director of a new research center he had founded in California, the Jonas Salk Institute for Biological Studies, now called the Salk Institute. There, Salk promoted socially responsible biological research, including investigations into an AIDS vaccine, until his death from heart failure in 1995. Among Salk's many worldwide honors was the Presidential Medal of Freedom in 1977, the highest honor the United States can give to a civilian.

David
SATCHER

born 1941
MEDICINE

* **anemia** disease marked by the reduction of oxygen-carrying material in the blood

David Satcher, an African American physician, scholar, and public health advocate, became the 16th Surgeon General of the United States and Assistant Secretary for Health in 1998. As Surgeon General, Satcher plays an important role in educating Americans about health issues and policies.

Born on a small farm near Anniston, Alabama, Satcher almost died from whooping cough at age two. A vaccine for the disease was available, but his poor family had little access to medical care. A local doctor, the only African American physician in the community, saved his life. This man's dedication inspired Satcher to become a family doctor.

Satcher graduated first in his class at a racially segregated high school in Alabama and then attended Morehouse College in Atlanta, Georgia, earning his B.S. in 1963. He later attended Case Western Reserve University in Cleveland, Ohio, becoming the first African American at the school to earn both Ph.D. and M.D. degrees.

In the 1970s Satcher held teaching and administrative positions at the Charles F. Drew Postgraduate Medical School, the King-Drew Sickle Cell Center, and the School of Public Health at the University of California at Los Angeles. During these years, he researched sickle-cell anemia* and opened a free clinic in Los Angeles.

In 1979 Satcher returned to Atlanta and became chairman of the department of community medicine and family practice at the Morehouse College Medical School. Later he served as president of Meharry Medical College in Nashville, Tennessee. During his time in Nashville, Satcher recruited many faculty members and improved the college's academic standing. He also put the school on a firm financial footing.

In 1993 Satcher became director of the Centers for Disease Control and Prevention (CDC) in Atlanta, Georgia. There he worked to increase the rates of childhood immunization and improve the nation's ability to deal with infectious diseases. He also instituted a system to detect and prevent foodborne illnesses, increased the CDC's emphasis on disease prevention, and highlighted the importance of physical activity for good health. Satcher launched a controversial program aimed at the prevention of violence. He called violence a public health problem as well as a criminal justice issue. He also served as administrator of the Agency for Toxic Substances and Disease Registry. There he worked to prevent adverse effects on human health caused by exposure to hazardous substances in the environment.

Charles Scott
SHERRINGTON
1857–1952
NEUROPHYSIOLOGY

* **physiology** science that deals with the functions of living organisms and their parts

Charles Scott Sherrington was a pioneer in the modern science of neurophysiology, the study of the physiology* of the nervous system. In 1932 he and fellow scientist Edgar Adrian won the Nobel Prize in physiology or medicine for their discoveries concerning the function of the nervous systems of vertebrates (animals with spines).

Life and Career

Sherrington's work spanned a period of nearly 50 years, comprised a long history of research into the function of the nervous system, and set the stage for new investigations by future scientists. His colleagues considered Sherrington to be "the supreme philosopher of the nervous system" and the one who "almost single-handedly crystallized the special field of neurophysiology."

Background and Education. Sherrington was born in London, England, the son of Anne Brooks and James Norton Sherrington. When he was still a young child, his father died. His mother married Dr. Caleb Rose, who lived in Ipswich, and his home was a gathering place for artists and scholars. Early exposure to these people and their ideas gave Sherrington a lifelong interest in philosophy, history, and poetry, as well as science.

Sherrington attended school in Ipswich. Encouraged by his stepfather to take up the study of medicine, he began his medical training at St. Thomas's Hospital in London. A few years later the family's financial situation improved, and Sherrington entered medical school at Gonville and Caius College at Cambridge University. He studied physiology under instructors who passed on to him their strong interest in determining how anatomical structures are related to physiological functions.

Sherrington received his bachelor's degree in 1883 and his medical qualification two years later. He traveled to Germany to study and conduct research with leading scientists such as Rudolf Virchow and Robert Koch at the University of Berlin. Virchow was the foremost German physician of his time and an outspoken advocate for medical research. Scientists regard Koch as the founder of modern bacteriology, the science that deals with microscopic organisms called bacteria that can cause infection and disease. Studying with these important figures gave Sherrington superb training in physiology, morphology (the study of the structure of animals and plants), histology (the study of the structure of animal and plant tissues, which can only be seen with a microscope), and pathology (the study of diseases and their effects on organisms).

Early Career. After completing his studies, Sherrington was appointed to lecture in physiology at St. Thomas's Hospital. In 1891 he began a four-year stint as physician-superintendent of the Brown Institution, a London animal hospital. The rest of his scientific career involved experimental research on animals. In 1895 Sherrington became a professor of physiology at the University of Liverpool.

Sherrington's scientific work can be divided into two broad phases. The first began in the 1880s and continued until 1906, when he published his most important and influential work. The second part of his career spanned the period from the publication of *The Integrative Action of the Nervous System* until 1932, when he received the Nobel Prize.

During the first period, Sherrington investigated movement in animals, focusing on reflexes, which are automatic, unconscious, or involuntary responses to a stimulus. They occur when nerve impulses cause a muscle or gland to react without the participation of the conscious or decision-making mind. A classic example of a reflex motion is the knee jerk, in which a tap on the knee of a seated person causes the lower leg to jerk forward. Sherrington decided to explore how the nervous system governs such reflexes.

When Sherrington began his work, information and ideas about the anatomy and physiology of the nervous system had developed over centuries but were far from unified or organized. Scientists had not yet begun to piece together a total theory of the anatomy and physiology of the nervous system. Techniques for studying reflexes were imprecise, and the field lacked experimentally based concepts to aid scientists in their evaluation of the role of animal reflexes. Sherrington decided to investigate the

Charles Scott Sherrington studied the workings of the nervous system in mammals. His work influenced the development of techniques in brain surgery as well as the treatment of nervous disorders such as paralysis.

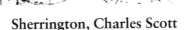

Lost in His Work?

During World War I Charles Sherrington lent his talents to the government. One summer day he departed from home on a bicycle, and everyone thought he had gone off on a cycling holiday. Instead he had cycled to the industrial city of Birmingham where he worked under an assumed name in a factory that made artillery shells. As an unskilled laborer, he was able to study firsthand the effects of industrial fatigue.

physiology of the spinal cord—one of the major components of the nervous system—and its involvement in reflex movements. To do so he spent ten years painstakingly mapping the distribution of nerve bundles that originate in the spinal cord.

This work produced three major contributions to neuroanatomy. The first was Sherrington's mapping of motor pathways, the tracks of nerve impulses involved in movement. The second established the fact that muscles contain sensory nerves that detect and communicate information. The third breakthrough traced the distribution of nerves from the spinal cord across the skin.

Along with this anatomical work, Sherrington continued to study the activity of the nervous system, using cats, dogs, and monkeys. In a long series of experiments, he studied reflex motions in living animals whose brains had been removed. These studies proved that such movements originated in the nervous system outside the brain.

The most important theme in Sherrington's work until 1900 was his study of how nerves and nerve impulses affect antagonistic muscles, which are pairs of muscles whose actions oppose each other. He discovered a principle, sometimes called Sherrington's law, which states that whenever a nerve impulse excites or stimulates a muscle, the opposing muscle is inhibited, which means that it is blocked or prevented from acting. This principle, also known as reciprocal innervation, was "the clue to the whole system of traffic control in the spinal cord and throughout the central [nervous system] pathways," according to Edgar Adrian, with whom Sherrington later shared the Nobel Prize.

Sherrington coined many of the concepts and terms that have come to be part of the common vocabulary of nervous system research. In 1897, for example, he proposed the term *synapsis* or *synapse* to refer to the gap between the ends of nerve cells, discovered in the 1880s by the Spanish scientist Santiago RAMÓN Y CAJAL.

Integrative Action

By 1900 Sherrington had put together the major elements of his main achievement, the concept that he called integrative action. He began introducing some of the research data and thoughts in his publications, which included textbooks, papers, and a series of ten guest lectures he delivered at Yale University in New Haven, Connecticut, in 1904.

Sherrington's complex presentations at Yale were hard to follow, even for those familiar with his work, and as the lecture series progressed the audiences grew smaller and less enthusiastic. However, when Sherrington published the lectures in 1906 under the title *The Integrative Action of the Nervous System,* his fellow scientists were more easily able to follow his thoughts, and they recognized the book as a major event in the development of neurophysiology. In 1947, when the fifth edition of the book was published, a reviewer for the *British Medical Journal* wrote of its "permanent value" as "a product of sustained thought upon what is essentially—though only [Sherrington's] genius revealed it as such—a single problem—namely, the mode of nervous action."

Sherrington's book reviewed work by other investigators and summarized his own research and ideas. In the book, he explains the concept of integrative action as having three main points: the nervous system, which plays a major role, possibly the key role, in enabling a complex multicellular organism to function as an integrated whole; the reflex, which is the basic unit of nervous system integration; and simple reflexes that can combine into complex ones by occurring at the same time or in a series. Starting with these points, Sherrington demonstrated in detail the basic theme of integrative action—the nervous system organizes what would otherwise be merely a collection of organs into a coordinated individual organism. He described simple reflexes controlled by the spinal cord and continued on to explain the complex patterns of reflex muscle management that, in animals, are guided by the brain.

Another key feature of the work was Sherrington's description of three different groups of sense organs: the exteroceptors, whose function is to gather information about the outside world using sight, hearing, smell, and touch; the interoceptors, which respond to taste; and the proprioceptors, which sense events or conditions inside an organism. A good example of proprioceptive action is the way sensory nerves within an animal's muscles control the reflex actions that maintain the animal's posture and balance against the force of gravity, even in animals whose brains have been removed.

The Oxford Years. After publishing *The Integrative Action,* Sherrington remained active as a researcher, teacher, writer, and well-known member of the international scientific community. In 1913 he left Liverpool for Oxford University, where he worked as a professor of physiology until his retirement in 1935.

World War I interrupted Sherrington's research, as it did for many scientists who were summoned to help Great Britain's war effort. Sherrington threw himself into government work, some of which drew on his neurological expertise. During the war he investigated the causes of industrial fatigue, a condition that reduced factory workers' efficiency or made them more likely to have accidents.

At Oxford, Sherrington measured, tested, and reviewed the concepts of how muscles are supplied with nerves and integrative action. New laboratory techniques enabled him to measure muscle tension with greater accuracy than earlier. Using these advanced techniques, he could measure the processes that excited and inhibited the movement of muscles, balancing them against each other and expanding his knowledge of reflexes.

Sherrington also published major works on the stretch reflex, which is the basic reflex used in standing, and on the excited and inhibited states in the central nervous system. He proved that inhibition is separate from excitation, although the two are similar and follow the same laws.

The Motor Unit and the Nobel Prize. Sherrington's last major contribution to neurophysiology was the concept of the motor unit. Called a spinal motoneuron, the motor unit is a cell emerging from the spinal cord with branches that control and coordinate the actions of more than 100 muscle

Animal Testing

The lab rat and the guinea pig are fixtures in popular culture, but in recent decades some people have protested that using animals in clinical studies and experiments is inhumane. They claim that people have no right to exploit or inflict pain on animals. Supporters of animal testing maintain that millions of lives are saved each year because of drugs, treatments, and techniques developed through animal testing. Without such testing, they say, people and animals both would suffer needlessly. In 1998 more than 1.2 million animals were used in scientific research in the United States.

fibers. Although the concept is simple, it took years of difficult research by Sherrington and his colleagues to map these motor units and observe their function.

In 1932 Sherrington received the Nobel Prize in physiology or medicine specifically for isolating and analyzing the motor unit. He shared the award with Edgar Adrian of Cambridge University, who had analyzed the activity of single motor units. Many felt that Sherrington's award was long overdue, perhaps because the Nobel committee had difficulty singling out a specific discovery for the prize. Much of the value of Sherrington's work lies in its wide scope, his awareness that all of his varied research was interrelated, and his search for unifying principles.

Sherrington's Activities and Philosophy. By the time of his death in 1952, Sherrington was a widely recognized scientist. In addition to his theories and his many years of carefully gathered data on nervous system functions, his legacy included the invention of laboratory instruments and surgical procedures and techniques.

Throughout his life Sherrington also was active in circles outside the laboratory and the lecture room. He was interested in sports, and during his years in London, he regularly participated in Sunday morning parachute jumps off the tower of St. Thomas's Hospital. He was active in many scientific organizations and served as the president of London's Royal Society from 1920 to 1925. In 1922 the British government made him a knight in recognition of his scientific achievements. After retiring from Oxford, he served as a trustee of the British Museum and a governor of Ipswich School, where he had attended grammar school. He also advised the town of Ipswich on museums and health services. At the time of his death, Sherrington was a member of more than 40 scientific academies, and he had received honorary degrees from 22 universities.

Although science occupied much of his time and energy, Sherrington never lost his fondness for philosophy and the arts. In his scientific work, he was driven to explain organized, purposeful actions, including human behavior. He believed that reflexes and physiological actions together formed only a small part of the integrated human whole. In a philosophical work called *Man on His Nature,* published in 1941, Sherrington quoted the sixteenth century French physician Jean Fernel, who wrote, "our task, now that we have dealt with the excellent structure of the body, cannot stop there, because man is a body and a mind together." Sherrington, who studied the operations of the nervous system so closely, always tried to understand the relationship between the mind and the body.

Like Fernel and the French philosopher René Descartes, who is credited with proposing the philosophical position known as mind-body dualism, Sherrington held that the mind is distinct from the physical body. He believed that humans are the product of natural forces, but he also felt that neurophysiology could not completely explain mind and thought. He considered the link between the mind and body the most baffling problem of human existence.

In his foreword to the 1947 edition of *The Integrative Action,* Sherrington summed up years of thought about the roles and relations of the body and the mind. He identified three levels of integration. On the first level, physiological processes such as nervous system reflexes make the body's organs into a "unified machine." On the second level, a mental integrative system creates an aware, thinking, and active individual consciousness. On the third level, the body and the mind are linked in "the final and supreme integration completing the individual." Sherrington could not describe or locate exactly where or how the physical body and the mind came together, but neither could he find any reason to suggest that humankind's being rested on only one or the other as a fundamental principle. Instead, he believed that mind and body together form a complete being. (*See also* **Pavlov, Ivan Petrovich.**)

Hans SPEMANN

1869–1941
EMBRYOLOGY

* **embryo** organism at the early stages of development before birth or hatching

Hans Spemann was a remarkable theorist and researcher in embryology—the study of the development of organisms from fertilization to birth or hatching. He probed deeply into the questions of how an organism's embryo becomes exactly that organism—why a frog embryo* becomes a frog, and how it develops limbs and a nervous system. Yet he never allowed himself to get lost in philosophical mysteries. He created specific experiments with clear questions and precise technical procedures.

Impressions on a Young Scientist. Spemann was the eldest of four children of a well-known book publisher in Stuttgart, Germany. His father's family included several lawyers, and many members of his mother's family were doctors. As a result, Spemann grew up in a large house with a fine library and received a good education. Although his first interest was classical literature and philosophy, he decided to study medicine. After completing a year of military service in the cavalry, he entered the University of Heidelberg.

At the university he formed a friendship with a scientist a few years older named Gustaf Wolff. Wolff had begun experiments on the embryos of newts (small salamanders), and he showed Spemann an astonishing result: when the lens of the newt embryo's eye was removed, a new lens grew—not from the tissues that created the original lens, but from the retina at the back of the eye. This phenomenon held a great challenge for Spemann, motivating and influencing his life's work. From Wolff, Spemann received his favorite choice of experimental animal, a fine example of planned and well-executed experiments, and a somewhat mystical way of thinking about biology.

In 1908 Spemann received his doctoral degree from the University of Würzberg. Thereafter he taught and conducted research at the university. During World War I he served as the director of the Kaiser Wilhelm Institute for Biology in Berlin-Dahlem. In 1919 he became a professor at Freiburg im Breisgau, where he remained for the rest of his life. During all these years, he worked closely with his students and took their contributions quite seriously.

Eyes, Eggs, and Embryos. Spemann's work, like Wolff's experiments, began with the eye of amphibians such as newts, but he went a step further,

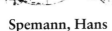

asking how the original lens was generated from the embryo in the first place. Through careful observation, he found that at a certain developmental stage, an outgrowth from the embryo's brain pushes to the embryo's outer layer of cells—the ectoderm—and ultimately becomes an eye. Spemann used a tiny, hot needle to burn and kill the cells of the outgrowth, believing that the embryo would develop without an eye.

To carry his research further, he designed a set of extremely small surgical tools, mostly from glass, to operate on eggs and embryos only a millimeter or two in diameter. In so doing, Spemann pioneered the field of microsurgery, itself a major contribution to science. Using the small instruments, Spemann removed the cells that would become the lens and replaced them with cells from elsewhere on the ectoderm. He found that the retina developed normally and caused the foreign ectoderm cells to turn into a lens, proving that the retina is responsible for the development of the lens.

Spemann also began another important study. He used a very thin human hair to encircle and squeeze newt eggs just after they had been laid. He found that if he pulled the hair tight enough to cut the egg in half, each half developed into a whole embryo, or one half formed a whole embryo and the other half became a shapeless mass of cells. However, if he squeezed the egg to create a dumbbell shape, the embryo sometimes developed with a single tail and two heads. Thus, half an egg never produced half an embryo—it always produced either a whole embryo (or body part) or nothing at all.

However, when Spemann carried out the same experiment at a later stage in the embryo's development, before the formation of organs and body parts, he noted that each half of the embryo simply produced half a newt. He concluded that at some stage between these two developmental points something had determined that certain parts of the embryo would become certain parts of the newt.

Spemann avoided the profound philosophical question of how this determination occurs. Instead, he set a more manageable question: what specific event happens before the determination and may be said to cause it? He found that the key was in the mesoderm, the layer of cells in the embryo that developed beneath the ectoderm. Using his microsurgical tools, Spemann showed that when any part of the ectoderm came into contact with the mesoderm, it turned into nerve cells—specifically, the organs of the central nervous system. Yet if the cells of the ectoderm that would normally turn into nerve cells were not allowed to touch the mesoderm, they would not form nerve cells.

In later experiments Spemann made another major discovery. Working with embryos in advanced stages of development, he found that the determination for what cells would become a certain organ came from the cells themselves, and not from the surrounding tissues. For example, when he transferred the cells that would become a particular newt organ onto the part of a frog embryo that would create that organ in the frog, he found that the organ created was one that would normally be found in a newt, not a frog. This discovery implied that the cells themselves contained the prescription for their own development.

The Open Door

Hans Spemann's work showed that animal cells determine their own identity, a fact now explained in terms of genetics—that the proteins called DNA, grouped in genes and chromosomes in the cells, carry the instructions for creating a living organism. However, Spemann never seemed to follow his thoughts toward such a conclusion. Meanwhile, across the Atlantic Ocean, Thomas Hunt Morgan was pioneering these ideas. However, because communication between Spemann's colleagues and Morgan's was very poor, the connection was not made until late in Spemann's life.

* **physiology** science that deals with the functions of living organisms and their parts

Spemann received the 1935 Nobel Prize in physiology* or medicine for his work. He ended his career at Freiburg im Breisgau, retiring in 1938. He died in his country home nearby three years later.

Edward Lawrie
TATUM

1909–1975
BIOCHEMISTRY, GENETICS

* **genetics** branch of biology that deals with heredity

* **physiology** science that deals with the functions of living organisms and their parts

* **enzyme** any of numerous complex proteins that are produced by living cells and catalyze specific biochemical reactions at body temperature

* **microbiology** study of microscopic organisms

* **biochemistry** science that deals with chemical compounds and processes occurring in living organisms

* **metabolism** physical and chemical processes involved in maintaining life

Edward Lawrie Tatum made important contributions to the study of genetics*. Tatum and two colleagues, George BEADLE and Joshua LEDERBERG, shared the 1958 Nobel Prize in physiology* or medicine for research that showed that genes govern the structure of enzymes* and control the biochemical reactions that take place in living organisms. Tatum also contributed to studies of sexual reproduction in bacteria, work that helped make bacteria a focus of genetic research.

Early Career. Tatum was born in Boulder, Colorado. He had a twin brother, Elwood, who died soon after birth. His father was a physician who also served as a professor at the University of Wisconsin in Madison, where the family settled when Edward Tatum was in his mid-teens.

Encouraged by his father's medical background and stimulated by the intellectual atmosphere of the university community, Tatum turned his attention to science. Educated throughout at the University of Wisconsin, Tatum received his B.A. in chemistry in 1931, an M.S. in microbiology* in 1932, and a doctoral degree in biochemistry* in 1934. Tatum's thesis for his doctoral degree concerned research he had conducted into the nutrition and metabolism* of bacteria, a subject that laid the foundation for his later work.

The same year that Tatum received his doctoral degree, he married a fellow student, June Alton, with whom he had two daughters. Five years later the family moved to the Netherlands after Tatum received an offer to study at the University of Utrecht. Tatum felt his studies in Holland lacked direction, however, and he returned to the United States the following year. He accepted a position as research associate in the Department of Biological Sciences at Stanford University in Palo Alto, California. In 1941 he was made an assistant professor at Stanford, a position he held for four years.

Tatum worked on several projects at Stanford. He continued his research into the nutrition of microorganisms and the biology of their cells. In his role as a teacher, he prepared a new course of study in biochemistry for graduate students. He also collaborated with a colleague, George Beadle, a professor of biology and genetics, forming a partnership that resulted in Tatum's most famous scientific contribution.

Learning How Genes Function. For some time Beadle had been investigating the connection between genes and the biochemical processes that occur in all living organisms. He wanted to determine whether genes control those processes and, if so, how they do it. To help him in his research, Beadle hired Tatum as an associate.

Earlier Tatum, Beadle, and another colleague had worked for some time with fruit flies, studying the mutations* of eye color in these insects, which are widely used in laboratory experiments. Once Beadle and Tatum joined forces, however, they shifted their experimental focus to *Neurospora*

* **mutation** relatively permanent change in the structure of a material

* **mutant** abnormal or atypical form of an organism produced by a mutation, or alteration, of its genetic material

* **amino acid** class of compounds that function as the building blocks of proteins

Making Mutants

A mutant is an organism with abnormal characteristics caused by a gene that has mutated, or changed, from its normal form. Organisms in nature undergo mutations all the time. Radiation, chemicals, and other random influences can cause the genetic material of a plant or animal to mutate. When that material is passed to the organism's offspring, it affects the offspring's development. Sometimes the results are significant. Tatum and Beadle needed mutated bread molds for their research, but they did not want to wait for mutants to appear naturally. They bombarded mold colonies with X rays, and the colonies then produced a high percentage of mutants.

crassa, a type of pink bread mold. They concentrated their research on efforts to establish the link between specific genes and the biochemical reactions that they control.

The standard procedure for this type of research was to look for mutant* examples of the organism in the laboratory and try to determine which gene was mutated and what chemical reaction that gene controlled. Beadle and Tatum took a different approach. They began with known chemical reactions and worked backward to determine which gene controlled the reaction. They chose bread mold because it has a short life span and it reproduces quickly. In addition, techniques for analyzing its genes had already been developed.

Beadle and Tatum placed mutant forms of bread mold—each of which had suffered genetic damage—on various kinds of culture media, which are substances known to nourish the growth of microorganisms. By observing whether the mutant bread molds lived or died on certain culture media, Beadle and Tatum discovered that some of the mutants had lost the ability to carry out certain essential biochemical functions, such as producing amino acids* or vitamins.

In their experiments they noticed that one strain of mutant mold flourished only in cultures to which they added biotin, or vitamin B6, but that unmutated mold did not require biotin to grow. Tatum and Beadle believed that the mutated mold had lost its ability to produce biotin through internal biochemical processes. The gene affected in the mutation, therefore, controlled that particular process. Because such processes depend on the presence of enzymes in the cells, Tatum and Beadle concluded that the affected gene regulated the production of the enzyme required to make B6.

Together they established a number of points about the biochemistry of cells. Their most crucial finding was that each mutation affected an organism's ability to perform a single chemical process, governed by one enzyme. This became known as the one gene, one enzyme theory, which became significant in genetic research. Their studies also showed that all biological processes could be resolved into a series of individual sequential chemical reactions, or pathways.

Another important finding concerned the mutant forms of bread mold that they used in their research. They artificially created the mutants and crossbred mutant strains with normal strains of mold. When they analyzed the offspring of these breedings, they found that the offspring had inherited the new mutations, which were genuine genetic alterations. In this manner Tatum and Beadle proved that artificially created mutants are identical to naturally occurring mutants.

Later Career. In 1945 Tatum left Stanford to spend a semester at Washington University in St. Louis, Missouri. He then moved to Yale University in New Haven, Connecticut, where he spent three years, first as an assistant professor of botany and then as a professor of microbiology.

At Yale, Tatum collaborated on experimental work with Joshua Lederberg, then a graduate student. Tatum employed techniques he had used on bread mold—methods of creating mutations and examining biochemical reactions—and applied them to bacteria. Working with Lederberg, he discovered that the *Escherichia coli (E coli)* bacteria reproduce sexually—in

Whether working with bread mold or bacteria, Edward Tatum sought to learn how genes, the units of heredity, operate at the cellular level in an organism. His work helped lay the foundations of the modern science of molecular genetics.

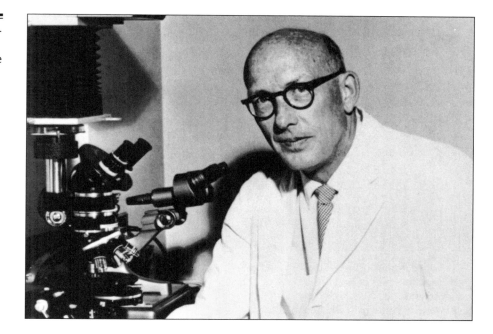

other words, that the genetic material of a bacterium combines genes inherited from two parents. This was significant because it demonstrated the continuity of life from microorganisms to higher plants and animals. Because of this breakthrough other researchers began focusing on bacteria in their quest to gain more knowledge of how genes regulate cellular biochemistry. As a result of the efforts of Tatum, Beadle, and Lederberg, bacteria became the main source of information concerning the genetic control of biochemical processes in the cell.

Tatum returned to Stanford in 1948. He remained there for nine years, serving as professor of biology and later of biochemistry, before joining the staff of the Rockefeller Institute for Medical Research, now known as Rockefeller University, in New York City. Tatum held his position as professor at the Rockefeller Institute until his death in 1975.

In 1953 Tatum received the Remsen Award from the American Chemical Society in recognition of his contributions to biochemistry. Five years later the Nobel Prize committee honored Beadle, Tatum, and Lederberg. Beadle and Tatum shared half of the award for their discovery of how genes influence organisms by controlling enzymes. Lederberg received the other half of the award for demonstrating that bacteria reproduce sexually.

Helen Brooke
TAUSSIG

1898–1986
MEDICINE

The founder of pediatric cardiology*, Helen Brooke Taussig is best known for discovering the cause of death of so-called blue babies. Doctors had assumed that these infants died from heart failure, but Taussig discovered that they died because their blood was deprived of oxygen as a result of insufficient circulation to the lungs.

Taussig was born in Cambridge, Massachusetts. Her father was a professor of economics at Harvard University and a cofounder of the Harvard

After her retirement Helen Taussig continued her activism in causes that affected children and their health. She also began to engage in debates in which she fought for scientists' rights to conduct experiments on animals and advocated women's rights to chose to terminate pregnancies.

* **cardiology** study of the heart and its functions in health and disease

* **congenital** existing at birth

School of Business Administration. Her mother, who died when Taussig was still a young girl, was interested in botany and zoology. Illness and a learning disability, later identified as dyslexia, complicated Taussig's early education. Nevertheless, she attended several small private schools and graduated from the Cambridge School for Girls in 1917.

Taussig enrolled at Radcliffe College but transferred to the University of California at Berkeley, where she earned a B.A. in 1921. Her father encouraged her to pursue a degree in public health because the educational opportunities in medicine were very limited for women at the time. Taking his advice, Taussig entered Harvard University's School of Public Health, where women could take courses but not work toward a degree.

Taussig next studied anatomy at Boston University. She then applied to the medical school at Johns Hopkins University in Baltimore, Maryland, where she earned her medical degree in 1927 and served as a pediatric intern. Three years later, she became head of the Pediatric Cardiac Clinic, part of the children's division at the Johns Hopkins University Hospital. She held this position until her retirement in 1963. Treating hundreds of children whose hearts had been damaged by disease or congenital* defects, she developed new methods of observation that led to a better understanding of pediatric heart problems.

After discovering the cause of "blue babies," Taussig and her colleague, a surgeon named Alfred Blalock, devised a surgical procedure, known as the Blalock-Taussig shunt. In the years that followed, the surgery saved the lives of thousands of infants, brought Taussig increasing fame, and influenced a whole generation of physicians. Her research also spurred the development of many other treatments for common heart problems.

In 1959 she became the first woman in the history of Johns Hopkins University to gain a position as full professor. Taussig gained further recognition in the 1960s, when she examined the increasing incidence of European children born with severely deformed limbs. She investigated the problem and found that most of these children had been born to women who had taken a drug called thalidomide during pregnancy to counteract nausea. She played a key role in banning the use of the drug in the United States. Taussig retired in 1963, but she remained active in children's health and social issues. She received many awards and honors, including being named the first female president of the American Heart Association. She died in an automobile accident in 1986.

Nikolay Ivanovich
VAVILOV

1887–1943

BOTANY, AGRONOMY, GENETICS

* **genetics** branch of biology that deals with heredity

Nikolay Ivanovich Vavilov was an outstanding Russian scientist whose extensive research produced important breakthroughs in the fields of plant breeding and genetics*. His father was a factory owner, but Vavilov and his siblings pursued scientific careers. His brother Sergei, a physicist, served as president of the Soviet Academy of Sciences. After receiving his bachelor's degree at the Moscow Agricultural Institute, Vavilov traveled to England to study immunity in plants, particularly wheat. When World War I began, he returned to Russia, where he completed his master's degree. He went on to teach genetics, selection, and agronomy (a branch of

agriculture) at the university level and served as the head of several government institutes of agriculture.

Vavilov's scientific success was built on his extensive specimen collecting expeditions. Between 1920 and 1940, he traveled across five continents, during more than 180 expeditions, and collected nearly 250,000 plant specimens, which he distributed to experimental stations throughout the Soviet Union. His study of these specimens led to his most important theoretical contributions. The first was his law of homologous series in heredity variation, in which he stated that many of the same variants and mutations* occur in closely related plant species. The more closely related the species, the more variants they shared in common. He produced a table to classify the different species and their variations. Just as the periodic table of the elements in chemistry predicted the existence of undiscovered elements, Vavilov believed his table could act as a guide to predict the existence of undiscovered plant forms based on the known forms and their variants. Vavilov later modified his theory to distinguish between genetic variations and variations in phenotypic, or outward, traits. He strongly supported the validity of the law and discovered several new plant forms based on his theory.

Vavilov's other significant contribution was his identification of the ancient centers of the world where most cultivated plants originated. He closely studied many species of grains and fruits and mapped the locations in which variant forms of those plants were found. Based on this work Vavilov located seven centers of civilization around the world from which more than 600 species of cultivated plants originated. His discovery of plant centers has greatly benefited botanical researchers.

Vavilov enjoyed the support of the Soviet government for many years and became prominent and influential. However, in the 1930s, he fell out of favor with the Soviet government when he refused to adapt his scientific ideas to Marxism*. One of his most vocal critics was Trofim Lysenko, a scientist whose theories on plant genetics and the inheritance of acquired characteristics received the political support of the state. In 1941 Vavilov was imprisoned because of these attacks and because of his refusal to adopt the Lysenko program. He died in prison two years later. After the death of Soviet dictator Josef Stalin in 1953, Vavilov's case was reopened at the request of his family. Two years later the Soviet state restored Vavilov's reputation and published most of his writings, many of which had not been printed during his lifetime.

* **mutation** relatively permanent change in the structure of a material

* **Marxism** social, political, and economic principles advocated by philosopher Karl Marx

---

Julius
WAGNER VON JAUREGG

1857–1940

PSYCHIATRY

The Austrian psychiatrist Julius Wagner von Jauregg's main contributions to science involved determining the causes behind two common psychological problems, cretinism* and general paresis*. He also discovered that syphilis, a sexually transmitted disease, could be cured by infecting patients with malaria. Wagner von Jauregg studied medicine at the University of Vienna and worked at a clinic in Vienna. During that time he met Sigmund FREUD, who also attended the university. Despite strong differences of opinion about scientific matters, the two became lifelong friends.

Wagner von Jauregg, Julius

* **cretinism** thyroid deficiency that causes arrested mental and physical development

* **general paresis** brain disease marked by mental deterioration, speech disturbances, and progressive muscular weakness

Fighting Goiter in Graz

In the late 1880s, the people of the city of Graz, Austria, were experiencing an epidemic of goiter, a condition marked by swelling of the thyroid gland. Around the same time, Wagner von Jauregg had been examining the effectiveness of using iodine tablets for various treatments. Based on his research, he concluded that taking small amounts of iodine on a regular basis would help prevent goiter. At his request the Austrian government adopted the policy of selling iodine salts in regions where the disease was common.

* **physiology** science that deals with the functions of living organisms and their parts

* **parasite** organism that lives on or within another organism from whose body it obtains nutrients

* **neurology** study of the structure, function, and disorders of the nervous system

After receiving his medical degree in 1883, Wagner von Jauregg went to work at the university's psychiatric clinic. While serving as an assistant at the clinic, he conducted experiments in which the thyroid glands of cats were removed. This procedure produced spasms, convulsions, and aggressive behavior in the animals. In 1889 he took a post as professor of psychiatry at the University of Graz in Austria. There he conducted additional studies of the function of the thyroid gland, which convinced him that impaired thyroid function causes cretinism.

Following this work, Wagner von Jauregg turned to the study of general paresis. He examined psychiatric patients who had contracted diseases that produced high fevers. He noticed that their mental state, which was troubled prior to contracting the disease, improved greatly after the fever passed. He concluded that psychotic behavior, including general paresis, might also be treated by inducing fever. However, when he injected patients with tuberculosis, he only achieved partial success in curing their paresis. These efforts were interrupted in 1893, when he accepted a position as director of Vienna's Psychiatric and Neurological Clinic. For the next six years, he also served on the Austrian board of health and promoted laws to provide more humane treatment for the mentally ill.

In the mid-1910s, Wagner von Jauregg returned to his studies of paresis. During the intervening years, little progress had been made in treating the disease, which affected about 15 percent of all mental patients, particularly those who had contracted syphilis. Victims usually died within three to four years. Wagner von Jauregg resumed his fever-treatment research by injecting patients with blood taken from people infected with malaria. He had considered using malaria in his earlier studies but abstained because there was no cure for the disease. However, with the development of an effective quinine cure for malaria in 1917, his experiment was much safer.

The syphilis patients he treated showed significant improvement after their fevers passed. In some cases they were cured completely. However, he could not explain how the fevers cured patients. Some physicians believed that the high temperatures killed the bacteria that caused syphilis. Others speculated that the malaria infection boosted the patient's immune system, which then could fight off the bacteria.

Because of these studies, fever therapy became a widely used treatment until the discovery of penicillin. In 1927 Wagner von Jauregg earned the Nobel Prize in physiology* or medicine for developing fever therapy. The treatment also provided new knowledge about malarial parasites*. He proved that victims infected with one form of malaria might not show symptoms for up to 40 weeks after exposure to the disease.

Wagner von Jauregg spent the rest of his career as director of the Psychiatric and Neurological Clinic in Vienna, building it into an outstanding school of psychiatry and neurology*. Much of his success at the clinic stemmed from his willingness to tolerate approaches and ideas that differed from his own. He fostered an atmosphere in which the many branches of psychological thinking came together. As a result, the clinic trained some of the most important figures in the early history of psychiatry. Wagner von Jauregg retired in 1928, but he remained active, publishing nearly 80 scientific papers before his death in 1940.

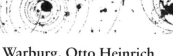

Otto Heinrich
WARBURG

1883–1970

BIOCHEMISTRY

* **biochemist** person who specializes in the science that deals with chemical compounds and processes occurring in living organisms

The German scientist Otto Heinrich Warburg is considered to be the most accomplished biochemist* of all time because of the number and importance of his discoveries. He was also one of the most controversial scientists of his day. The radical nature of many of his findings often led to widespread criticism of his research by his colleagues. Warburg, however, did not let these problems deter him from his work. Consequently, he left an unmatched legacy of knowledge in the field of biochemistry.

Life and Career

Warburg led a conventional and uneventful life until his early 30s, achieving little scientific distinction before World War I. However, after the war he embarked on a remarkable career, creating an unsurpassed record of accomplishment during the last 50 years of his life.

Early Life and Career. Warburg was born in the German town of Freiburg im Breisgau but moved to Berlin at age 13 when his father was appointed the chair of physics at Berlin University. He grew up in comfortable surroundings and had the opportunity to meet many of the leading German scientists of the day when they visited his parents. He studied at the University of Berlin, where he received a doctorate in chemistry in 1906, and at the University of Heidelberg, where he earned a doctorate in medicine in 1911.

Research Methods. Warburg conducted his earliest scientific work under the guidance of the prominent chemist Emil Fischer, who taught him to appreciate experimental rigor. Fischer required Warburg to repeat his procedures many times to ensure that they were carried out properly. This experimental method remained a strong influence on Warburg's future research. As a mature scientist, Warburg repeated his experiments between 20 and 100 times before he published his results, ensuring that his data were not only error-free but also easily reproducible by anyone familiar with his methods. At a time when theoretical scientists often dismissed those who performed experiments as mere technicians, Warburg accepted that label gladly. It reflected his dedication to careful procedures and precise observation. Near the end of his life, he summed up his approach, saying that "a scientist must have the courage to attack the great unsolved problems of his time, and solutions usually have to be forced by carrying out innumerable experiments without much critical hesitation."

In 1913 Warburg was chosen as a member of the Kaiser Wilhelm Institute for Biology in Berlin. When World War I began the following year, Warburg served as a cavalry officer on the Russian front. Before the war ended, Albert Einstein wrote to persuade Warburg to return to the Kaiser Wilhelm Institute. Warburg had been an active researcher there before the war, but it was only afterward that he achieved his greatest professional successes. In fact, when he left his unit near the end of the war, his fellow officers joked that he would "return to feeding sea urchins," referring to the research on respiration in sea urchin eggs that Warburg had conducted before the war. Little did they know that Warburg's later career would

The Other Half

Warburg's personal assistant, Jacob Heiss, was an integral part of his personal and professional life. From 1918 until Warburg's death, Heiss managed Warburg's professional activities, reviewed his scientific papers, and acted as his financial adviser and consultant on a variety of subjects on a daily basis. Although the two men had very different personalities, they worked well together. Warburg, who never married, made Heiss his only heir.

take him to the very top of his profession. In 1931 Warburg received the Nobel Prize in physiology* or medicine for his research on respiratory enzymes*. The same year, he was also named head of the Max Planck Institute for Cell Physiology (formerly the Kaiser Wilhelm Institute). He served in this post for the rest of his life. Warburg was an active man who remained fit, riding his horse every morning. He remained mentally active as well and published scientific papers until the year of his death.

Scientific Accomplishments

Warburg was a prolific researcher who investigated many areas in biochemistry. However, his work in cellular respiration, photosynthesis, and cancer research probably represent his most outstanding contributions to biochemistry.

Cellular Respiration. In the early 1920s, Warburg began a series of investigations of cellular respiration. At the time, scientists knew that during respiration the body converts lactic acid into carbon dioxide and water, while consuming oxygen. Warburg wanted to find out exactly how this process worked. To do so, however, he needed a tool to measure the rate at which human tissue consumes oxygen. He designed the Warburg manometer* to measure the change in the pressure of carbon dioxide and oxygen in the blood. The invention of the manometer was in itself an outstanding accomplishment, and it remained the standard tool for measuring metabolic reactions until the invention of the oxygen electrode around 1970.

Warburg was convinced that cellular respiration occurs at normal temperature and that it takes place with the aid of enzymes. He set out to investigate the nature of these enzymes by identifying the substances that affect the rate of oxygen consumption by the body. Many years earlier, the French biologist Claude Bernard had shown that carbon monoxide (CO) inhibits the action of hemoglobin, an iron-rich protein in red blood cells that carries oxygen throughout the human body. Normally, the iron in hemoglobin binds to oxygen molecules in the lungs and the oxygen is transported by the hemoglobin through the bloodstream to the rest of the body. However, CO, when it is present, binds more strongly to the iron in hemoglobin than does oxygen, breaking any bonds between oxygen and iron.

While experimenting with yeast cells, Warburg discovered that CO inhibits respiration in cells as well. Because CO breaks the bond between iron and oxygen in hemoglobin, Warburg reasoned that the enzyme present during cell respiration must also contain iron. He knew that compounds of CO and iron could be split when exposed to light. When he exposed cells respiring in CO and oxygen to alternating periods of light and darkness, he found that cellular respiration ceased during the dark periods and resumed when the cells were exposed to light. This proved further that iron was a component of the enzyme he was investigating.

Warburg then exposed the cells to various wavelengths of light. This enabled him to determine that the absorption spectrum* of the enzyme when it was bound to CO was similar to the spectrum for hemoglobin when it was bound to CO. Further studies identified the main enzyme responsible for cellular respiration as iron oxygenase. For this discovery, Warburg received the 1931 Nobel Prize in physiology or medicine. He later showed that the coloration of both blood and plant chlorophyll comes from this enzyme.

Photosynthesis. Warburg spent nearly 50 years investigating various aspects of photosynthesis, the process by which plants convert sunlight into energy and release oxygen. He made his first major discovery in this area when he found that, under the right conditions, photosynthesis can occur with almost perfect thermodynamic* efficiency. His early research proved that the conversion of light energy into chemical energy could take place with an efficiency of about 65 percent. Later, with improved experimental conditions, he showed that this figure was almost 100 percent. However, many researchers objected to this finding because they were unable—or unwilling—to reproduce the conditions under which Warburg conducted his experiments. When he invited various researchers to come to Germany and observe the experiments themselves, no one took his offer.

Cancer Research. Warburg's cancer research probably held the most relevance and interest for a wider audience, but it was more intensely criticized than his other efforts. Several years after he returned to the Kaiser Wilhelm Institute, Warburg discovered that cancer cells produced a great deal of lactic acid from glucose*. In lab experiments he noticed that this occurred both in the body and in test tubes—with or without the presence of oxygen—and that it varied greatly from one type of cancer to another.

* **thermodynamic** referring to the physics of the relationship between heat and other forms of energy

* **glucose** natural sugar found in many fruits and animal tissues

The number and magnitude of Otto Warburg's discoveries rank him as the most accomplished biochemist of all time. He was also a pioneer in scientific methodology and believed in using simple but new variations in experimental conditions.

167

* **fermentation** chemical reaction in which complex organic compounds are split into relatively simple substances

* **differentiated** referring to the process whereby cells, tissues, and structures are specialized to perform certain functions

Ordinary cells, by contrast, did not produce lactic acid from glucose in the presence of oxygen. He also noticed that this significant increase in lactic acid production was accompanied by injured cell respiration, leading Warburg to conclude that cancer occurs in two phases. In the first phase, cellular respiration is injured and cells struggle to maintain their normal structure. During this struggle some cells die from lack of energy, while others replace the lost energy with energy from fermentation*. Because this is a less sophisticated form of energy, the second phase of cancer develops when highly differentiated* body cells become undifferentiated cells. These cells grow uncontrollably, creating tumors that spread throughout the body. He concluded that cancer occurs when glucose replaces oxygen as a source of cellular energy. As Warburg wrote, "The prime cause of the plague is the plague bacillus, but secondary causes of the plague are filth, rats, and the fleas that transfer the plague bacillus from rats to man. . . .Cancer, above all other diseases, has countless secondary causes. But, even for cancer, there is only one prime cause. . . . There is no disease whose prime cause is better known."

Based on his findings, Warburg recommended the consumption of large amounts of the active groups of various enzymes that promote cellular respiration, including iron and the B vitamins. He announced his recommendations in a lecture he delivered in 1966, immediately sparking controversy and criticism.

Such criticism might have intimidated or discouraged others, but Warburg was secure in the knowledge that his discoveries were the product of hard work. His attitude toward criticisms of his work is reflected in one of his favorite quotations by the scientist Max Planck: "A new scientific truth is often accepted, not as a result of opponents becoming convinced and declaring themselves won over, but rather by the opponents dying off, and the oncoming generation of scientists becoming familiar with the new truth right from the start." This philosophy proved true for Warburg. Although he often failed to convince colleagues during his lifetime, his work and his reputation have withstood the test of time.

WATSON AND CRICK

James Dewey Watson
born 1928
MOLECULAR BIOLOGY

Francis Harry Compton Crick
born 1916
MOLECULAR BIOLOGY

James Dewey Watson and Francis Harry Compton Crick discovered the molecular structure of DNA* in 1953. By determining the structure of DNA, they were able to explain how genes duplicate themselves to pass on genetic* information from parent to offspring. Many scientists consider Watson and Crick's work to be one of the most important breakthroughs in modern biology. For their efforts, the two shared the 1962 Nobel Prize in physiology* or medicine with English physicist Maurice WILKINS.

Lives and Careers

It would be hard to imagine a more unlikely pairing than Watson and Crick. Nationality, temperament, and scientific background separated the two men, but together they formed a remarkable working relationship that contributed greatly to their success.

* **DNA** deoxyribonucleic acid, the material in chromosomes that carries genetic information from ancestor to offspring

* **genetic** relating to genes, the basic units of heredity that carry traits from ancestors to offspring

* **physiology** science that deals with the functions of living organisms and their parts

* **mutation** relatively permanent change in the structure of a material

* **bacteriologist** specialist who studies microscopic organisms called bacteria that can cause infection and disease

* **nucleic acid** class of complex chemicals, including DNA and RNA, that is found in all living cells and viruses

* **biochemistry** science that deals with chemical compounds and processes occurring in living organisms

Watson's Life and Career. Born in Chicago, Illinois, Watson displayed the first indication of his intellect at age 12. His neighbor produced a radio show called *Quiz Kids,* in which contestants answered difficult questions for prizes, and Watson was selected to appear on the show. His gift became even more apparent three years later when he graduated from high school at age 15 and enrolled at the University of Chicago under a special program. Watson showed much more enthusiasm for his hobby of bird-watching than for any of his studies. Although his professors recall his seeming indifference in class, he still received top grades. Later, in his autobiography, Watson said that genetics was the one subject that held his interest in college. Consequently, he decided to do graduate work in that area, but his habits did not impress the administrators at Harvard University or the California Institute of Technology. Both schools turned down his application to their graduate programs. He enrolled at the University of Indiana, which was an important center of genetic research.

The faculty at Indiana included Hermann Joseph MULLER, who had done pioneering work in genetics by studying *Drosophila,* the fruit fly, and X-ray–induced mutation*. However, Watson felt that the new breakthroughs in genetics would come from other research. He decided instead to work with the bacteriologist* Salvador Luria on bacteriophages, viral organisms that can infect bacteria. This work showed Watson that DNA affects the hereditary transmission of traits from parent to offspring. It also convinced him that scientists must learn more about nucleic acids* to fully understand genes. After earning his Ph.D. in 1950, at the urging of Luria, Watson went to Copenhagen, Denmark, for further research in biochemistry*. He spent a year there before transferring to the Cavendish Laboratory in Cambridge, England. It was there that he met Francis Crick, who was studying the three-dimensional structure of large organic molecules. The two men formed a close friendship and working partnership. Within two years they discovered the structure of DNA, which enabled scientists to understand how traits from a parent are passed to an offspring. This stands as one of the most important discoveries in the history of genetics. It was also the starting point for a great deal of modern research in molecular biology and biochemistry.

Two years after their historic discovery, Watson left Cavendish to take a teaching position at Harvard, where he stayed for more than 20 years. In 1968 he was named director of the Laboratory of Quantitative Biology in Cold Spring Harbor, New York. Watson split his time between Cold Spring Harbor and Harvard, but eight years later he resigned his teaching position and dedicated his efforts to the laboratory. When he arrived at Cold Spring Harbor, the laboratory was struggling to survive, but under Watson's leadership it became one of the world's leading cancer research centers. From 1988 to 1992, he served as head of the newly established Human Genome Project, which hoped to map and sequence the entire human genetic composition. However, Watson had invested money in several biotechnology companies that stood to profit from this work, and he was eventually forced to resign his position because of potential conflicts of interest. He currently serves as president of the Cold Spring Harbor facility.

Watson and Crick

* **X-ray diffraction** observational technique based on the fact that X rays bend when they encounter obstacles

* **RNA** ribonucleic acid, a cellular molecule similar to DNA that is involved in the production of proteins in the cell

Crick's Life and Career. Francis Crick grew up in London and developed an early interest in physics, chemistry, and mathematics. He attended University College of London University, where he majored in physics. World War II interrupted his work on a Ph.D., and Crick joined the British Admiralty Research Laboratory. There, he helped develop magnetic and acoustic mines for the British Navy, remaining with the laboratory for two years after the end of the war. During this time he read a book by the Austrian physicist Erwin Schrödinger titled *What is Life? The Physical Aspects of the Living Cell.* The book urged scientists to investigate genes at the molecular level, and it stimulated Crick to think of applying his training in physics to the study of biology. Crick switched his career path from physics to biology and went to work at the Strangeways Research Laboratory in Cambridge, England. Over the next two years, he learned biology, organic chemistry, and X-ray diffraction*. The latter technique proved instrumental in the discovery of the structure of DNA.

In 1949 Crick transferred to the Cavendish Laboratory in Cambridge, the site of important X-ray diffraction studies. He soon met Watson and began the collaboration that unlocked the mystery of DNA, which was just the first of Crick's achievements in molecular biology. Several years later, building on his work with Watson, he discovered that DNA guides the development of proteins in cells by transmitting genetic information to RNA*, which then passes the information to the proteins. He found that this process can be reversed, with RNA sending genetic information back to DNA. His discovery was vital in understanding so-called retroviruses such as HIV, the virus that causes AIDS. Crick reached another milestone when he demonstrated how the sequence of bases in the genetic code of DNA specifies which proteins are created in cells.

Crick left Cambridge in 1976 to join the staff at the Salk Institute for Biological Studies in California, where he became interested in studies on

Heeding Mother's Advice

Francis Crick claims that he was interested in science for as long as he could remember. He claims that receiving a set of encyclopedias as a child helped stimulate his interest. After reading many articles on astronomy, chemistry, and biology, he decided to become a scientist. However, he told his mother he worried that by the time he grew up, everything would already have been discovered. She reassured him that much would remain for him to discover, although she could not have guessed how important his discoveries would become.

* **posthumous** occurring after the death of an individual

* **phosphate** mineral compound containing phosphorus and oxygen

the workings of the brain. Since that time he has been particularly interested in the phenomena of consciousness and dreaming. Crick has received more attention, however, for his support of the unconventional theory of panspermia. Crick's version of the theory argues that technologically sophisticated alien cultures "seeded" life on earth millions of years ago by sending unmanned rockets containing microorganisms. Like Watson, Crick has received many awards and honors in addition to the Nobel Prize.

Discovering the Structure of DNA

Watson, the prodigy from Chicago, was 12 years younger than Crick, but he already had earned a doctorate. Watson was brash and ambitious, a single man looking for adventure and fame. Crick, who had recently married, had an outgoing personality, as well as an unmistakable laugh and loud voice. When Watson arrived at Cambridge in 1951, he and Crick hit it off instantly. They got along so well that they were assigned an office together so they would not disturb the other researchers. Two colleagues from King's College, London, Maurice Wilkins and Rosalind FRANKLIN, proved instrumental in Watson and Crick's famous discovery. Although Wilkins's role in uncovering the structure of DNA earned him scholarly acclaim, Franklin's contribution went largely unrecognized, in part because she died before the Nobel Prize was awarded to the other three in 1962. (The Nobel Foundation does not award prizes posthumously*.)

Building on Early Foundations. Watson and Crick built their research on a series of discoveries made during the preceding half century and added their own scientific contributions. Scientists had been aware for some time that all cells contain nucleic acids. They also knew that these acids are composed of a sugar, a phosphate*, and several bases that consist largely of carbon and nitrogen atoms. The most important bases had also been identified as adenine, cytosine, guanine, thymine, and uracil. The next major breakthrough was the discovery of two types of nucleic acid, RNA and DNA. Researchers had found only two differences between them: the sugar in RNA (ribose) has one less oxygen atom than the sugar in DNA (deoxyribose), and the base uracil in RNA is replaced by thymine in DNA. Seven years before Watson and Crick met, the Canadian biologist Oswald AVERY showed that DNA was the main agent in the cell that carries genetic information, not proteins as many scientists had previously believed. Avery's discovery was controversial for many years, but Watson and Crick were among those who supported his conclusions. Soon after they met, the pair decided to build a model of the DNA molecule.

One of the first obstacles that Watson and Crick encountered was that the DNA molecule was too small to be observed by standard methods. However, it could be viewed using the X-ray diffraction technique that Crick had studied at Strangeways. In the technique, an object is bombarded with X rays, which are scattered by the object in such a way as to reveal its structure. Before coming to Cambridge, Watson had seen a rough image of DNA produced with this technique but it was not clear

The DNA Double Helix

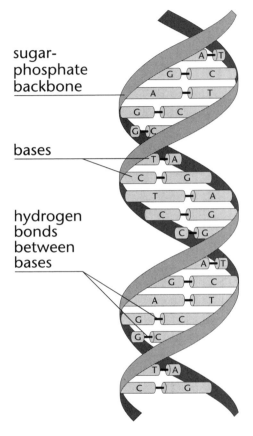

sugar-
phosphate
backbone

bases

hydrogen
bonds
between
bases

All the information needed to make a human being is present in the tangled threads of the DNA's double helix. DNA directs development and maintains the life of an organism by instructing cells to make proteins. The long DNA molecules are packaged into chromosomes on which genes are arranged like beads on a string. The DNA molecule is called a double helix because of its spiral backbones, which are made up of sugar and phosphate. Adenine (A) always pairs with thymine (T), and cytosine (C) always pairs with guanine (G), ensuring that the sequence of bases along one backbone mirrors, or complements, the sequence of the other backbone. The complementary nature makes the mispairing of bases—which could cause a damaging mutation—unlikely.

enough to give a precise indication of its structure. Watson and Crick soon solved this problem with the aid of the X-ray diffraction work of Wilkins and Franklin.

False Starts and Secret Help. Wilkins and Franklin were both engaged in research at a laboratory in King's College. Franklin made the best X-ray diffraction images of DNA available at the time. Shortly after Watson arrived at Cambridge, Franklin gave a lecture in which she stated that the DNA molecule was a big helix (a spiral) with a backbone of sugar and phosphate on the outside. The next day Watson and Crick built a model of the molecule, but because Watson did not take notes at the lecture, they constructed it with the backbone on the inside. They showed the model to Franklin, who explained their error and noted that their model accounted for only a small portion of the water in the molecule. When the head of the Cavendish laboratory learned of the incident, he ordered Watson and Crick to leave DNA research to the researchers at King's College. Crick returned to work on his Ph.D., but Watson continued his study of bacteria.

Little more than a year later, the chemist Linus Pauling claimed that he was close to discovering the structure of DNA. Watson and Crick believed that Pauling had beaten them to the punch. However, when Watson and Crick concluded that Pauling's model contained critical flaws, it renewed their hope. They went to a local pub to toast Pauling's failure and rededicated themselves to solving the problem. At this point they received crucial help from Wilkins that opened the door to the solution.

Wilkins had been experimenting with X-ray crystallography, and he showed Watson and Crick some of the images he had taken, as well as several made by Franklin. Although Franklin was an excellent scientist, she faced severe discrimination as a woman in what was considered a man's profession. Rather than working with her as a research partner, Wilkins treated her as his assistant. She resented his attitude and refused to share her results with him unless he changed his behavior toward her. Meanwhile, Wilkins had grown close to Watson, who provided Wilkins with a sympathetic ear for his complaints against Franklin. In early 1953 Wilkins showed Watson one of Franklin's X-ray images of DNA without her permission. This was the final piece of the puzzle that Watson and Crick needed.

The Double Helix. The image Watson saw proved that the molecule was a helix, and Watson realized that it most likely consisted of two chains of DNA. He returned to the laboratory, where he and Crick began to build models of the possible structure. They reversed their earlier model, placing the sugar-phosphate backbone on the outside of the molecule. However, one key question remained: how do the four bases in DNA—adenine, cytosine, guanine, and thymine—fit together inside the backbone? They turned to the research of Austrian-born American chemist Edwin Chargaff of the Rockefeller Institute, which showed that the DNA molecule contained equal amounts of adenine and thymine, as well as equal amounts of cytosine and guanine.

Watson and Crick still had to determine the precise arrangement of these bases within the molecule. They built large models of the molecule to test various structures. After experimenting with many configurations, Watson came to an important conclusion. In his book *The Double Helix,* he recalled that "an adenine-thymine pair held together by two hydrogen bonds was identical in shape to a cytosine-guanine pair." This realization provided the final key to the structure of DNA.

In the Watson and Crick model, the DNA molecule takes the shape of a double helix (similar to a spiral staircase or a flexible ladder), with the outside "railings" of the staircase made of sugar and phosphate. The inner "rungs" of the staircase consist of pairs of bases joined by double hydrogen bonds and connected to the sugar-phosphate "railings." Each base on one side of the staircase is joined to a complementary base on the other side—adenine joined to thymine, cytosine joined to guanine. This structure enables DNA from the parent to reproduce itself exactly in the offspring.

As cells divide during reproduction, the DNA molecule in each cell unzips itself by breaking the hydrogen bonds between the bases. Each new cell receives one unzipped half of the DNA molecule. Because each base can only pair with its complementary partner, the unzipped strand of DNA acts as a template for the creation of the other complementary half of the molecule. Because adenine only pairs up with thymine and cytosine can only be paired with guanine, there is only one way that the molecule can be reproduced in the new cell. This ensures that the structure of the offspring's DNA is an exact copy of that of the parent's DNA.

Watson and Crick had followed several false trails before discovering the correct model for DNA. But their perseverance paid off, and Watson knew they had determined the structure of DNA because, as he wrote, "the structure was too pretty not to be true."

Triumph and Controversy. Watson and Crick celebrated their discovery the same way that they celebrated Pauling's failure—by going to a pub, where they announced that they had discovered "the secret of life." In 1953 they published their findings in two issues of the journal *Nature,* in which they suggested that the structure of DNA provided an explanation for the mechanism by which genetic material copied itself. In the years that followed, experimental testing confirmed the validity of their discovery, and in 1962 Watson, Crick, and Wilkins received the Nobel Prize in physiology or medicine for their work. However, Franklin, whose X-ray images provided the crucial evidence in Watson and Crick's discovery, failed to receive any credit. She had died in 1958, four years before Watson, Crick, and Wilkins received the Nobel Prize, which is only awarded to living individuals.

Adding insult to injury, Watson painted an unflattering portrait of Franklin in his autobiographical account of the discovery, *The Double Helix*. Many of her colleagues criticized the account as inaccurate. Written in an unscientific tone, the book heaped contempt on the scientific establishment, saying, "A goodly number of scientists are not only narrow-minded and dull but also just stupid." Although Crick has publicly disagreed with much of what Watson wrote in that book, one fact is beyond dispute: their discovery was not only the most important breakthrough in biology during the twentieth century, but it was also the foundation on which the science of molecular biology stands.

Eyes on the Prize?

Although Watson and Crick worked closely, Watson's account of their collaboration in *The Double Helix* did not always ring true to Crick. In the book, Watson claims that the prospect of gaining fame and glory by winning a Nobel Prize motivated the team. However, Crick later said that he never thought about winning a Nobel Prize. "My impression," he said, "was that we were just, you know, mad keen to solve the problem." He also said that it only occurred to him several years after the discovery that "this is just the sort of thing people get prizes for."

Wilkins, Maurice Hugh Frederick

Maurice Hugh Frederick
WILKINS

born 1916

BIOPHYSICS

* **biophysicist** person who specializes in biophysics, the study of the structures and processes of organisms using the methods of physics

* **DNA** deoxyribonucleic acid, the material in chromosomes that carries genetic information from ancestor to offspring

* **X-ray diffraction** observational technique based on the fact that X rays bend when they encounter obstacles

* **biochemist** person who specializes in the science that deals with chemical compounds and processes occurring in living organisms

* **physiology** science that deals with the functions of living organisms and their parts

* **isotope** one of two or more forms of the same element

* **ultrasonic** relating to a frequency of sound above the range of human hearing

* **genetics** branch of biology that deals with heredity

* **nucleic acid** class of complex chemicals, including DNA and RNA, that is found in all living cells and viruses

The New Zealand-born biophysicist* Maurice Hugh Frederick Wilkins played an important role in unraveling the mysteries of the structure of DNA*, one of the building blocks of life. Molecules of DNA contain the information that enables hereditary traits to pass from one generation to the next and controls the production of proteins. His X-ray diffraction* work with DNA proved crucial to the research of American biochemist* James Watson and English biophysicist Francis Crick, the scientists who discovered the structure of the DNA molecule in 1953. For their work, Wilkins, Watson, and Crick jointly received the Nobel Prize in physiology* or medicine in 1962.

Early Life and Career. Born in Pangaroa, New Zealand, Wilkins was the son of an Irish physician who worked for the School Medical Service. At age six Wilkins was sent to Great Britain to attend the King Edward VI School in Birmingham. He later attended St. John's College at Cambridge University, where he received a degree in physics in 1938.

After graduating from Cambridge, Wilkins went to Birmingham University, where he continued his studies and worked as a research assistant in the physics department. He earned his doctoral degree in 1940 after completing a thesis on light emission at low temperatures. His theories on this subject were put to good use in World War II, when Wilkins applied his ideas to improving the developing technology of radar.

During the war Wilkins also worked on the separation of uranium isotopes*. In 1944 he moved to the University of California at Berkeley, where he continued this research on isotopes as part of the Manhattan Project—the secret wartime program to produce an atomic bomb.

Wilkins returned to England after the war as a lecturer at the University of St. Andrews in Scotland. Like many physicists who had worked on military projects during the war, Wilkins became disillusioned with nuclear physics and the use of science for military purposes. In searching for other beneficial areas of research, he became interested in biophysics and in the application of physics to the understanding of life.

In 1946 Wilkins and his former professor John Randall helped establish the biophysics unit at the Medical Research Council at King's College in London. The goal of this center was to merge the fields of physics and biology. Wilkins became assistant director of the Medical Research Council Unit in 1955 and served as its director from 1970 to 1980. He also played a leading role in establishing a department of biophysics at King's College, where he served as professor of molecular biology from 1963 to 1970 and professor of biophysics from 1970 to 1981. Thereafter Wilkins retired and accepted the honorary position of professor emeritus.

Research in Biophysics and DNA. Wilkins's research at the Medical Research Council began with studies on the effects of ultrasonic* waves on genetics*. After several years he turned his attention to developing a special reflecting microscope that used ultraviolet rays to study nucleic acids* in cells. That research led to his groundbreaking work on DNA.

Molecules of DNA were relatively easy to isolate, but their seemingly complicated structure made them difficult to study. In his initial research

Maurice Wilkins participated in two of the 20th century's most notable scientific efforts: the development of the atomic bomb and the discovery of the structure of DNA. His expertise in X-ray diffraction was essential to both projects.

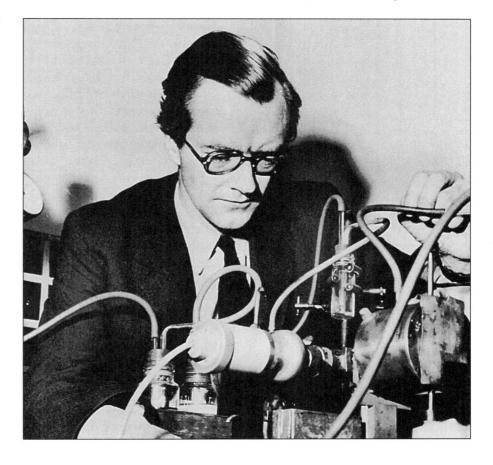

* **crystalline** composed of tiny crystals

on DNA, Wilkins used a microscope that illuminated DNA molecules, hoping to observe their structure through the reflection of light. Using this method he observed that the DNA molecule had a fiberlike shape.

A generation earlier, scientists had shown that X rays could be used to determine the spacing between atoms and the different chemical units of fiberlike molecules. Other important facts, such as the size of the units, could be determined from the details of diffraction. Wilkins assumed that X-ray diffraction could also be used to observe and analyze DNA. He prepared crystalline* samples of DNA and subjected them to X-ray analysis. In theory, the spacing of the individual atoms in the DNA should have caused the X rays to bend, or diffract, into a distinct pattern. However, Wilkins's X-ray diffraction experiments showed distinct patterns that suggested that the DNA molecule was shaped like a spiral, or helix. He also noticed that compounds within the DNA that contained nucleic acids seemed to form a regular pattern resembling steps or the rungs of a ladder. Wilkins concluded that the molecule of DNA was a double helix composed of two strands.

Wilkins shared his finding with Watson and Crick, who had already theorized that the DNA molecule was a double helix with two strands. However, Wilkins's work was crucial to the determination of the molecular structure of DNA, and it confirmed that their idea was correct. All three scientists shared the Nobel Prize for the discovery.

Who Deserves Credit? There is controversy among scientists over who deserves credit for the research that led to the discovery of the structure of DNA. Many give the credit to Wilkins, but another individual may be equally deserving. British biochemist Rosalind FRANKLIN did research on DNA at the same laboratory as Wilkins, and photos taken using her technique were much clearer and showed more detail than the X rays that Wilkins took. Wilkins and Franklin were quite competitive, and although they were colleagues, their professional relationship was strained. Wilkins showed Franklin's photos and other data to Watson and Crick, who based their conclusions on the two sets of photos. Unfortunately for Franklin, few women received the respect they deserved within the scientific community at the time. Moreover, she died before Watson, Crick, and Wilkins received their Nobel Prize, and the Nobel Foundation does not award the prize posthumously*.

Wilkins continued his research with nucleic acids and later began working with RNA* as well. RNA is a substance found in cells that delivers the genetic instructions in DNA to the places in cells that are responsible for manufacturing protein. Through his work Wilkins showed that RNA also has a spiral structure like DNA. He has earned many awards, and he has received several honorary doctorates. In 1959 he was named a Fellow of the Royal Society, and the following year he received the Albert Lasker Award. (*See also* **Watson and Crick.**)

* **posthumous** occurring after the death of an individual

* **RNA** ribonucleic acid, a cellular molecule similar to DNA that is involved in the production of proteins in the cell

Ian
WILMUT

born 1944

EMBRYOLOGY

* **embryologist** scientist who studies the development of an egg and sperm into an embryo, an organism at the early stages of development before birth or hatching

* **genetic** relating to genes, the basic units of heredity that carry traits from ancestors to offspring

The Scottish embryologist* Ian Wilmut is best known for his groundbreaking work in cloning, the process by which an identical copy of an organism is created using a cell from that organism and fusing its nucleus with a recipient egg cell's nucleus. Wilmut made history in 1996 when he was part of a team that cloned a mammal, a lamb named Dolly, from the fully formed cells of an adult sheep. This historic achievement proved that animals could be cloned from adult cells, but it also set off a public debate about the benefits and dangers of cloning and other forms of genetic* engineering.

Born in Hampton Lucey, England, Wilmut attended the University of Nottingham and received a Ph.D. in animal genetics in 1971 from the University of Cambridge. For his doctoral thesis he investigated the effects of freezing on pig semen. Two years after earning his doctoral degree, he successfully created a calf—which he named Frosty—from a frozen embryo.

In 1974 Wilmut went to work for the Animal Research Breeding Station near Edinburgh, Scotland, now known as the Roslin Institute. Since then Wilmut has remained at the institute, performing research on genetic engineering and cloning. His years of hard work at the institute reached their apex in 1996 with the successful cloning of Dolly.

While working on the insertion of genes into sheep embryos in the mid-1980s, Wilmut pondered the possibility of cloning mammals from differentiated adult cells (specialized cells that form after a certain stage in the development process of embryos). These cells are programmed to become, for example, nerve, bone, or skin cells. Successful cloning had been accomplished before this time but only from undifferentiated cells at the embryonic stage or from the adult cells of plants and lower animals such as frogs. All previous attempts to clone mammals from adult cells had resulted in failure.

In 1990 Wilmut and his colleague, biologist Keith CAMPBELL, began work on cloning mammals. After five years of work, Wilmut and Campbell succeeded in cloning two Welsh mountain sheep—named Megan and Morag—from differentiated embryo cells. With this achievement, the two scientists had pioneered a technique that halted the development of embryo cells at a stage just before the nucleus is transferred to the fertilized egg cells. The technique enabled Wilmut and Campbell to synchronize the growth cycles of the embryo and egg cells, which made successful cloning easier and more reliable.

Using this process Wilmut and Campbell attempted to clone a mammal from adult cells. They used cells from the mammary gland of a pregnant adult sheep. Wilmut and Campbell then inserted the cells into another sheep's unfertilized egg cell, whose nucleus had been removed. They implanted the resulting embryo into a third sheep, which served as surrogate mother and gave birth to Dolly after the normal gestation period for sheep—about 148 days. Continuing their studies, in 1997, Wilmut and Campbell produced Polly, a sheep cloned from fetal skin cells that had been genetically altered to contain a human gene.

The announcement of the successful cloning of Dolly set off an international debate on the ethics and future of cloning research, particularly on the implications of cloning human cells. Wilmut believes that cloning can be used to improve livestock and as a source of valuable human proteins for medical purposes. He also feels that cloning is particularly useful for the study of genetic diseases, such as diabetes and Parkinson's disease, for which there are presently no cures. Others think that cloning might one day produce animal organs that would be suitable for transplanting into humans, helping to save lives. Still others maintain that cloning might be used to save endangered species.

Critics, however, question the ethics of using animals in this way. Even more troubling for many people, including Wilmut, is the possibility of cloning humans. Despite criticism, the process of cloning will no doubt develop further as scientists probe the experimental limits of life.

Edmund Beecher
WILSON
1856–1939
CYTOLOGY, EMBRYOLOGY, GENETICS

* **evolution** historical development of a biological group such as a species

Edmund Beecher Wilson was one of the most important biologists of the late 1800s and early 1900s. His extensive investigation of the structure and function of cells led to many of the key findings that form the bases of current theories of cell biology and its role in reproduction and evolution*. Modern biologists are still investigating many of the problems that Wilson studied. His groundbreaking textbook, *The Cell in Development and Inheritance,* published in 1896, is a valuable resource because many of the problems it posed remain unresolved. Wilson made outstanding contributions to the theoretical and experimental aspects of biology as well as to the gathering of knowledge and education in that field.

Life and Career

Wilson was born in 1856, three years before the publication of *The Origin of Species,* the famous book in which the English biologist Charles Darwin outlined his theory of evolution by natural selection*. At the time biology was not an experimental science but one dominated by the study of natural history. However, Wilson's work played a central role in changing the orientation of the discipline.

Early Life and Career. Wilson was one of five children, whose father served as a judge in Illinois. When Wilson was three years old, his family moved to Chicago after his father became a circuit court judge. Throughout his youth Wilson divided his time between his parents' home and the home of his mother's sister in Geneva, Illinois. During that time he cultivated two interests—living things and music—that captivated him for the rest of his life. While in Geneva, he spent much time collecting specimens that he stored in a special room set aside in his aunt's house. When Wilson was 16, his uncle suggested he take over as the master of a local school that Wilson's brother had run the previous year.

This experience whetted Wilson's appetite for learning and he decided to enroll at Antioch College, a small institution in Ohio that his cousin, Samuel Clarke, attended. At Antioch, Wilson received his first exposure to formal instruction in zoology, botany, and chemistry. Meanwhile, Clarke had entered the Sheffield Scientific School at Yale University, which he also recommended to Wilson. Because Wilson lacked the proper educational background to enter Yale, he spent a year studying at the University of Chicago and enrolled at Yale at the age of 19. He had had his first encounter with the studies of heredity and evolution at Yale. Shortly thereafter, he transferred to the newly founded Johns Hopkins University in Baltimore, again following his cousin's example.

The years that Wilson spent at Johns Hopkins set the course of his future work. He began his first original investigations under the direction of teachers who emphasized the importance of research and pointed out the many unsolved problems in the field of biology. After receiving his Ph.D. in 1881, Wilson spent a year abroad, traveling to England, Germany, and Italy, and working with many prominent biologists. The most important part of the trip for Wilson's future development as a biologist was the time he spent at the zoological station in Naples, Italy, where his thoughts about future biological research gained shape.

After he returned to the United States, Wilson spent a year teaching at Williams College in Massachusetts, followed by a year as a lecturer at the Massachusetts Institute of Technology. He then took a post as head of the biology department at Bryn Mawr College in Pennsylvania, where he remained until 1891 when he was appointed chair of the zoology department at Columbia University. Before taking the position at Columbia, Wilson spent another year in Europe, this time focused on working with the famous zoologist Theodor Boveri in Munich and the experimental embryologists* Hans Driesch and Curt Herbst in Naples. During this and later trips, Wislon spent considerable time at marine stations.

* **natural selection** theory that within a given species, individuals best adapted to the environment live longer and produce more offspring than other individuals, resulting in changes in the species over time

* **embryologist** scientist who studies the development of an egg and sperm into an embryo, an organism at the early stages of development before birth or hatching

Later Life and Career. At Columbia, Wilson performed his most important research and published *The Cell in Development and Inheritance.* He was a popular professor who taught his students to view biology as a combination of such fields as heredity, evolution, and embryology, which departed from the traditional approach that treated these areas separately. During his years at Columbia, Wilson also worked at marine research stations, most prominently the Marine Biological Laboratory at Woods Hole, Massachusetts. He felt that the study of living organisms, particularly marine life-forms, was important for a true understanding of biology.

Wilson remained an active researcher for many years, and toward the end of his life he spent a great deal of time preparing a revised edition of his book. Published when Wilson was 69, the new edition won an award from the National Academy of Sciences of the United States as well as a gold medal from the Linnean Society of London. Wilson retired from his position at Columbia in 1928 and died 11 years later at the age of 82.

Scientific Accomplishments

Wilson's active career spanned almost 70 years, and it can be divided accordingly by his main interests at different stages of his life. The first stage lasted from his college years to the time he took over the zoology department at Columbia when he focused on descriptive embryology and morphology*. In his first dozen years at Columbia, he studied experimental embryology, including the organization of the egg and the effects of various substances on reproductive processes within the cell. During the final stage of his career, which lasted until his death, he was concerned with heredity, examining how the Austrian geneticist* Gregor Mendel's theory of transmission of traits related to cytology*, the determination of sex, and evolution.

His overriding concern in all of these studies was to determine how an individual organism develops from an egg. He searched for the specific biological mechanisms by which traits pass from parents to children, and he tried to understand how that process occurs in the developing embryo. Wilson pioneered the study of how activity at the cellular level influences development. He examined interactions between the cell nucleus and the cytoplasm*, between the egg and sperm, between layers of embryonic tissue, and between the embryo and its environment. He realized that knowledge of the structure, functions, and organization of the cell was necessary to understand the problems in tissues and organisms. Wilson's emphasis on the cell's role in heredity and evolution marked the beginning of a new era of reproductive biology and genetics.

Descriptive Embryology and Morphology. Wilson's earliest important work involved the family of sea creatures called *Renilla,* which includes jellyfish and coral. Among other findings, he noted differences in the first appearance of cell division within the eggs of these creatures. The noted biologist T.H. Huxley recognized Wilson's work and asked him to read the paper reporting his findings to the Royal Society of London. Following his work with *Renilla,* Wilson collaborated with William Sedgwick, a close friend from his days at Yale and Johns Hopkins, to write a textbook

* **morphology** branch of anatomy that deals with the form and structure of animals and plants

* **geneticist** scientist who specializes in genetics, the science of heredity

* **cytology** branch of biology that deals with the structure, function, and life history of cells

* **cytoplasm** organic and inorganic substances outside the cell's nuclear membrane

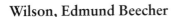

A Wealth of Talents

A dedicated scientist, Edmund Wilson had interests that ranged far from the field of biology. He was an outstanding musician and was once called the best amateur cellist in New York. His daughter shared his musical gifts, enjoying a career as a professional cellist. Wilson loved sailing and he served as captain on many scientific expeditions and pleasure cruises out of Woods Hole, Bermuda, and other places. He also had a gift for languages. He spoke German, French, Italian, Spanish, and Arabic, as well as English.

titled *General Biology,* which was published in 1886. Most biology textbooks of the day focused on classifying organisms and exploring their evolutionary development. However, Wilson and Sedgwick's book presented biology from a chemical and physical standpoint, emphasizing the importance of an organism's individual atoms and molecules in determining the properties of the organism itself. The book also tried to demonstrate how all organic processes involved an interaction between an organism and the environment.

Thereafter, Wilson turned to the study of early development in earthworms. He was particularly concerned with tracing the origin of the mesoderm, a layer of embryonic tissue that eventually forms the muscles, connective tissues, urinary and genital organs, and blood vessels. He discovered that certain cells were specifically assigned early in the development process to form the mesoderm and that all mesodermal tissue originated from these cells. He called this a mosaic pattern of development. He found, however, that the earthworm was not suitable for his studies because it was difficult to trace the cells through several stages of division. A colleague at Johns Hopkins pointed out that cellular division in marine worms of the family *Nereis* was precise, regular, and easier to trace. Wilson spent the next five years studying cell division in marine worms, producing discoveries that had a profound influence on biology as well as on his career.

Wilson wanted to determine the pattern by which cell division occurs in an organism. To do so, he had to study the cell-by-cell development of embryos from fertilization of the egg to the formation of the blastula, a hollow ball of cells from which the embryo grows. Wilson developed a method called cell lineage, in which he observed the division of an individual cell and noted the exact location of all the daughter cells produced during the process. This enabled him to follow the pattern of cell division and to determine the ancestry of every cell in the blastula.

Armed with this knowledge, Wilson proved that animals with three layers of reproductive cells could be classified into groups based on the formation patterns of their mesoderm. One group showed the mosaic pattern he discovered in earthworms. The other group (including higher animals and humans) showed a pattern in which the mesoderm originates in pouches in the digestive tract of the gastrula, the stage of embryonic development following the blastula. Wilson showed that cell lineage provided a way to establish similarities between different organisms during the development of the embryo that were often not noticeable in later stages of development.

Wilson's work on cell lineage led him to believe that the problem of tracing similarities between organisms was more difficult than suspected at the time. Although their cell division patterns were similar, he noticed that large groups of animals showed important differences during embryonic development. For example, some structures that grew to be very similar in later stages of development derived from quite different types of embryonic cells. Consequently, cell lineage could only suggest very broad evolutionary relationships between organisms. Wilson realized that because the process of embryonic development is evolutionary, an organism's current pattern of development does not necessarily correspond to the patterns of development experienced by earlier forms of the organism. In his future work, Wilson turned from an emphasis on morphology to a study of processes at the cellular level to understand evolution.

Experimental Embryology and Cytology. The time he spent working with Theodor Boveri in Munich influenced the next phase of Wilson's career. Boveri had reached the conclusion that the nucleus, and particularly the chromosomes* in the nucleus, was the key factor in determining an organism's heredity. He also believed that the chromosomes specifically influenced development, a point that he demonstrated experimentally some years later. The other important influence on Wilson at this time was the experimental embryology of Hans Driesch and Curt Herbst at Naples. Both men were exploring the mosaic theory of development proposed by the German anatomist Wilhelm Roux. Roux stated that hereditary material in a parent cell is divided qualitatively among the daughter cells during cell division. In other words, the material that leads to development of muscle cells is divided equally among the daughter cells, as is material that produces liver cells and bone cells. Roux believed that each type of cell had only one type of determinant—muscle cells had only muscle determinants, and bone cells had only bone determinants.

According to Roux the various organs and tissues of the adult organism develop from these specific types of hereditary material. However, Driesch had performed experiments in which he isolated cells from young embryos at various stages of development and found that each could develop into a normal organism. This contradicted Roux's theory and emphasized that the embryonic process was much more flexible than had been imagined. It also suggested that each cell contained all the hereditary material necessary to create a new organism and was not restricted in the way Roux had imagined. The disagreement between the theories of Roux and Driesch focused Wilson's attention on the mechanism by which cells differentiate into tissues, organs, and systems. This question turned Wilson away from studies of morphology and toward work in experimental embryology.

Unlike many of his colleagues, Wilson refused to take sides in the debate between the supporters of Roux and those of Driesch. Wilson's work with *Nereis* had shown him that developmental processes are determined and yet flexible and that they show the effects of interaction between heredity and environment. After several years of study, Wilson began to agree with Driesch because he had accounted for the facts of embryonic development more thoroughly and consistently than had Roux. Driesch had also considered the exact process of cell differentiation* as more than simply the segregation of hereditary material among daughter cells. Wilson reasoned that the key to the regularity and flexibility of cell differentiation must be found in the organization of the cytoplasm, the cellular material that lies outside of the nucleus. Because each daughter cell receives the same number and type of chromosomes as the parent cell, he thought that differentiation must be controlled by variations in the cytoplasm. He proposed that the cytoplasm was preorganized, so that the different substances responsible for the development of various tissues and

* **chromosome** structure in the cell that contains the DNA (genes) that transmit unique genetic information

* **differentiation** process whereby cells, tissues, and structures are specialized to perform certain functions

181

organs are located in specific parts of the cytoplasm. Many biologists criticized this theory, arguing that it pushed back the problem of differentiation by one step. Instead of occurring in the embryo, in Wilson's theory differentiation took place in the cytoplasm of the egg. Moreover, his theory still failed to explain the mechanism by which differentiation took place. Later work showed that, although the cytoplasm does show local variations, it has little to do with differentiation in many species.

Stimulated by his work with Boveri, Wilson began extensive research into the cellular processes associated with cell division, particularly those involving the development of the egg. He focused on studying the movement of chromosomes, especially the formation of structures known as spindles. Just before a cell divides, its chromosomes are differentiated, segregated, and then distributed along an axis between the two centers of cytoplasm that will become two different cells after division. This axis, called a spindle, contains a distinct region at each end called a pole. In Wilson's day, the accepted theory said that these poles were formed when centrosomes—material from chromosomes of the sperm and egg—fuse together, divide, and move through the cytoplasm. Through close observation Wilson determined that the replication of centrosomes was unrelated to the replication of chromosomes. He said that both centrosomes and chromosomes doubled in response to some basic rhythm in the cell's activity. He proved this by examining the activity of fragments of fertilized mollusk eggs. He observed that the same rhythmic changes occurred in the egg fragments as in the portion of the egg that contained the nucleus, although the two parts of the egg had been physically separated.

The Role of the Nucleus

While he was pursuing his work on the cytology of cell division, Wilson prepared the first edition of *The Cell in Development and Inheritance*. The book was an outstanding compilation of information on cell biology and structure. It also presented Wilson with an opportunity to present his view that a basic understanding of all aspects of the cell was essential for better understanding the basic processes of evolution, including heredity, variation, and differentiation.

Chromosomes and Heredity. Wilson was convinced that the nucleus was the center of hereditary information and that chromatin, a substance contained in the chromosomes, was its active agent. He also believed that the nucleus controlled the cytoplasm through chemical processes. However, he had too little information about the chemistry of chromatin to find out how the nucleus exerted this control to determine the character of the cytoplasm. He also realized that the cytoplasm influences the nucleus as well and that this interaction between the two determines the development of an organism. The nucleus and the cytoplasm perform different functions that complement each other and must be understood in relation to one another.

Wilson next turned his attention to seeking connections between the work of Gregor Mendel and cytology, the study of the structure and functions of the cell. Mendel was the first to propose that specific hereditary traits were determined by genetic factors known as genes. His work was largely ignored during his lifetime but was rediscovered in 1900. It was one of Wilson's students, Walter Sutton, who first made the connection between cytology and Mendel's work. Sutton was studying synapsis, a process during which two homologous chromosomes (those containing the same sequence of genes) are paired during division of reproductive cells. When a reproductive cell divides, half of its chromosomes go to one of the daughter cells and the other half go into the other daughter cell. Sutton found that the chromosomes that divide during this process are members of homologous pairs, not simply two random chromosomes from the same cell. Each chromosome could thus be considered either the counterpart of one of Mendel's factors or a structure that carries such a factor.

Working from clues provided by the work of another former student, Wilson set out to see if an unpaired chromosome present in the males of some animal species might determine sex inheritance. Wilson called this unpaired chromosome the X chromosome. His work led him to conclude that females normally have two X chromosomes (XX pattern), while males normally have an X and a Y chromosome (XY pattern). These chromosome pairs separate during the production of egg and sperm cells, so that all egg cells have a single X chromosome and a sperm may have either an X or a Y chromosome. If a sperm with an X chromosome fertilizes the egg, the offspring will be female (XX); if the egg is fertilized by a sperm with a Y chromosome, the offspring will be male (XY). This discovery, also made independently by the Bryn Mawr College biologist Nettie Stevens, proved that chromosomes determined sex. It also marked the first time that a specific pair of chromosomes was linked with hereditary traits.

During the years following this work, Wilson published a series of studies that outlined his theory on the role of chromosomes in sex determination. Among his findings was that the size of X and Y chromosomes in insect species varied greatly. In some they were nearly identical in size, while in others the Y was much smaller or nonexistent. He also found different patterns that included XXY in females and X but no Y in males. He attributed these cases to the failure of the X and Y chromosomes to split during the formation of sperm cells. These findings led him to suggest that the Y chromosome had degenerated over the course of history so that it contained either inactive chromatin or chromatin that was also found in other chromosomes. Wilson was the first to recognize that the Y chromosome has little hereditary function in determining sex or any other trait. He proposed that the difference between the X and Y chromosomes may be due to a chemical substance contained in or associated with the X chromosome that influences the development of the organism.

Based on Wilson's findings, his colleague and friend Thomas Hunt MORGAN developed a chromosome theory of inheritance. Morgan's work supported Wilson's theory that chromosomes determined sex, and that the presence or absence of certain traits was determined by the sex of the individual. Wilson, in turn, actively supported Morgan's work. Although he still had no proof that genes were actually a part of chromosomes, he believed that such a conclusion was consistent with the data and offered the

Sources of Inspiration

Two men who greatly influenced Wilson's career were his teacher and mentor William Keith Brooks and the German biologist Theodor Boveri. Both touched Wilson on a spiritual and creative level, and they also appealed to his scientific side. Brooks encouraged Wilson to read the work of philosophers such as Aristotle and David Hume. This led him to ponder life's deeper questions, not merely record and classify life. Wilson developed a strong personal and professional relationship with Boveri and considered him "far more than a brilliant scientific discoverer and teacher. He was a many-sided man, gifted in many directions, an excellent musician, a good amateur painter, and we found many points of contact outside of the realm of science."

* **Golgi bodies** network of structures in living cells that is active in the modification and transport of proteins

* **mitochondria** structure inside a cell that contains the enzymes necessary for energy production

best explanation for it. One theory that Morgan's work seemed to support was the idea that, during the division of sperm or egg cells, chromosomes actually come together and wrap around each other to share genetic information. Wilson showed that this coming together (called synapsis) really occurred, but the actual exchange of chromosome parts was not proven for many years.

Beyond the Chromosome. Following his work on chromosomes, Wilson set out to determine what other parts of the cell affect heredity. He studied various structures within the cytoplasm of scorpions and insects, including Golgi bodies* and mitochondria*. Both of these structures increase in size and break apart so that each daughter cell receives an equal number of them each time the cell divides. However, these bodies are all very similar and do not possess the genetic individuality of chromosomes. In studying the cytoplasm, Wilson repeated his earlier view that it was impossible to make clear distinctions about the effects of the nucleus and cytoplasm in heredity. He argued that scientists must study both of them to determine the precise ways in which the nucleus and cytoplasm affect each other. Over time Wilson came to see the cell as a structure that is constantly changing. It is always building itself up and tearing itself down to maintain a balance between stability and change, heredity and variation, and maintenance and differentiation. He determined that the only constant in cell life is the basic organization of molecules and the relations between them that produce life.

By the early 1920s so much new information had been gathered about cytology that Wilson decided to revise his textbook. Like the previous editions, the third edition (titled *The Cell in Development and Heredity*) related the ideas of heredity, cellular structure and function, and development to evolution and adaptation. The central question of evolution was how hereditary variations occur. Wilson agreed with Darwin that heredity was controlled at the level of the cell. By showing that heredity was a phenomenon controlled by the chromosomes, Wilson provided experimental support for Mendel's ideas about heredity. This was a key element in forming a comprehensive theory of evolution in the 1930s.

Despite his support of Darwin's basic ideas, Wilson disagreed with many particular features of his theory. He felt Darwin placed too much emphasis on the accumulation of small variations, which Darwin could not prove were inherited, as a vehicle of evolutionary change. Without making a distinction between inherited and acquired variations, Darwin failed to provide a mechanism to explain the origin of adaptations. Wilson also felt that Darwin placed too much importance on random chance in the origin of species. Regardless of his disagreements with aspects of Darwin's theory, however, Wilson ultimately admitted that it was "the one really simple and intelligible explanation of organic adaptation . . . that has thus far been placed in our hands."

Wilson's Scientific Methodology. Wilson's early training in morphology did not prevent him from quickly adopting an experimental and quantitative approach to biology. He believed that until that time, the great weakness of biologists was their tendency to speculate and construct

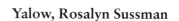

theories without facts. Wilson believed that the only way to reach true conclusions was to observe carefully, construct hypotheses based on observation, and conduct experiments to confirm or disprove hypotheses. The process of forming hypotheses was crucial to the experimental process because experiments had to be designed to test a specific proposition. Unless hypotheses were tested by experimentation, they led to oversimplified or misleading ideas. His emphasis on experimentation was rooted in the belief that biologists must understand the chemical interactions that occur within the cell before they can understand the nature of life.

The other key idea in Wilson's methodology was his belief that science was not simply an accumulated body of facts but a process of reasoning, understanding, and testing that understanding by observing the natural world. He felt that one should always explore new ideas and unresolved issues but never propose untested solutions. He instilled in his students the idea that science is the activity of humans who do not accept ideas at face value. It is a creative process that, although based in theory, is only valuable when applied to practical problems.

Rosalyn Sussman
YALOW

born 1921

MEDICINE, PHYSICS

* **pharmacological** relating to pharmacology, the science dealing with the preparation, uses, and effects of drugs

Rosalyn Yalow developed a sensitive yet simple means to measure small amounts of substances in blood or other bodily fluids. Because of her work, scientists can determine the concentrations of hormones, vitamins, enzymes, and drugs in a person's body.

The American medical physicist Rosalyn Sussman Yalow helped develop radioimmunoassay (RIA), a technique used to measure small amounts of biological and pharmacological* substances in blood or other bodily fluids. Now in widespread use, RIA helps medical professionals diagnose and monitor health problems by measuring the concentrations of hormones*, viruses, enzymes*, vitamins, drugs, and other substances in the body.

Born in the Bronx, New York, Yalow is the daughter of Russian and German immigrants who instilled in her a great enthusiasm for education. While attending Walton High School in the Bronx, she became interested in science, especially chemistry. However, her focus shifted to physics during her undergraduate years at Hunter College in New York.

185

* **hormone** internally secreted substance transported by body fluids to stimulate the functions of organs or tissues

* **enzyme** any of numerous complex proteins that are produced by living cells and catalyze specific biochemical reactions at body temperature

* **isotope** one of two or more forms of the same element

* **metabolism** physical and chemical processes involved in maintaining life

* **insulin** hormone produced by the pancreas that is used in the treatment of diabetes

* **physiology** science that deals with the functions of living organisms and their parts

* **posthumous** occurring after the death of an individual

Yalow graduated with a B.A. in 1941 and went to study physics at the University of Illinois, where she was the only woman in the College of Engineering. She worked as a teaching assistant in the school. After earning her Ph.D. in physics at Illinois in 1945—only the second woman in the school's history to do so—Yalow moved back to New York City to work as an assistant engineer at a private research laboratory. The following year she began teaching physics at Hunter College, the women's section of the College of the City of New York, where she remained for four years.

Yalow also worked as a part-time consultant for a hospital run by the Veterans Administration (VA). Her work for the VA included research on the medical uses of radioactive substances. In 1950 Yalow left Hunter and took a full-time position with the VA.

At the Veterans Administration, Yalow began doing research with Solomon Berson, a physician who specialized in internal medicine. Working together, they began investigating the medical applications of radioactive isotopes*. Their research led to the discovery of new ways of using such isotopes in the measurement of blood volume, the study of iodine metabolism*, and the diagnosis of thyroid disease.

Yalow and Berson also used radioactive isotopes to investigate adult-onset diabetes. It was through their studies of the insulin* levels of people with diabetes that Yalow and Berson developed their groundbreaking radioimmunoassay technique, which used radioactive isotopes to measure small amounts of insulin in the blood. In the years following the discovery of this technique, radioimmunoassay has found hundreds of other applications. Using this technique, scientists can quickly and precisely detect and measure very small concentrations of enzymes, hormones, and hundreds of other substances in blood or other bodily fluids.

A trailblazer for women in the field of physics, Yalow has won many honors and awards. In 1977 she won the Nobel Prize in physiology* or medicine for her development of the RIA technique. (Berson died in 1972 and could have shared the prize, but the Nobel Foundation does not make awards posthumously*.) In 1976 she became the first woman to win the Albert Lasker Prize for basic medical research. Thereafter, she taught and continued her research at several universities and institutes.

Robert Mearns
YERKES

1876–1956

COMPARATIVE PSYCHOLOGY

Robert Mearns Yerkes was a pioneer in the study of the psychology of nonhuman primates, especially monkeys and apes. The research laboratory he founded in Orange Park, Florida, later named the Yerkes Regional Primate Research Center in his honor, is the world's leading site for research in primate behavior.

Yerkes grew up in rural Pennsylvania where his close relationship with animals influenced his choice of career. He attended Ursinus College before enrolling at Harvard University, where he earned his Ph.D. in psychology in 1902. By that same year, he had launched his scientific career with publications and was appointed instructor in psychology at Harvard. Although he had wanted to be a physician, his interest in laboratory research led him away from a career in medicine.

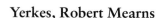

Yerkes was one of the first psychologists to study the behavior of animals in the laboratory rather than in the field. He began by working with invertebrates (animals without backbones) but soon turned his attention to studying sensation, instinct, imitation, and learning in vertebrates (animals with backbones). A study in which he examined the behavior of a dancing mouse was key to establishing mice and rats as the animals used in psychological research. He was convinced, however, that the study of apes would be of greater importance to psychology because apes were the animals most closely related to humans.

Yerkes served on Harvard's faculty until the United States entered World War I in 1917. For the next two years, he was in charge of psychological testing of army personnel. The extensive testing brought psychology out of its academic isolation and made it a part of the mainstream world. After the war Yerkes headed programs run by the government's National Research Council that examined the characteristics of human migration. The studies were intended to help develop the country's immigration laws. Throughout the 1920s and 1930s, he served on many committees that had a significant impact on American science.

In 1924 Yerkes left the National Research Council and joined Yale University's new Institute of Psychology to work with nonhuman primates. Five years later, he founded an experimental laboratory in Florida. Around the same time, Yerkes and his wife published a groundbreaking book titled *The Great Apes: A Study of Anthropoid Life*. For many years, this work remained the standard for information on the biology and psychology of monkeys and apes. Yerkes served as head of the research center for 12 years and retired from the university in 1944.

During his career, Yerkes provided strong leadership and organizational skills not only to the lab but also to the whole field of psychology. He was the founding editor of the *Journal of Animal Behavior*, president of the American Psychological Association, and later a leading figure in reforming the structure of that organization. He continued his research even after his retirement, playing an active role in organizing psychology's contribution to the defense effort during World War II.

GLOSSARY

A

abscess   localized collection of pus in the body surrounded by an inflamed area

absorption spectrum   measure of material's absorption of light at different wavelengths

acetylcholine (ACh)   substance that transmits nerve impulses and forms salts that lower blood pressure

action potential   temporary change in the electric charge on the surface of a nerve or muscle cell that occurs when the cell is stimulated

alkaloid   group of naturally occurring organic bases containing nitrogen, such as caffeine, morphine, and nicotine

amino acid   class of compounds that function as the building blocks of proteins

anemia   disease marked by the reduction of oxygen-carrying material in the blood

anesthetic   substance that causes loss of sensation with or without loss of consciousness

anthropologist   scientist who specializes in the study of human beings, especially in relation to origins and cultural characteristics

anthropology   study of human beings, especially in relation to origins and cultural characteristics

anthropometrist   one who studies measurements of the human body to determine differences and similarities among cultural groups

antibacterial   referring to substances that hinder the growth of bacteria, microscopic organisms that can cause infection and disease

antibiotic   any chemical substance produced by various microscopic organisms that hinders the growth of or destroys other harmful microorganisms

antibody   protein produced by the immune system to neutralize the presence of a foreign protein in the body

antiserum   serum containing antibodies; used to treat, or give temporary protection against, certain diseases

archaeological   referring to the scientific study of material remains of past human cultures, usually by excavating ruins

archaeology   scientific study of material remains of past human cultures, usually by excavating ruins

autonomic nervous system   part of the nervous system that supplies the smooth and cardiac muscles and glandular tissues with nerves and controls involuntary actions; consists of the sympathetic and parasympathetic nervous systems

B

bacteriological   related to the study of bacteria, microscopic organisms that can cause infection and disease

bacteriologist   specialist who studies microscopic organisms called bacteria that can cause infection and disease

bacteriology   science that deals with bacteria, microscopic organisms that can cause infection and disease

biochemist   person who specializes in the science that deals with chemical compounds and processes occurring in living organisms

biochemistry   science that deals with chemical compounds and processes occurring in living organisms

biophysicist   person who specializes in biophysics, the study of the structures and processes of organisms using the methods of physics

biophysics   study of the structures and processes of organisms using the methods of physics

C

cadaver   dead body, especially one intended for dissection

cannibalism   eating of the flesh of an animal by another animal of the same kind; also eating of human flesh by another human

Glossary

cardiac   of, near, or related to the heart

cardiology   study of the heart and its functions in health and disease

cerebral cortex   outer layer of the gray tissue of the brain that is responsible for higher nervous functions

chromosome   structure in the cell that contains the DNA (genes) that transmit unique genetic information

clinical   related to the observation and treatment of disease in actual patients rather than in artificial experiments

coagulation   transformation of a liquid into a semi-solid or solid mass; clotting

Communist   referring to Communism, a social system in which land, goods, and the means of production are owned by the state or community rather than by individuals

congenital   existing at birth

coronary thrombosis   blood clot that develops in a cavity of the heart

corpuscle   blood cell

cretinism   thyroid deficiency that causes arrested mental and physical development

crystalline   composed of tiny crystals

culture (noun)   microorganisms, such as bacteria or tissue, grown in a specially prepared nutrient substance for scientific study

culture (verb)   to grow microorganisms, such as bacteria or tissue, in a specially prepared nutrient substance for scientific study

cytogenetics   study of heredity based on techniques used to examine the formation, structure, and function of cells

cytological   relating to cytology, the branch of biology that deals with the structure, function, and life history of cells

cytologist   specialist in the branch of biology that deals with the structure, function, and life history of cells

cytology   branch of biology that deals with the structure, function, and life history of cells

cytoplasm   organic and inorganic substances outside the cell's nuclear membrane

D

differentiated   referring to the process whereby cells, tissues, and structures are specialized to perform certain functions

differentiation   process whereby cells, tissues, and structures are specialized to perform certain functions

diuretic   substance that increases the flow of urine

DNA   deoxyribonucleic acid, the material in chromosomes that carries genetic information from ancestor to offspring

E

electrophysiology   branch of physiology that deals with the basic mechanisms by which electric currents are generated within living organisms

embryo   organism at the early stages of development before birth or hatching

embryologist   scientist who studies the development of an egg and sperm into an embryo, an organism at the early stages of development before birth or hatching

embryology   branch of biology that deals with embryos, organisms at the early stages of development before birth or hatching, and their development

endocrinology   study of the physiology of the endocrine glands, which secrete hormones into the bloodstream

entomologist   specialist in entomology, a branch of science dealing with insects

enzyme   any of numerous complex proteins that are produced by living cells and catalyze specific biochemical reactions at body temperature

ethnologist   one who practices ethnology, the study of the division of humans into races and their origin, distribution, relations, and characteristics

ethnology   study of the division of humans into races and their origin, distribution, relations, and characteristics

eugenics   study of improving human heredity by means of genetic control

evolution   historical development of a biological group such as a species

extract   solution that contains the essential components of a more complex material

F

fermentation   chemical reaction in which complex organic compounds are split into relatively simple substances

G

gastric   of or relating to the stomach

gastrointestinal   relating to or affecting the stomach and intestines

general paresis   brain disease marked by mental deterioration, speech disturbances, and progressive muscular weakness

genetic   relating to genes, the basic units of heredity that carry traits from ancestors to offspring

geneticist   scientist who specializes in genetics, the science of heredity

genetics   branch of biology that deals with heredity

genome   set of chromosomes that contains the genetic information of an organism

glucose   natural sugar found in many fruits and animal tissues

Golgi bodies   network of structures in living cells that is active in the modification and transport of proteins

H

helix   spiral or coil

hematology   study of the formation, structure, and diseases of the blood

hemoglobin   protein in red blood cells that carries oxygen to the tissues of the body

hemophilia   disease characterized by the delayed clotting of blood

histamine   compound found in mammalian tissues that is released during allergic reactions and causes the dilation of blood vessels, the contraction of smooth muscle, and the stimulation of gastric acid secretion

histologist   scientist who studies the structure of tissues at the microscopic level

histology   branch of anatomy that deals with the minute structure of animal and plant tissues, observable only through a microscope

hormone   internally secreted substance transported by body fluids to stimulate the functions of organs or tissues

humanism   system of thought in which human interests and values are of primary importance

humoral   having to do with bodily fluids

I

immunology   science that deals with the immune system, which protects the body from foreign substances, cells, and tissue by causing an immune response

inoculate   to introduce a disease agent into an animal or plant to produce a mild form of the disease and render the organism immune

inoculation   introduction of a disease agent into an animal or plant to produce a mild form of the disease and render the organism immune

insulin   hormone produced by the pancreas that is used in the treatment of diabetes

invertebrate   animal without a backbone

isotope   one of two or more forms of the same element

L

legume   edible family of plants, including peas and beans, that carries seeds in pods

lymphatic system   system of vessels that produces lymph, a fluid that removes bacteria and proteins from tissues and supplies white blood cells

M

manometer   instrument for measuring the pressure of gases and vapors

Marxism   social, political, and economic principles advocated by philosopher Karl Marx

Marxist   person who follows the social, political, and economic principles advocated by Karl Marx

meiosis   special method of cell division to produce reproductive cells that contain half the number of chromosomes found in all other cells of the body

metabolism   physical and chemical processes involved in maintaining life

microbe   microscopic organism

Glossary

microbiologist   scientist who studies microscopic life-forms, such as bacteria and viruses

microbiology   study of microscopic organisms

microorganism   plant, animal, or bacterium so small that it can only be seen through a microscope

microscopy   skilled scientific use of a microscope

mitochondria   structure inside a cell that contains the enzymes necessary for energy production

monocotyledon   class of plants with seeds that contain only one leaf, leaves that have parallel veins, and flower structures that are arranged in groups of three

morphology   branch of anatomy that deals with the form and structure of animals and plants

mutant   abnormal or untypical form of an organism produced by a mutation, or alteration, of its genetic material

mutation   relatively permanent change in the structure of a material

myocardium   muscle tissue of the heart

N

natural selection   theory that within a given species, individuals best adapted to the environment live longer and produce more offspring than other individuals, resulting in changes in the species over time

naturalist   one who studies objects in their natural settings

neurologist   scientist who specializes in neurology, the study of the structure, function, and disorders of the nervous system

neurology   study of the structure, function, and disorders of the nervous system

neuron   specialized cell that transmits nerve impulses

neurophysiologist   specialist in neurophysiology, a branch of physiology that deals with the nervous system

neurophysiology   branch of physiology that deals with the nervous system

neurosis   mental disorder with no obvious organic cause that involves anxiety, phobia, or other abnormal behavior; *pl.* neuroses

neurosurgery   surgery performed on any part of the nervous system, including the brain, spinal cord, and nerves

nucleic acid   class of complex chemicals, including DNA and RNA, that is found in all living cells and viruses

O

oceanography   science that deals with oceans and marine biology

omnivore   animal whose natural diet consists of both meat and plants

ornithologist   one involved in ornithology, the scientific study of birds

oscilloscope   device that measures periodic changes in electric voltage or current

oxidation   chemical reaction in which oxygen combines with another substance

oxidize   to combine with oxygen

P

paleoanthropologist   one who studies or practices paleoanthropology, the study of fossilized humans and their ancestral and related forms

paleobotanist   scientist who studies extinct or prehistoric plants

paleontology   study of extinct or prehistoric life, usually through the examination of fossils

parasite   organism that lives on or within another organism from whose body it obtains nutrients

parasitologist   one who specializes in parasitology, the branch of biology that deals with organisms that live on or within another organism from whose body they obtain nutrients

parasitology   branch of biology that deals with parasites, organisms that live on or within another organism from whose body they obtain nutrients

parasympathetic nervous system   part of the nervous system that calms the body, reducing breathing and slowing the pulse rate

pathogen   agent that causes disease, such as a bacterium or virus

pathological   of or relating to pathology, the study of diseases and their effects on organisms

pathologist   specialist in the study of diseases and their effects on organisms

pathology   study of diseases and their effects on organisms

pepsin   one of the enzymes in gastric juice that breaks down proteins during digestion

pernicious anemia   severe form of anemia caused by the failure of the intestines to absorb vitamin B_{12}

pharmacological   relating to pharmacology, the science dealing with the preparation, uses, and effects of drugs

pharmacology   science dealing with the preparation, uses, and effects of drugs

phosphate   mineral compound containing phosphorus and oxygen

physiological   of or relating to physiology, the science that deals with the functions of living organisms and their parts

physiologist   one who specializes in physiology, the science that deals with the functions of living organisms and their parts

physiology   science that deals with the functions of living organisms and their parts

pituitary gland   gland whose secretions control the actions of other glands and influence growth and metabolism

platelet   minute particle in blood that assists in clotting

poliomyelitis   viral disease that causes paralysis and deterioration of muscle tissue, often resulting in permanent disability or death; also called infantile paralysis

polymer   chemical compound composed of small molecules linked together to form larger molecules with repeating structures

posthumous   occurring after the death of an individual

psychic   of or relating to the psyche (mind or soul); phenomenon outside the realm of physical science or knowledge

psychoanalysis   method of treating emotional disorders in which the patient is encouraged to talk freely about personal experiences

pulse pressure   difference in blood pressure between when the heart contracts and when it relaxes

pulse wave   increase in arterial blood pressure that occurs when the heart contracts

Puritan   of or relating to the Puritans, a Protestant group of the 1500s and 1600s that advocated reformation of the Church of England and a strict moral code

R

radiology   branch of medicine that uses radiant energy, in the form of X rays and radium, to diagnose and treat disease

Rh factor   genetically determined protein in the blood of humans and some animals; named for the rhesus monkey, in which the protein was first detected

rheumatoid arthritis   inherited condition that cripples the joints, especially in the hands and feet, often developing in early adulthood

RNA   ribonucleic acid, a cellular molecule similar to DNA that is involved in the production of proteins in the cell

S

semipermeable membrane   biological divider that allows certain molecules to pass through freely while preventing others from crossing, creating different concentrations of molecules on each side of the membrane

serology   study of the properties and reactions of serums, clear watery fluids in animal bodies

serum   clear liquid that separates from the blood after the blood cells clot

silicosis   buildup of fibrous tissue in the lungs caused by inhaling silica dust over a long period of time

socialism   economic or political system based on the idea that the state or groups of workers should own and control the means of production and distribution of goods

sphygmomanometer   instrument for measuring arterial blood pressure

steroid   class of organic compounds that form the building blocks for cholesterol and certain hormones and play an important role in the body's functions

streptococcal   referring to the spherical *Streptococcus* bacterium that causes disease in humans and domestic animals

sulfates   chemical compounds containing sulfur and oxygen

Glossary

sympathetic nervous system part of the nervous system that excites the body, increasing breathing and pulse rate to prepare an animal to fight or flee danger

synthesize to create artificially

T

taboo prohibition imposed by social custom

tetanus infectious disease marked by contractions of the voluntary muscles; also known as lockjaw

thermodynamic referring to the physics of the relationship between heat and other forms of energy

thermodynamics physics of the relationship between heat and other forms of energy

thorax part of the body between the neck and the diaphragm

tissue culture technique of growing body tissue in the laboratory outside the organism

toxicity degree of being toxic or poisonous

traumatic shock disturbances in the body's circulation and metabolism in response to severe physical injury

typhus bacterial disease transmitted by body lice that causes severe fever, headache, and delirium

U

ultrasonic referring to a frequency of sound above the range of human hearing

urea compound found in urine and other body fluids that is synthesized from ammonia and carbon dioxide

V

vagus nerve either of a pair of nerves that arise in the brain and supply the organs with nerve fibers

vertebrate animal with a backbone

virologist scientist who studies the microscopic disease-causing agents called viruses, their effects, and methods of controlling them

virulent extremely poisonous

vivisection practice of dissecting or cutting into the body of a living animal for the purpose of scientific investigation

X

X-ray diffraction observational technique based on the fact that X rays bend when they encounter obstacles

SUGGESTED READINGS

History

Allen, Garland, E. *Life Sciences in the Twentieth Century.* New York: Wiley Publishing, 1975.

Bass, Thomas A. *Reinventing the Future: Conversations with the World's Leading Scientists.* Reading, Mass.: Addison-Wesley, 1994.

Benson, Keith R., Jane Maienschein, and Ronald Rainger, eds. *The Expansion of American Biology.* New Brunswick, N.J.: Rutgers University Press, 1991.

Bud, Robert T. *The Uses of Life: A History of Biotechnology.* Cambridge, England: Cambridge University Press, 1994.

Carlson, Elof A. *The Gene: A Critical History.* Philadelphia: W.B. Saunders, 1966.

Coleman, William, and Camille Limoges, eds. *Studies in History of Biology.* 7 vols. Baltimore, Md.: Johns Hopkins University Press, 1977–1984.

Crick, Francis. *Of Molecules and Men.* Seattle: University of Washington Press, 1966.

——-. *What Mad Pursuit: A Personal View of Scientific Discovery.* New York: Basic Books, 1988.

Dunn, L.C. *A Short History of Genetics.* New York: McGraw-Hill, 1965.

Ghiselin, M.T. *The Triumph of the Darwinian Method.* Berkeley: University of California Press, 1969.

Gilbert, Scott F., ed. *A Conceptual History of Modern Embryology.* Baltimore, Md.: Johns Hopkins University Press, 1994.

Hamburger, Viktor. *The Heritage of Experimental Embryology: Hans Spemann and the Organizer.* Oxford, England: Oxford University Press, 1988.

Hughes, A. *A History of Cytology.* London: Abelard-Schuman, 1959.

Hunter, Graeme K. *Vital Forces: The Discovery of the Molecular Basis of Life.* San Diego, Calif.: Academic Press, 2000.

Jacob, François, and Betty E. Spellman, trans. *The Logic of Life: A History of Heredity.* Princeton, N.J.: Princeton University Press, 1993.

Jaenicke, R., and G. Sennenza, eds. *History of Biochemistry.* New York: Elsevier, 1983.

Journal of the History of Biology. Cambridge, Mass.: Harvard University Press, Dordrecht, Netherlands: Kluwer, 1968–present.

Judson, Horace Freeland. *The Eighth Day of Creation: Makers of the Revolution in Biology.* Plainview, N.Y.: Cold Spring Harbor Laboratory Press, 1996.

Kay, Lily E. *Who Wrote the Book of Life: A History of the Genetic Code.* Palo Alto, Calif.: Stanford University Press, 2000.

Lagerkvist, Ulf. *DNA Pioneers and Their Legacy.* New Haven, Conn.: Yale University Press, 1998.

Lee, Thomas F. *Gene Future. The Promise and Perils of the New Biology.* New York: Plenum, 1994.

Leicester, Henry M. *Development of Biochemical Concepts from Ancient to Modern Times.* Cambridge, Mass.: Harvard University Press, 1974.

Magner, Lois N. *A History of the Life Sciences.* New York: Marcel Dekker, 1994.

Maienschein, Jane. *Transforming Traditions in American Biology, 1880-1915.* Baltimore, Md.: Johns Hopkins University Press, 1991.

Morange, Michel, and Matthew Cobb, trans. *A History of Molecular Biology.* Cambridge, Mass.: Harvard University Press, 2000.

Olby, Robert C. *The Path to the Double Helix: The Discovery of DNA.* London: Macmillan, 1974.

Stern, Curt, and E.R. Sherwood. *The Origin of Genetics: A Mendel Sourcebook.* San Francisco: W.H. Freeman, 1966.

Stevens, Peter F. *The Development of Biological Systematics.* New York: Columbia University Press, 1994.

Wilmut, Ian, Colin Tudge, and Keith Campbell. *The Second Creation: Dolly and the Age of Biological Control.* New York: Farrar, Straus, and Giroux, 1999.

Biographies

Allen, Garland E. *Thomas Hunt Morgan: The Man and His Science.* Princeton, N.J.: Princeton University Press, 1978.

Suggested Readings

Clark, Ronald William. *J.B.S., The Life and Work of J.B.S. Haldane*. New York: Oxford University Press. 1984.

De Kruif, Paul. *Microbe Hunters*. San Diego, Calif.: Harcourt Brace, 1996.

Di Gregorio, Mario. *T.H. Huxley's Place in Natural Science*. New Haven, Conn.: Yale University Press, 1984.

Du Temple, Lesley A. *Jacques Cousteau*. Minneapolis, Minn.: Lerner Publications, 2000.

Fossey, Dian. *Gorillas in the Mist*. Boston: Houghton Mifflin Company, 1983.

Gillispie, Charles C., ed. *The Dictionary of Scientific Biography*. 16 vols. New York: Charles Scribner's Sons, 1970–1980.

Grinstein, Louise S., Carol A. Biermann, and Rose K. Rose, eds. *Women in the Biological Sciences: A Bio-bibliographical Sourcebook*. Westport, Conn.: Greenwood Press, 1997.

Hamilton, Alice, and Norah Hamilton. *Exploring the Dangerous Trades: The Autobiography of Alice Hamilton, MD*. Boston: Northeastern University Press, 1985.

Holmes, Frederic Lawrence. *Hans Krebs: The Formation of a Scientific Life 1900–1933*. 2 vols. New York: Oxford University Press, 1991–1993.

Keller, Evelyn Fox. *A Feeling for the Organism: The Life and Work of Barbara McClintock*. San Francisco: W.H. Freeman, 1983.

Lear, Linda. *Rachel Carson: Witness for Nature*. New York: Holt, 1997.

McMurry, Linda O. *George Washington Carver: Scientist and Symbol*. New York: Oxford University Press, 1981.

Pauly, Philip. *Controlling Life: Jacques Loeb and the Engineering Ideal*. New York: Oxford University Press, 1987.

Profitt, Pamela, ed. *Notable Women Scientists*. Farmington Hills, Mich.: Gale Group, 1999.

Sayre, Anne. *Rosalind Franklin and DNA*. New York: Norton, 1978.

Watson, James D. *The Double Helix: A Personal Account of the Discovery of DNA*. New York: Scribner, 1998.

On-line Resources

Gene School '99. *Gives a basic background of genetics and its applications, covers current developments in genetic technology, and contains an interactive educational component.*

http://library.thinkquest.org/28599

International Society for the History, Philosophy, and Social Studies of Biology. *Official web site for the organization, containing membership information, newsletters, research in the history of science, educational resources, and links to other relevant web sites.*

http://www.phil.vt.edu/ishpssb/

Molecular Biology Notebook On-line. *Web site generated by the Association of Applied Biologists that provides an overview of basic concepts in cell and molecular biology.*

http://www.iacr.bbsrc.ac.uk/notebook/courses/guide/

National Center for Biotechnology Information. *Web site supported by the National Institutes of Health that contains informative databases in molecular biology, biochemistry, and genetics. Also includes a taxonomy browser and links to special projects, such as the human genome project.*

http://www.ncbi.nlm.nih.gov

Neuroscience for Kids. *Provides information, educational activities, and current news concerning various aspects of the nervous system, as well as links to other web sites about neuroscience.*

http://faculty.washington.edu/chudler/neurok.html

The Nobel Institute. *Official web site of the Nobel Institute, containing a time line of important world events since 1833, when Alfred Nobel was born, biographies of Nobel Prize winners in all fields, and a transcript of the presentation speeches. Provides links to various universities and institutes around the world.*

www.nobel.se

Women in Developmental Biology. *Contains biographical information on various female figures in the field of developmental biology, as well as links to other web sites covering women in science and the history of science.*

http://web.mit.edu/afs/athena.mit.edu/org/w/womens-studies/www/dev-bio/

Zoological Record, BIOSIS and the Zoological Society of London, Biographies of Biologists. *Provides links to numerous web sites with biographical information about important figures in the history of biology.*

http://www.york.biosis.org/zrdocs/zoolinfo/biograph.htm

PHOTO CREDITS

INDEX

Page numbers in **boldface** refer to the main entry on a subject.
Page numbers in *italics* refer to illustrations, figures, and tables.

Index

Index

Index